GEOGRAPHIA

GLASGOW
ATLAS

Geographia, part of John Bartholomew & Son Ltd, was founded over 70 years ago. This Geographia street atlas is one of a new and up to the minute series of street atlases, each one of which has clear easy to read mapping and a full street index based on the National Grid.

The greatest care and attention is taken when we produce these atlases but, if you find any errors, we would be grateful to hear from you.

If you wish to send us information relating to this product, please contact:-

The Chief Cartographer,
Geographia Limited,
105/107 Bath Road,
Cheltenham,
Glos. GL53 7LE

First Edition 1986
Second Edition 1987
Third Edition 1988
Fourth Edition 1989
Fifth Edition 1989

Published by Geographia, an imprint of John Bartholomew & Son Ltd, Duncan Street, Edinburgh EH9 1TA.

Printed in Great Britain by Bartholomew & Son Ltd.
RAN B/N2904

Contents

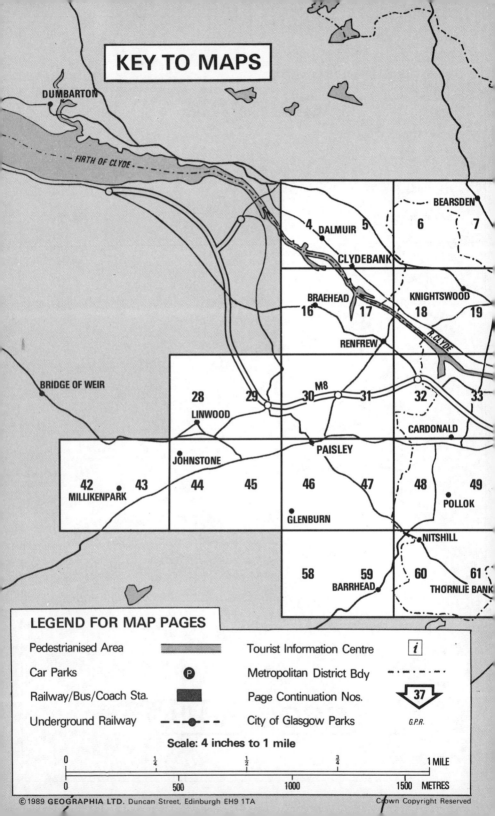

KEY TO MAPS

DUMBARTON

FIRTH OF CLYDE

BEARSDEN

4 DALMUIR 5 | 6 | 7

CLYDEBANK

BRAEHEAD | KNIGHTSWOOD
16 | 17 | 18 | 19

RENFREW | R. CLYDE

BRIDGE OF WEIR

28 | 29 | 30 M8 | 31 | 32 | 33
LINWOOD

CARDONALD

PAISLEY

JOHNSTONE

42 | 43 | 44 | 45 | 46 | 47 | 48 | 49
MILLIKENPARK | POLLOK

GLENBURN

NITSHILL

58 | 59 | 60 | 61
BARRHEAD | THORNLIE BANK

LEGEND FOR MAP PAGES

Pedestrianised Area	Tourist Information Centre	i
Car Parks	(P)	Metropolitan District Bdy	— · — · —
Railway/Bus/Coach Sta.	Page Continuation Nos.	37
Underground Railway	— ● —	City of Glasgow Parks	G.P.R.

Scale: 4 inches to 1 mile

0   ¼   ½   ¾   1 MILE

0   500   1000   1500   METRES

Strathclyde Transport

Rail Network

Personal Information

Name	Address	Tel. No.	Notes
	Post Code		
	Post Code		
	Post Code		
	Post Code		
	Post Code		
	Post Code		
	Post Code		
	Post Code		
	Post Code		
	Post Code		

Personal Information

Name	Address	Tel. No.	Notes
	Post Code		
	Post Code		
	Post Code		
	Post Code		
	Post Code		
	Post Code		
	Post Code		
	Post Code		
	Post Code		
	Post Code		

Personal Information

Name	Address	Tel. No.	Notes
	Post Code		
	Post Code		
	Post Code		
	Post Code		
	Post Code		
	Post Code		
	Post Code		
	Post Code		
	Post Code		
	Post Code		

Personal Information

Name	Address	Tel. No.	Notes
	Post Code		
	Post Code		
	Post Code		
	Post Code		
	Post Code		
	Post Code		
	Post Code		
	Post Code		
	Post Code		
	Post Code		

Personal Information

Name	Address	Tel. No.	Notes
	Post Code		
	Post Code		
	Post Code		
	Post Code		
	Post Code		
	Post Code		
	Post Code		
	Post Code		
	Post Code		
	Post Code		

Personal Information

Name	Address	Tel. No.	Notes
	Post Code		
	Post Code		
	Post Code		
	Post Code		
	Post Code		
	Post Code		
	Post Code		
	Post Code		
	Post Code		
	Post Code		

Glasgow

Local Information Guide

Contents

City of Glasgow
Local Information Guide

Useful information

Area of City 76 sq. miles

Population (Glasgow District)
(1980 estimate) 781,694.

Early Closing Days
Tuesday with alternative of Saturday.
Most of the shops in the central area
operate six-day trading.

Electricity 240 volts A.C.

Emergency Services
Police, Fire and Ambulance. Dial 999
on any telephone.

Licensing Hours
Public Houses
Daily (except Sundays) 11 a.m. to
2.30 p.m. and 5 to 11 p.m. (many
open continuously 11 a.m. to
11 p.m.)
Sundays, 12.30 to 2.30 p.m. and 6.30
to 10.30 p.m.
Restaurants, Hotels and Public
Houses with catering facilities, same
as above but can be extended for
drinks with meals.

Information Bureau
Tourist Information Centres:
35–39 St. Vincent Place
Glasgow. 041-227 4880

Town Hall, Abbey Close
Paisley. 041-889 0711

Glasgow Airport 041-848 4440

Travel Information Centre
St. Enoch Square
Open Monday–Saturday 9.30 a.m.
to 5.30 p.m. 041-226 4826 (Monday
to Saturday 7 a.m. to 12 midnight,
Sunday 9 a.m. to 9 p.m.) for City
services, ferry services, local airlines,
train and express services. Free
timetables are available.

Help & Advice
British Broadcasting Corporation
Queen Margaret Drive, G12.
041-339 8844

British Council
6 Belmont Crescent, G12.
041-339 8651

British Telecom Scotland

Glasgow Area
Marland House, 40 George Street
Glasgow G1 1BA
All Enquiries 041-220 1234 or dial
100 and ask for FREEFONE BT
GLASGOW.

Chamber of Commerce
30 George Square, G2.
041-204 2121

Citizens Advice Bureau
212 Bath Street, Glasgow G2 4HW.
041-331 2345/6/7/8
119 Main Street, Glasgow G40 1HA.
041-554 0336

27 Dougrie Drive, Castlemilk,
Glasgow G45 9AD 041-634 0338
139 Main Street (Town Hall)
Rutherglen G73 4HG 041-647 5100
66 Main Street, Barrhead
041-881 2032/880 7686
Civic Centre, East Kilbride
East Kilbride 21295
1143 Maryhill Road, Glasgow G20
041-946 6373/4
46 Township Centre, Easterhouse,
Glasgow G34 9DS 041-771 2328

Consumer Advice Centre
St. Enoch House, 1 St. Enoch Square
Glasgow G1 4BH. 041-204 0262

Customs and Excise
21 India Street, G2.
041-221 3828

H.M. Immigration Office
Admin Block D, Argyll Avenue
Glasgow Airport
Tel. 041-887 4115

Housing Aid and Advice
Shelter, 53 St. Vincent Crescent
Glasgow G3 8NQ. 041-221 8995/6

Legal Aid and Advice
Castlemilk Advice & Law Centre
27 Dougrie Drive, Glasgow G45.
041-634 0338

Law Centre
30 Dougrie Drive
041-634 0313

Lost Property
Strathclyde Passenger Transport
Executive
St. Enoch Underground Station
Tel. 041-248 6950 (City Buses)
12 West George Street G32
041-332 6811. (Underground)
Other Buses—Office of Bus Company.
Trains—Station of arrival.
Elsewhere in City—Strathclyde Police
Lost Property Department,
173 Pitt Street, G2
041-204 2626

Passport Office
Northgate 96 Milton Street
Glasgow G4. Tel. 041-332 0271

**Registrar of Births, Deaths and
Marriages**
1 Martha Street, G1. 041-227 6343
Hours – Monday to Friday 9.15 a.m.
to 4.15 p.m., Friday evenings
5.30 p.m. to 7.15 p.m.
Births must be registered within
twenty-one days, deaths within eight
days, and marriages within three
days. The Registrar should be
consulted at least one month before
intended date of marriage.

**Royal Scottish Society for the
Prevention of Cruelty to Children**
15 Annfield Place, G31.
041-556 1156

**RNID–
Royal National Institute for the
Deaf**
9a Clairmont Gardens, Glasgow
G3 7LW. 041-332 0343

Samaritans
218 West Regent Street, Glasgow
G2 4DQ. 041-248 4488

**Scottish Society for the Mentally
Handicapped**
13 Elmbank Street, Glasgow G2.
041-226 4541

Scottish Television
Cowcaddens. G2. 041-332 9999

**Society for the Prevention of
Cruelty to Animals**
15 Royal Terrace, G3.
(Business Hours)   041-332 0716
(After Hours)   041-204 2626

Newspapers

Morning Daily
Daily Record
Anderston Quay, G3.   041-248 7000

Glasgow Herald
195 Albion Street, G1. 041-552 6255

Scottish Daily Express
Park Circus Place, G3. 041-332 9600

The Scotsman
78 Queen Street, G1.   041-221 6485

Evening Daily
Evening Times
195 Albion Street, G1. 041-552 6255

Weekly
Scottish Sunday Express
Park Circus Place, G3. 041-552 3550

Sunday Mail
Anderston Quay, G3.   041-248 7000

Sunday Post
144 Port Dundas Road, G4.
041-332 9933

Parking

Car parking in the central area of Glasgow is controlled. Parking meters are used extensively and signs indicating restrictions are displayed at kerbsides and on entry to the central area. Traffic Wardens are on duty.

British Rail Car Parks
(Open 24 hours)
Central Station
Queen Street Station

Multi-Storey Car Parks
(Open 24 hours)
Anderston Cross: Cambridge Street: George Street: Mitchell Street: Port Dundas Road: Waterloo Street.

(Limited Opening)
Charing Cross
Sauchiehall Street Centre

Surface Car Parks
Carrick Street: Holland Street: Ingram Street: McAlpine Street: North Frederick Street: Albion Street: Oswald Street: St. Enoch: Shuttle Street: Wemyss Street.

Post Offices

Head Post Office
George Square, G2.   041-248 2882
Open Monday to Friday 9 a.m. to 5.30 p.m. Saturdays 9 a.m. to 12.30 p.m. Closed Sunday.

Branch Offices
85–91 Bothwell Street, G2.
4 Dixon Street, G1.

216 Hope Street, G2.
533 Sauchiehall Street, G3.

Cables can be handed in to any Post Office doing telegraph business.

Taxis

Fares by Distance
For one person of 14 years of age or over for a distance not exceeding 1 mile – 80p
sixth of a mile or part thereof 10p.
Minimum fare – 80p

Waiting Time
for each completed period of two minutes – 10p. Hires beginning or ending between 12 midnight and 6.00 a.m. – surcharge 20p.
Where there is more than 1 person of 14 years of age or over an extra charge of 5p per person for the whole journey is made. The maximum number of persons to be carried at any time not to exceed 5. Under no circumstances will passengers be charged separate fares. An additional charge is made for luggage exceeding 56 lb. (25½ kilos), prams and bicycles.

Complaints
Any complaints about taxis should be taken up with the Town Clerk's Office, Licensing Department, City Chambers, Glasgow.
Tel.041 227 4535 or any Police Station

Note
Fares and conditions apply to meter taxis within the boundary of the City of Glasgow. A surcharge of ⅓ of the meter fare is added if the taxi is hired to travel to a place beyond the boundary and within a distance of 8 miles from the Head Post Office, George Square. Persons wishing to travel beyond the 8 miles should obtain an estimate.

Local Government
Strathclyde Regional Council
Strathclyde House, 20 India Street
Glasgow G2 4PF
041-204 2900

District Councils:
Argyll & Bute
District Council Headquarters
Kilmory, Lochgilphead PA31 8RT
0546 2127

Bearsden & Milngavie
Municipal Building, Boclair
Bearsden G61 2TQ
041-942 2262

Clydebank
Council Offices, Rosebery Place
Clydebank G81 1TG
041-941 1331

Clydesdale
Clydesdale District Offices
Lanark ML11 7JT
0555 61331

Cumbernauld & Kilsyth
Council Offices, Bron Way
Cumbernauld G67 1DZ
02367 22131

Cummock & Doon Valley
Council Offices, Lugar
Cumnock KA18 3JQ
0290 22111

Cunninghame
Cunninghame House
Irvine KA12 8EE
0294 74166

Dumbarton
Crosslet House
Dumbarton G82 3NS
0389 65100

East Kilbride
Civic Centre
East Kilbride G74 1AB
035-52 28777

Eastwood
Council Offices
Eastwood Park, Rouken Glen Road
Rouken Glen, Giffnock
Glasgow G46 6UG
041-638 6511
041-638 1101

Glasgow City
City Chambers
Glasgow G2 1DU
041-221 9600

Hamilton
Town House
102 Cadzow Street
Hamilton ML3 6HH
0698 282323

Inverclyde
Municipal Buildings
Greenock PA15 1LY
0475 24400

Kilmarnock & Loudoun
Civic Centre
Kilmarnock KA1 1BY
0563 21140

Kyle & Carrick
Burns House
Burns Statue Square
Ayr KA7 1UT
0292 281511

Monklands
Municipal Buildings
Dunbeth Road
Coatbridge ML5 3LF
0236 24941

Motherwell
PO Box 14
Civic Centre
Motherwell ML1 1TW
0698 66166

Renfrew
Municipal Buildings
Cotton Street
Paisley PA1 1BU
041-889 5400

Strathkelvin
PO Box 4
Council Chambers
Kirkintilloch
Glasgow G66 1PW
041-776 7171

History & Development

The City of Glasgow began life as a makeshift hamlet of huts huddled round a 6thC church, built by St Mungo on the banks of a little salmon river — the Clyde. It was called Gleschow, meaning 'beloved green place' in Celtic. The cathedral was founded in 1136; the university, the second oldest in Scotland, was established in the 15thC; and in 1454 the flourishing mediaeval city wedged between the cathedral and the river was made a Royal burgh. The city's commercial prosperity dates from the 17thC when the lucrative tobacco, sugar and cotton trade with the New World flourished. The River Clyde, Glasgow's gateway to the Americas, was dredged, deepened and widened in the 18thC to make it navigable to the city's heart.

By the 19thC, Glasgow was the greatest shipbuilding centre in the world. From the 1820s onwards, it grew in leaps and bounds westwards along a steep ridge of land running parallel with the river. The hillside became encased in an undulating grid of streets and squares. Gradually the individualism, expressed in one-off set pieces characteristic of the 18thC and early 19thC, gave way to a remarkable coherent series of terraced squares and crescents of epic proportions — making Glasgow one of the finest of Victorian cities. But the price paid for such rapid industrialisation, the tremendous social problems manifest in the squalor of some of the worst of 19thC slums, was high. Today the city is still the commercial and industrial capital of the West of Scotland. The most notorious of the slums have been cleared but the new buildings lack that sparkling clench-fisted Glaswegian character of the 19thC. Ironically, this character was partially destroyed when the slums were cleared for it wasn't the architecture that had failed, only the bureaucrats, who designated such areas as working class ghettos.

Districts
Little remains of mediaeval Glasgow,

which stood on the wedge of land squeezed between the cathedral and the River Clyde. Its business centre was The Cross, a space formed by the junction of several streets — the tall, square Tolbooth Steeple, 1626, in the middle. Opposite is Trongate, an arch astride a footpath, complete with tower and steeple salvaged from 17thC St Mary's Church — destroyed by fire in 1793. The centre of 20thC Glasgow is George Square, a tree-lined piazza planned in 1781 and pinned down by more than a dozen statues including an 80-foot-high Doric column built in 1837 to carry a statue of Sir Walter Scott. Buildings of interest: the monumental neo-Baroque City Chambers 1883-88 which take up the east side and the Merchants' House 1874, on the west. To the south of the square, in a huddle of narrow streets, is the old Merchant City. Of interest here is the elegant Trades House, 85 Glassford Street, built by Robert Adam in 1794. An elegant Ionic portico stands on a rusticated ground storey flanked by domed towers. Hutcheson's Hospital, 158 Ingram Street, is a handsome Italianate building designed by David Hamilton in 1805. Nearby is Stirling's Library, originally an 18thC private residence, it became the Royal Exchange in 1827 when the Corinthian portico was added. To the north west is Kelvingrove, Victorian Glasgow at its best. Built around a steep saddle of land, landscaped by Paxton in 1850 and lined along its edge with handsome terraces.

Last but not least are the banks of the River Clyde. From Clyde Walkway on the north bank you can see: the Suspension Bridge of 1871 with its pylons in the form of triumphal arches; the old clipper ship, C. V. Carrick, a contemporary of the Cutty Sark, moored by Victoria bridge; 17thC Merchants' Steeple; the Gothic Revival St Andrew's R.C. Cathedral of 1816; the church, built 1739, in nearby St Andrew's Square is a typical copy of London's St Martin-in-the-Fields.

Buildings & Shops

Interesting buildings

Victorian Glasgow was extremely eclectic architecturally. Good examples of the Greek Revival style are Royal College of Physicians 1845, by W. H. Playfair and the Custom House 1840, by G. L. Taylor. The Queen's Room 1857, by Charles Wilson, is a handsome temple used now as a Christian Science church. The Gothic style is seen at its most exotic in the Stock Exchange 1877, by J. Burnet. The new Victorian materials and techniques with glass, wrought and cast iron were also ably demonstrated in the buildings of the time. Typical are: Gardener's Stores 1856, by J. Baird; the Buck's Head, Argyle Street, an amalgam of glass and cast iron; and the Egyptian Halls of 1873, in Union Street, which has a masonry framework. Both are by Alexander Thomson. The Templeton Carpet Factory 1889, Glasgow Green, by William Leiper, is a Venetian Gothic building complete with battlemented parapet.

Glasgow University

The great genius of Scottish architecture is Charles Rennie Mackintosh whose major buildings are in Glasgow. In the Scotland Street School 1904-6, he punctuated a 3-storey central block with flanking staircase towers in projecting glazed bays. His most famous building — Glasgow School of Art 1897-9 — is a magnificent Art Nouveau building of taut stone and glass; the handsome library, with its gabled facade, was added later in 1907-9.

Stirling's Library

Galleries & museums

Scotland's largest tourist attraction, The Burrell Collection, is situated in Pollok Country Park, Haggs Road and has more than 8,000 objects, housed in an award-winning gallery. The Art Gallery and Museum, Kelvingrove Park, Argyle Street, a palatial sandstone building with glazed central court, has one of the best municipal collections in Britain; superb Flemish, Dutch and French paintings, drawings, prints, also ceramics, silver, costumes and armour, as well as a natural history section. Provand's Lordship c1471, in Castle Street, is Glasgow's oldest house and now a museum of 17th-18thC furniture and household articles. Pollok House, Pollok Country Park, a handsome house designed by William Adam in 1752, has paintings by William Blake and a notable collection of Spanish paintings, including works by El Greco. The Museum of Transport, housed in Kelvin Hall, Bunhouse Road, has a magnificent collection of trams, cars, ships models, bicycles, horse-drawn carriages and 7 steam locos. The People's Palace, The Green, built 1898 with a huge glazed Winter Garden, has a lively illustrated history of the city. But the oldest museum in Glasgow is the Hunterian Museum, University of Glasgow, University Avenue, opened in 1807, it has a fascinating collection of manuscripts, early printed books, as well as some fine archaeological and geological exhibits. 400-year-old Haggs Castle, St Andrew's Drive, is now a children's museum with practical demonstrations and exhibits showing how everyday life has changed over the centuries.

Streets & shopping

The Oxford Street of Glasgow is Sauchiehall (meaning 'willow meadow') Street. This with Buchanan Street and Argyle Street is the main shopping centre. Here you will find the department stores, boutiques and general shops. All three streets are

Sheriff Court

partly pedestrianised, but the most exhilarating is undoubtedly Buchanan Street. Of particular interest is the spatially elegant Argyll Arcade 1828, the Venetian Gothic-style Stock Exchange 1877, and the picturesque Dutch gabled Buchanan Street Bank building 1896. In Glasgow Green is The Barrows, the city's famous street market, formed by the junction of London Road and Kent Street. The Market is *open weekends*. Some parts of the city have *EC Tue*.

Art Gallery & Museum Kelvingrove

Cathedrals & Churches

Glasgow Cathedral is a perfect example of pre-Reformation Gothic architecture. Begun in 1238, it has a magnificent choir and handsome nave with shallow projecting transepts. On a windy hill to the east is the Necropolis, a cemetery with a spiky skyline of Victoriana consisting of pillars, temples and obelisks, dominated by an 1825 Doric column carrying the statue of John Knox. Other churches of interest: Lansdowne Church built by J. Honeyman in 1863; St George's Tron Church by William Stark 1807; Caledonian Road Church, a temple and tower atop a storey-high base, designed by Alexander Thomson in 1857; a similar design is to be found at the United Presbyterian Church, St Vincent Street, 1858, but on a more highly articulated ground storey; Queen's Cross Church 1897 is an amalgam of Art Nouveau and Gothic Revival by the brilliant Charles Rennie Mackintosh.

Churches within the central area of Glasgow are:

Church of Scotland
Glasgow Cathedral
Castle Street
Renfield St. Stephen's Church
262 Bath Street
St. George's Tron Church
165 Buchanan Street
St. Columba Church (Gaelic)
300 St. Vincent Street

Baptist
Adelaide Place Church
209 Bath Street

Congregational
Hillhead Centre
1 University Avenue

Episcopal Church of Scotland
Cathedral Church of St. Mary
300 Great Western Road, G4.

First Church of Christ Scientist
1 la Bell Place, Clifton Street, G3.
(off Sauchiehall Street)

Free Church of Scotland
265 St. Vincent Street

German Speaking Congregation
Services held at 7 Hughenden Terrace, G12.

Greek Orthodox Cathedral
St. Luke's, 27 Dundonald Road, G12.

Jewish Orthodox Synagogue
Garnethill, 29 Garnet Street

Methodist
Woodlands Church
229 Woodlands Road

Roman Catholic
St. Andrew's Cathedral
190 Clyde Street
St. Aloysius' Church
25 Rose Street

Unitarian Church
287 St. Vincent Street

United Free
Wynd Church,
427 Crown Street, G5.

Glasgow Cathedral

Entertainment

As Scotland's commercial and industrial capital, Glasgow offers a good choice of leisure activities. The city now has 6 theatres where productions ranging from serious drama to pantomime, pop and musicals are performed. The Theatre Royal, Hope Street, is Scotland's only opera house and has been completely restored to its full Victorian splendour. The Scottish National Orchestra gives concerts at the City Hall, Candleriggs, every *Sat night in winter,* while the Kelvin Hall is the venue for the proms in *Jun.* Cinemas are still thriving in Glasgow, as are the many public houses, some of which provide meals and live entertainment. In the city centre and Byres Road, West End, there is a fair number of restaurants where traditional home cooking, as well as international cuisines, can be sampled. More night life can be found at the city's discos and dance halls — Tiffany's, Sauchiehall Street and the Plaza, Eglinton Toll. Outdoors, apart from the many parks and nature trails, there is Calderpark Zoological Gardens, situated 6 miles from the centre between Mount Vernon and Uddingston. Here you may see white rhinos, black panthers and iguanas among many species. Departing from Stobcross Quay, you can also cruise down the Clyde in 'P.S. Waverley' – the last sea-going paddle-steamer in the world.

Cinemas

Cannon Cinema, 380 Clarkston Rd, G44.
041-637 2641
Cannon Film Centre–
326 Sauchiehall St, G2.   041-332 9513
(Admin Dept), 326 Sauchiehall St, G2
041-332 1592
326 Sauchiehall St, G2.   041-332 1593
Caledonian Associated Cinemas Ltd–
Regent House, 72 Renfield St, G2
041-332 0606
Cannon Grand–
18 Jamaica St, G1.   041-248 4620
Glasgow Film Theatre–
12 Rose St, G3. (Box Off)   041-332 6535

Grosvenor Cinema–
Ashton Lane, G12.   041-339 4298
Kelburne Cinema–
(Manager), Glasgow Rd, Paisley
041-889 3612
Odeon Film Centre, 56 Renfield St, G2.
041-332 8701
Salon Cinema, Vinicombe St, G12.
041-339 4256

Halls

City Hall, Candleriggs, G1.
Couper Institute
86 Clarkston Road, G44.
Dixon Halls, 650 Cathcart Road, G42.
Govan Hall, Summertown Road, G51.
Kelvin Hall, Argyle Street, G3.
Langside Hall, 5 Langside Avenue, G41.
McLellan Galleries
270 Sauchiehall Street, G2.
Partick Hall, 9 Burgh Hall Street, G11.
Pollokshaws Hall
2025 Pollokshaws Road, G43.
Woodside Hall, Glenfarg Street, G20.

(More information about the above G.D.C. halls and others from the Director, Halls and Theatres Department, Candleriggs, G1. 041-552 1201).

Theatres

Citizens' Theatre
Gorbals Street.   041-429 0022
King's Theatre, Bath Street.
Mitchell Theatre and Moir Hall
Granville Street.
Pavilion Theatre
Renfield Street.   041-332 1846
Theatre Royal
Hope Street.   041-331 1234
Tron Theatre
38 Parnie Street.   041-552 3748
The Ticket Centre
Glasgow's Central Box Office for King's Theatre, Mitchell Theatre, Kelvin Hall, Citizen's Theatre, Theatre Royal and City Hall at Candleriggs, G1.
Open Monday to Saturday 10.30 a.m. to 6.30 p.m.
041-227 5511

Glasgow (Abbotsinch) Airport

Glasgow Airport is located eight miles West of Glasgow alongside the M8 motorway at Junction 28. It is linked by a bus service to Anderston Cross Bus Station, the journey time is 25 minutes and buses leave at 30 minute intervals. There is a frequent coach service linking the Airport with

ERSKINE

RUNWAY

BARNSFORD ROAD A726

RUNWAY

HELICOPTERS

LOGAN AIR

CAR PARK

BUTE ROAD

CAR PARK

ST ANDREWS

FLYING CLUBS

M8

GREENOCK 15 miles

A726

CAR HIRE

PLAYING FIELDS

FOOTBRIDGE

M8

29

A740

LINWOOD 3 miles

ST JAMES PARK PLAYING FIELDS

A726

all major bus and rail terminals in the City and a Coach/Air link to and from Prestwick Airport.

The Airport Terminal has a restaurant, grill, buffet, three bars, lounges, shop, post office and banking facilities.

Car parking is available with a graduated scale of charges.

The Airport telephone no is 041-887 1111.

Airlines

(Domestic Routes)
British Airways
66 Gordon Street
Glasgow G1
Reservations Tel: 041-332 9666
British Caledonian Airways
(contact British Airways)
British Midland
Glasgow Airport,
Paisley PAU PA3
Reservations Tel: 041-204 2436
Loganair Ltd.
Glasgow Airport (administration)
Tel: 041-889 3181.
Trident House, Renfrew Road, Paisley

Sport & Recreation

For both spectator and participant, football is Glasgow's favourite sport. Both Celtic and Rangers, Scotland's most famous rival teams, have their grounds within the City. Glasgow houses Scotland's national football stadium at Hampden Park.

Badminton

Scottish Badminton Union's Cockburn Centre, Bogmoor Place, G51.
041-445 1218

Bowling Greens

There are greens in all the main Parks. Information about clubs from the Scottish Bowling Association:
50 Wellington Street, G2.
041-221 8999.

Cricket Grounds

Cartha Haggs Road, G41.
Clydesdale Beaton Road, G41.
Huntershill Crowhill Road, Bishopbriggs.
Poloc Shawholm 2060 Pollokshaws Road, G43.
West of Scotland Peel Street, G11.

Football Grounds

Celtic Park (Celtic F.C.)
95 Kerrydale St. G40
Firhill Park (Partick Thistle F.C. & Clyde F.C.)
Firhill Rd. G20
Hampden Park (Queen's Park F.C.)
Somerville Dr., G42
Ibrox Park (Rangers F.C.)
Edmiston Dr., G51
Kilbowie Park (Clydebank F.C.)
Argyll Rd., Clydebank
Mertland
Kirkintilloch
St. Mirren Park (St. Mirren F.C.)
Love St., Paisley

Golf Courses

Glasgow District Council
9 holes
Alexandra Park
King's Park.
Knightswood, Lincoln Avenue, G13.
Ruchill, Brassey Street, G20.

18 holes
Lethamhill, Cumbernauld Road, Littlehill, Auchinairn Road, G64.
Linn Park.

(Charges displayed)
Dougalston Golf Course
Strathblane Road, Milngavie.
(Five miles from Glasgow).
Open to the public daily.
041-956 5750 for charges.

Putting Greens

There are putting greens in all main Parks.

Pitch & Putt

Courses at Alexandra Park, Bellahouston Park, Dawsholm, Queen's Park, Rouken Glen and several others.

Rugby Grounds

Balgray (Kelvinside Academicals)
Great Western Road, G12.

Garscadden (Glasgow University)
Garscadden Road South, G15.

Hughenden (Hillhead High School)
Hughenden Road, G12.

New Anniesland (Glasgow Acad.)
Helensburgh Drive, G13.

Old Anniesland (Glasgow High School F.P.)
Crow Road, G11.

Westerlands (Glasgow University)
Ascot Avenue, G12.

Sports Centres

Bellahouston
Bellahouston Drive, G52.
041-427 5454.

Burnhill
Toryglen Road, Rutherglen.
041-643 0327.

James Murray
Caledonia Road, Baillieston.
041-773 1656

Springburn
Millarbank Street, Springburn.
041-558 7358.

Helenvale
Outdoor Sports Complex
Helenvale Street, G31.
041-554 4109.

Swimming Baths

Glasgow District Council
Castlemilk, 137 Castlemilk Drive, G45.
Drumchapel, 199 Drumry Road East.
Easterhouse, Bogbain Road, G34.
Govan, Harhill Street, G51.
Govanhill, 99 Calder Street, G42.
North Woodside, Braid Square.
Pollokshaws (Dry-Land/Water Sports Complex) Ashtree Road, G43.
Rutherglen, 44 Greenhill Road, G73.
Shettleston, Elvan Street, G32.
Temple, Knightscliffe Avenue, G13.
Whitehill, Onslow Drive, G31.
Whiteinch, Medwyn Street, G14.
Whitevale, 81 Whitevale Street, G31.

Hours
Monday to Friday 9 a.m. to 9 p.m.
Saturday 9 a.m. to 1 p.m.
*Sunday 9 a.m. to 1 p.m.

Charges
Admission charges are minimal.
OAPs free at certain times.

Turkish Baths/ Sun Beds

available at:
Govanhill	041-423 0233
Pollokshaws	041-632 2200
Shettleston	041-778 1346

and Whiteinch, 041-959 2465

Men and women on separate days. Telephone direct to baths for more information.

Hours
(All the year round).
Monday to Friday 9 a.m. to 9 p.m.
Saturday 9 a.m. to 1 p.m.

SAUNA at:

Castlemilk,	041-634 8254
Drumchapel,	041-944 5812
Rutherglen,	041-647 4530
and Whitehill,	041-551 9969

Tennis

There are courts in all the main parks. Information about clubs from the Secretary of the West of Scotland Lawn Tennis Association:
Mr.N.Floyd, 1 Bocleir Road
Bearsden   041-942 0162

Weather

The City of Glasgow is on the same latitude as the City of Moscow, but because of its close proximity to the warm Atlantic Shores, and the prevailing westerly winds, it enjoys a more moderate climate. Summers are generally cool and winters mostly mild, this gives Glasgow fairly consistent summer and winter temperatures. Despite considerable cloud the City is sheltered by hills to the south-west and north and the average rainfall for Glasgow is usually less than 40 inches per year.

The following table shows the approximate average figures for sunshine, rainfall and temperatures to be expected in Glasgow throughout the year:

Weather Forecasts
For the Glasgow Area including Loch Lomond and the Clyde Coast:
Weatherline
041-246 8091 (Recording)
The Glasgow Weather Centre (Meteorological Office)
118 Waterloo Street, G2.
041-248 3451.

Month	Hours of Sunshine	Inches of Rainfall	Temperature °C		
			Ave. Max.	Ave. Min.	High/Low
Jan	36	3.8	5.5	0.8	−18
Feb	62	2.8	6.3	0.8	−15
Mar	94	2.4	8.8	2.2	21
Apr	147	2.4	11.9	3.9	22
May	185	2.7	15.1	6.2	26
June	181	2.4	17.9	9.3	30
July	159	2.9	18.6	10.8	29
Aug	143	3.5	18.5	10.6	31
Sept	106	4.1	16.3	9.1	−4
Oct	76	4.1	13.0	6.8	−8
Nov	47	3.7	8.7	3.3	−11
Dec	30	4.2	6.5	1.9	−12

Renfrew District

A selection of leisure, recreational and cultural attractions in Renfrew District:

Barrhead Sports' Centre

The Centre contains swimming-pools, sports halls, activity rooms and sauna suite. Bar and restaurant facilities add to the wide range of sporting and leisure activities available.

Barshaw Park, Glasgow Road, Paisley

The park is extensive with formal and informal areas. It adjoins the public golf course and incorporates a boating-pond, playgrounds, model "ride-on" railway and a nature corner.

Castle Semple Country Park, Lochwinnoch

Castle Semple Loch is a popular feature for sailing and fishing. Canoes, rowing boats and sailing boards for hire. Fishing permits available. Tel: Lochwinnoch 842882 or Bridge of Weir 614791.

Coats Observatory

The Observatory has traditionally recorded astronomical and meteorological information since 1882. Now installed with a satellite picture receiver, it is one of the best equipped Observatories in the country. Monday–Friday 2–5pm. Saturday 10am–1pm and 2–5pm. Also first Thursday in October–31st October 7–9.30pm. Tel: 041-889 3151.

Erskine Bridge

The bridge is an impressive high level structure opened by HRH Princess Anne in 1971 and provides a direct link from Renfrew District to Loch Lomond and the Trossachs. The bridge replaced the Erskine Ferry and affords extensive views up and down river to pedestrian users.

Finlayston Estate

Off the A8 at Langbank. The Estate is now a garden centre with woodland walks. The house has connections with John Knox and Robert Burns and is open April to August on Sundays from 2.30–4.30pm. At other times groups by appointment. Tel: Langbank 285.

Formakin Estate, By Bishopton

A group of buildings and landscaped grounds designed in the Arts and Crafts style at the turn of the century. Currently being restored, visitors can take a guided tour in small groups — only by appointment. Open Saturday and Sunday 11am–6pm. Tel: 0505 863400.

Gleniffer Braes Country Park, Glenfield Road, Paisley

1,000 breathtaking acres including Glen Park nature trail, picnic and children's play areas. Open dawn till dusk, the park affords extensive walks and spectacular views from this elevated moorland area, and contains an area reserved for model aero flying.

Houston Village

Houston was developed in the 18th century as an estate village. The traditional smiddy building, village pubs and terraced houses combine to create a quiet, sleepy atmosphere which has successfully survived the development of extensive modern housing on its periphery.

Inchinnan Bridges

Early 19th century stone bridges over the White Cart and Black Cart rivers close to St Conval's stone, and the site of the Inchinnan Church which houses the graves of the Knights Templar, whose order was introduced to Scotland in 1153 by King David I.

Johnstone Castle

The remnants of a 1700 building formerly a much larger structure but largely demolished in the 1950's. The castle has significant historical links with the Cochrane and Houston families, major landowners who were instrumental in the development of the Burgh of Johnstone.

Kilbarchan Village

A good example of an 18th century weaving village with many original buildings still fronting the narrow streets. A focal point is the steeple building in the square, orignally a school and meal market and now used as public meeting rooms.

Laigh Kirk, Paisley

Originally built in 1738, the Laigh Kirk is now being converted to an Arts Centre. A former minister later became Principal Witherspoon of Princetown University, the only clergyman to sign the American Declaration of Independence in 1776. Theatre, workshop, cafeteria and bar open daily 10am–11pm. For further information telephone 041-887 1010.

Linwood Sports' Centre

A modern sports' complex with a wide range of dry, indoor activity areas currently being complemented by extensive external facilities to cater for bowling, golf, hockey, rugby, cricket and tennis.

Lochwinnoch Village

An attractive rural village close to the Castle Semple Water Park, Muirshiel Country Park and the R.S.P.B. nature reserve, Lochwinnoch contains a small local museum with displays reflecting agricultural, social and industrial aspects of village life. Museum open Monday, Wednesday and Friday 10am–1pm, 2–5pm and 6–8pm. Tuesday and Saturday 10am–1pm and 2–5pm. Open most days throughout the year, visitors should telephone Lochwinnoch 842615.

Muirshiel Country Park

Four miles north of Lochwinnoch, the park features trails of varying length radiating from the Information Centre. Open daily 9am–8pm. Tel: Lochwinnoch 842803.

Paisley Town Trail

An easy-to-follow route taking in the town's historic and architecturally significant buildings. Visitors can spend an hour or two walking round the trail and referring to a printed guide and wall plaques on the main buildings.

Paisley Leisure Complex

Ultra-modern complex with extensive "fun" pool featuring artificial wave machine and water slides. Unique within the area, the complex is easily reached by public transport and has ample car parking. Monday–Saturday 10am–9.15pm, Sunday 10am–4.15pm. Tel: 041-889 4000.

Paisley Abbey

Birthplace of the Stewart Dynasty, the Abbey dates, in part, to the 12th century and features regimental flags, relics, the Barochan Cross and beautiful stained glass windows. Monday–Friday 10.30am–12.30pm, 1.30–3.30pm, Saturday 10am–12 noon, 1.30–3.30pm. Tel: 041-889 3630.

Paisley Town Hall

A Renaissance style building by the River Cart in the heart of Paisley, it features a slim clock tower and houses a Tourist Information Centre. It accommodates many exhibitions during the year and is also available for conferences and functions. Monday–Saturday 9am–5pm. Tel: 041-887 1007.

Paisley Museum and Art Gallery, High Street, Paisley

In addition to the world famous collection of Paisley shawls, the Museum traces the history of the Paisley pattern, the development of weaving techniques and houses collections of local and natural history, ceramics and paints. Monday–Saturday 10am–5pm. Tel: 041-889 3151.

Renfrew Town Hall

The Town Hall has a "fairy-tale" style to its 105 feet high spire and was the administrative centre of the Royal Burgh of Renfrew. Originally the principal town in the area, Renfrew was strategically placed on the River Clyde, and a passenger ferry continues to operate daily.

Robert Tannahill, Weaver Poet

The works of Tannahill ranks with those of Burns. Born 1774 he took his own life in 1810 and is buried in a nearby graveyard. Visitors can visit his early home, site of his death, and his grave, and read his works in Paisley Library.

Royal Society for Protection of Birds, Lochwinnoch

An interesting visitor centre with observation tower, hides, displays and gift shop. Open daily 10am–5.15pm. Tel: Lochwinnoch 842663.

Sma' Shot Cottages, Paisley

Fully restored and furnished artisan's house of the Victorian era; exhibition room displaying photographs plus artefacts of local interest. 18th century weaver's loomshop with combined living quarters. Open May–September, Wednesday and Saturday 1–5pm. Group visits arranged by appointment. Tel: 041-812 2513 or 041-889 0530.

The Clyde Estuary

Visitors travelling along the rural route of the Old Greenock Road above Langbank village at the western end of the District are able to take advantage of extensive views of the upper and lower Clyde Estuary, the Gareloch and the mountains beyond.

Thomas Coats Memorial Church

Open daily 2–4pm. Visitors should check in advance. Another gift from the Coats family to Paisley, the Church was built in 1894 and, constructed of red sandstone, is one of the finest Baptist Churches in the country. Tel: 041-889 9980.

Wallace Monument, Elderslie

The monument was erected in 1912 and marks the birthplace of the Scottish Patriot, Sir William Wallace. It stands adjacent to the reconstructed foundation plan of the adjacent Wallace Buildings which dated from the 17th century.

Weaver's Cottage, Kilbarchan

This cottage, built in 1723, houses the last of the village's 800 looms and demonstrations are still given. It contains displays of weaving and domestic utensils, with Cottage garden and refreshments. Open April 2–May 31 and September 1–October 31 on Tuesdays, Thursdays, Saturdays and Sundays 2–5pm, June 1–August 31 from 2–5pm daily.

The City of Glasgow has one of the most advanced, fully integrated public transport systems in the whole of Europe. The Strathclyde Transport network consists of; the local British Rail network, the local bus services and the fully modernised Glasgow Underground, with links to Glasgow Airport and the Steamer and Car Ferry Services.
Note: Although the information in this section is correct at the time of printing it should be checked before use.

Bus Services and Tours

Long Distance Coach Service
Scottish Citylink Coaches Ltd
041-332 9191

Shorter Journeys
Tel: 041-226 4836
(0700-2400 Mon-Sat; 0900-2100 Suns) for City Services and buses to Airdrie, Clydebank, Cumbernauld, Dumbarton, East Kilbride, Erskine, Hamilton, Johnstone, Kirkintilloch, Paisley, Wishaw
Buses leave from Anderston Cross Bus Station 041-248 7432.
for Ardrossan, Ayr, Blantyre, East Kilbride (via Busby), Edinburgh, Glasgow Airport, Gourock, Hamilton, Kilmarnock, Lanark, Largs, Motherwell, Paisley, Prestwick, Renfrew, Wemyss Bay, etc.
Buses leave from Buchanan Bus Station 041-332 7133.
for Aberfoyle, Airdrie, Bearsden, Blantyre, Callander, Clydebank, Crieff, Cumbernauld, Dundee, Dunfermline, East Kilbride (via

Bridgeton), Edinburgh, Glasgow Airport, Glencoe, Leven, Milngavie, Motherwell, Perth, St. Andrews, Stirling, etc.
Day and Half Day Tours
Scottish City Link
Buchanan Bus Station.
041-332 8055

Haldane's of Cathcart, Delvin Road, G44. 041-637 2234.

Strathclyde Buses Ltd.
197 Victoria Road, G42 7AD
041-636 3190
(Glasgow City Bus Tour and Glimpses of Charles R. Mackintosh Architecture with C.R.M. Society) 041-636 3195

British Rail

Passenger enquiries: 041-204 2844.
Sleeper reservations: 041-221 2305.

Central Station
Inter-City electric services for English destinations, including Carlisle, Preston, Liverpool, Manchester (3 hours 35 minutes), Leeds, Nottingham, Crewe, Birmingham (4 hours 20 minutes), London (Euston) (5 hours). Also connections for Wales and West of England.
Scottish destinations in South and West include Ayr (for Burns country), Kilmarnock, Dumfries, Stranraer (for Ireland via Larne), Ardrossan and Largs. Electric trains include Gourock and Wemyss Bay (for Clyde steamers).

Queen Street Station
Trains for scenic West Highland Line to Oban, Fort William and Mallaig. Steamer connections to the Islands. Inter-City expresses for Edinburgh, connecting with trains to England including Newcastle, York, London (King's Cross). Services for North and East Scotland, including Fife, Stirling, Perth, Dundee, Aberdeen, Inverness, Wick, Thurso, Kyle of Lochalsh.
Electric trains: Dumbarton, Balloch (for Loch Lomond), Helensburgh. City Rail Link Service bus connects Queen Street Station and Central Station.

Parks & Gardens

There are over 70 public parks within the city. The most famous is Glasgow Green. Abutting the north bank of the River Clyde, it was acquired in 1662. Of interest are the Winter Gardens attached to the People's Palace. Kelvingrove Park is an 85-acre park laid out by Sir Joseph Paxton in 1852. On the south side of the city is the 148-acre Queen's Park, Victoria Road, established 1857-94. Also of interest: Rouken Glen, Thornliebank, with a spectacular waterfall, walled garden, nature trail and boating facilities; Victoria Park, Victoria Park Drive, with its famous Fossil Grove flower gardens and yachting pond. In Great Western Road are the Botanic Gardens. Founded in 1817, the gardens' 42 acres are crammed with natural attractions, including the celebrated Kibble Palace glasshouse with its fabulous tree ferns, exotic plants and white marble Victorian statues.

The main public parks in Glasgow are:

Alexandra
671 Alexandra Parade, G31.

Bellahouston
Paisley Road West, G52.

Botanic Gardens
730 Gt. Western Road, G12.

Hogganfield Loch
Cumbernauld Road, G33.

Kelvingrove
Sauchiehall Street, G3.

King's
325 Carmunnock Road, G44.

Linn
Clarkston Road at Netherlee Road, G44.

Queen's
Victoria Road, G42.

Rouken Glen
Rouken Glen Road, G46.

Springburn
Broomfield Road, G21.

Tollcross
461 Tollcross Road, G32.

Victoria
Victoria Park Drive North, G14.

Kibble Palace

Strathclyde
Further Education

Anniesland College
Hatfield Drive, Glasgow, G12 0YE.
041-357 3969

Ayr College
Dam Park, Ayr, KA8 0EU.
Ayr (0292) 265184

Barmulloch College
186 Rye Road, Glasgow, G21 3JY.
041-558 9071/4

Bell College of Technology
Almada Street, Hamilton,
Lanarkshire, ML3 0JB.
Hamilton (0698) 283100

Cambuslang College
Janebank, Glasgow Road,
Cambuslang, Glasgow, G72 7BS.
041-641 6197

**Cardonald College of Further
Education**
690 Mosspark Drive, Glasgow,
G52 3AY.
041-883 6151/4

Central College of Commerce
300 Cathedral Street, G1 2TA.
041-552 3941

Clydebank College
Kilbowie Road, Clydebank,
Dunbartonshire, G81 2AA.
041-952 7771/6

Coatbridge College
Kildonan Street, Coatbridge,
Lanarkshire, ML5 3LS.
Coatbridge (0236) 22316

Cumberland College
Town Centre, Cumbernauld,
Glasgow, G67 1HU.
Cumbernauld (0236) 731811

**Glasgow College of Building and
Printing**
60 North Hanover Street, Glasgow,
G1 2BP.
041-332 9969

**Glasgow College of Food
Technology**
230 Cathedral Street, Glasgow,
G1 2TG.
041-552 3751

**Glasgow College of Nautical
Studies**
21 Thistle Street, Glasgow, G5 9XB.
041-429 3201

Glasgow College of Technology
Cowcaddens Road, Glasgow,
G4 0BA.
041-332 7090

James Watt College
Finnart Street, Greenock,
Renfrewshire, PA16 8HF.
Greenock (0475) 24433

Kilmarnock College
Holehouse Road, Kllmarnock,
Ayrshire, KA3 7AT.
Kilmarnock (0563) 23501

Langside College
50 Prospecthill Road, Glasgow,
G42 9LB.
041-649 4991

Motherwell College
Dalzell Drive, Motherwell,
Lanarkshire, ML1 2DD.
Motherwell (0698) 59641

Reid Kerr College, The
Renfrew Road, Paisley, Renfrewshire,
PA3 4DR.
041-889 4225/7

Springburn College
110 Flemington Street, Glasgow,
G21 4BX.
041-558 9001

Stow College
43 Shamrock Street, Glasgow,
G4 9LD.
041-332 1786

University of Glasgow
University Avenue, Glasgow
041-339 8855

University of Strathclyde,
16 Richmond Street, Glasgow,
G11XQ
041 552 4400

Hospitals

**Greater Glasgow Health Board
(Administration)
225 Bath Street, Glasgow G2 4JT
041-204 2755**

Acorn Street Psychiatric Day Hospital
23 Acorn Street, Bridgeton,
Glasgow G40 4AN
041-556 4789

Baillieston Health Centre
20 Muirside Road,
Glasgow G69 7AD
041-771 0871

Belvidere Hospital
London Road, Glasgow G31 4PG
041-554 1855

Birdston Hospital, Milton of Campsie
Glasgow G65 8BY
041-776 6114

Blawarthill Hospital
Knightswood, Glasgow G13 3TG
041-954 9547

Bridgeton Health Centre
201 Abercromby Street
Glasgow G40 2EA
041-554 1866

Broomhill & Lanfine Hospitals
Kirkintilloch, Glasgow G66 1RR
041-776 5141

Carsewell House (Psychiatric
Outpatient)
5 Oakley Terrace, Glasgow G31 2HX
041-554 6267

Canniesburn Hospital
Switchback Road, Bearsden,
Glasgow G61 1QL
041-942 2255

Charing Cross (Alcohol and Drug)
Day Hospital, 8 Woodside Crescent,
Glasgow G3 7UL
041-332 5463

Children's Home Hospital
Strathblane, Glasgow G63 9EP
0360 70203

Clydebank Health Centre
Kilbowie Road, Clydebank G81 2TQ
041-952 2080

Cowglen Hospital
Boydstone Road, Glasgow G53 7XJ
041-632 9106

Darnley Hospital
Nitshill, Glasgow G53 7RR
041-881 1005

David Elder Infirmary
503 Langlands Road, Glasgow G51 4DY
041-445 2466

Douglas Inch Centre for Forensic
Psychiatry, 2 Woodside Terrace,
Glasgow G3 7UY
041-332 3844

Drumchapel Hospital
129 Drumchapel Road,
Glasgow G15 6PX
041-944 2344

Duke Street Hospital
253 Duke Street, Glasgow G31 1HY
041-556 5222

Duntocher Hospital
Duntocher, Clydebank G81 5QU
Duntocher 74294

Easterhouse Health Centre
9 Auchinlea Road, Glasgow G34 9NT
041-771 0781

Elder Cottage Hospital
1A Drumoyne Drive, Govan
Glasgow G51 4AT
041-445 2466

Gartloch Hospital
Gartcosh, Glasgow G69 8EJ
041-771 0771

Gartnavel General Hospital
1053 Great Western Road,
Glasgow G12 07N
041-334 8122

Gartnavel Royal Hospital
1055 Great Western Road,
Glasgow G12 0XH
041-334 6241

Glasgow Dental Hospital and School
378 Sauchiehall Street
Glasgow G2 3JZ
041-332 7020

Glasgow Eye Infirmary
2 Sandyford Place, Glasgow G3 7NB
041-204 0721

Glasgow Homeopathic Hospital
1000 Great Western Road,
Glasgow G12 0AA
041-339 0382

Glasgow Royal Infirmary
84 Castle Street, Glasgow G4 0SF
041-552 3535

Glasgow Royal Maternity Hospital
Rottenrow, Glasgow G4 0NA
041-552 3400

Glasgow School of Chiropody
757 Crookston Road,
Glasgow G53 7UA
041-883 0418

Glasgow School of Occupational
Therapy, 29 Sherbrooke Avenue,
Glasgow G41 4ER
041-427 3032

Gorbals Health Centre
45 Pine Place, Glasgow G5 0BQ
041-429 6291

Govan Health Centre
295 Langlands Road
Glasgow G51 4BJ
041-440 1212

Govanhill Health Centre
223 Calder Street
Glasgow G42 7DK
041-424 3003

Knightswood Hospital
125 Knightswood Road,
Glasgow G13 2XG
041-954 9641

Lennox Castle Hospital
Lennoxtown, Glasgow G65 7LB
Lennoxtown 313000

Lenzie Hospital
Lenzie, Kirkintilloch
Glasgow G66 5DE
041-776 1208

Leverndale Hospital
510 Crookston Road
Glasgow G53 7TU
041-882 6255

Lightburn Hospital
Carntyne Road, Glasgow G32 6ND
041-774 5102

Maryhill Health Centre
41 Shawpark Street,
Glasgow G20 9DR
041-946 7151

Mearnskirk Hospital
Newton Mearns, Glasgow G77 5RZ
041-639 2251

Parkhead Health Centre
101 Salamanca Street,
Glasgow G31 5ES
041-556 5232

Philipshill Hospital
East Kilbride Road, Busby,
Glasgow G76 9HW
041-644 1144

Possilpark Health Centre
85 Denmark Street,
Glasgow G22 5EG
041-336 5311

Queen Mother's Hospital
Yorkhill, Glasgow G3 8SH
041-339 8888

Royal Beatson Memorial Hospital
132 Hill Street, Glasgow G3 6UD
041-332 0286

Royal Hospital for Sick Children
129 Drumchapel Road
Glasgow G15 6PX
041-944 2344

Royal Hospital for Sick Children
Yorkhill, Glasgow G3 8SJ
041-339 8888

Royal Samaritan Hospital for Women
69 Coplaw Street, Glasgow G42 7JF
041-423 3033

Ruchill Hospital
Bilsland Drive, Glasgow G20 9NB
041-946 7120

Rutherglen Health Centre
130 Stonelaw Road, Rutherglen,
Glasgow G73 2PQ
041-647 7171

Rutherglen Maternity Hospital
120 Stonelaw Road, Rutherglen,
Glasgow G73 2PG
041-647 0011

Shettleston Health Centre
420 Old Shettleston Road,
Glasgow G32 7LU
041-778 9191

Southern General Hospital
1345 Govan Road, Glasgow G51 4TF
041-445 2466

Springburn Health Centre
486 Springburn Road,
Glasgow G21 1TR
041-558 0101

Stobhill General Hospital
133 Balornock Road,
Glasgow G21 3UW
041-558 0111

Stoneyetts Hospital
Chryston, Glasgow G69 0JG
041-776 1026

Townhead Health Centre
16 Alexandra Parade
Glasgow G31 2ES
041-552 3477

Victoria Geriatric Unit
Mansionhouse Road,
Glasgow G41 3DX
041-649 4511

Victoria Infirmary
Langside, Glasgow G42 9TY
041-649 4545

Waverley Park Hospital
Kirkintilloch, Glasgow G66 2HE
041-776 2461

Western Infirmary
Dumbarton Road, Glasgow G11 6NT
041-339 8822

Woodilee Hospital
Lenzie, Glasgow G66 3UG
041-776 2451

Woodside Health Centre
Barr Street, Glasgow G20 7LR
041-332 9977

INDEX TO STREETS

General Abbreviations

NOTES

The figures and letters following a street name indicate the postal district and map square where the name will be found.

A street name followed by the name of another street in italics does not appear on the map, but will be found adjoining or near the latter.

Name	Ref	Page
Alcaig Rd. G52	N12	49
Alder Av., Lenz.	C22	12
Alder Ct., Barr.	R 8	59
Alder Pl. G43	P14	62
Alder Pl., John.	N 1	44
Alder Rd. G43	P14	62
Alder Rd., Cumb.	C 4	71
Alder Rd., Dalm.	C 6	4
Alderman Pl. G13	G11	19
Alderman Rd. G13	F 9	18
Aldersdyke Pl., Blan.	R26	68
Alderside Dr., Udd.	O27	57
Alexander St., Clyde.	E 7	5
Alexandra Av. G33	G23	25
Alexandra Av., Lenz.	D23	13
Alexandra Cross G31	K19	37
Duke St.		
Alexandra Ct. G31	K19	37
Roebank St.		
Alexandra Dr., Pais.	M 4	45
Alexandra Dr., Renf.	H 8	17
Alexandra Gdns., Lenz.	D23	13
Alexandra Par. G31	K19	37
Alexandra Park St. G31	K19	37
Alexandra Rd., Lenz.	D23	13
Alford St. G21	H17	22
Alfred Ter. G52	H14	20
Great Western Rd.		
Algie St. G41	O15	51
Alice St. G5	M17	52
Alice St., Pais.	N 6	46
Aline Ct., Barr.	Q 7	59
Allan Av., Renf.	J 9	32
Allan Pl. G40	M19	53
Allan St. G40	N19	53
Allander Gdns., Bish.	D18	10
Allander Rd., Bear.	D11	7
Allander St. G22	H17	22
Allands Av., Renf.	G 5	16
Allanfauld Rd., Cumb.	B 2	70
Allanton Av., Pais.	M 9	48
Allanton Dr. G52	L10	32
Allerton Gdns., Bail.	M24	55
Alleysbank G73	N19	53
Allison Dr. G72	P22	66
Allison Pl. G42	N16	51
Prince Edward St.		
Allison Pl. Gart.	H27	27
Allison St. G42	N16	51
Allnach Pl. G34	K27	41
Alloway Cres. G73	P18	64
Alloway Dr. G73	P18	64
Alloway Dr., Clyde.	D 8	5
Alloway Rd. G43	P14	62
Alma St. G40	L19	37
Almond Av., Renf.	J 9	32
Almond Cres., Pais.	N 3	45
Almond Dr., Lenz.	C22	12
Almond Rd. G33	G23	25
Almond Rd., Bear.	E11	7
Almond St. G33	J20	37
Almond Vale, Udd.	O28	57
Hamilton Vw.		
Alness Cres. G52	M12	49
Alpatrick Gdns., John.	M 1	44
Alpine Gro., Udd.	O27	57
Alsatian Av., Clyde	E 8	5
Alston La. G40	L18	36
Claythorn St.		
Altnacreag Gdns., Chr.	D28	15
Alton Gdns. G12	H14	20
Great George St.		
Alton Rd., Pais.	M 8	47
Altyre St. G32	M21	54
Alva Gate. G52	N12	49
Alva Gdns. G52	N12	49
Alva Pl., Lenz.	D24	13
Alyth Cres., Clark.	S16	63
Alyth Gdns. G52	M12	49
Alyth Gdns., Clark.	S16	63
Ambassador Way, Renf.	J 8	31
Cockels Loan		
Amisfield St. G20	G15	21
Amochrie Dr., Pais.	O 3	45
Amochrie Rd., Pais.	N 3	45
Amulree Pl. G32	M22	54
Amulree St. G32	L22	38
Ancaster Dr. G13	G12	19
Ancaster La. G13	F11	19
Great Western Rd.		
Anchor Av., Pais.	M 7	47
Anchor Cres., Pais.	M 7	47
Anchor Dr., Pais.	M 7	47
Anchor Wynd, Pais.	M 7	47
Ancroft St. G20	H16	21
Ancrum St. G32	L22	38
Anderson Dr., Renf.	H 8	17
Anderson Gdns., Blan.	R27	69
Station Rd.		
Anderson Quay G3	L15	35
Anderson St. G11	J13	34
Andrew Av., Lenz.	D23	13
Andrew Av., Renf.	H 9	18
Andrew Dr., Clyde.	F 8	17
Andrews St., Pais.	L 6	30
Anglegate G14	H11	19
Angus Av. G52	M11	49
Angus Av., Bish.	F20	23
Angus Gdns., Udd.	O27	57
Angus La. G64	E20	11
Angus Oval G52	M10	48
Angus Pl. G52	M10	48
Angus St. G21	H18	22
Angus St., Clyde.	F 9	18
Angus Wk., Udd.	O28	57
Annan Dr. G73	O20	53
Annan Dr., Bear.	D11	7
Annan Dr., Pais.	N 3	45
Annan Pl., John.	O08	43
Annan St. G42	O16	51
Annandale St. G42	M16	51
Annbank St. G31	L18	36
Anne Av., Renf.	H 8	17
Anne Cres., Lenz.	D23	13
Annette St. G42	N16	51
Annfield Gdns., Blan.	R26	68
Annfield Pl. G31	K18	36
Annick Dr., Bear.	E11	7
Annick St. G32	L22	38
Annick St. G72	P23	67
Anniesdale Av. G33	G23	25
Anniesland Cres. G14	G10	18
Anniesland Mansions G13	G12	19
Ancaster Dr.		
Anniesland Rd. G13	G11	19
Anniesland Rd. G14	G10	18
Anson St. G40	M18	52
Anson Way, Renf.	J 8	31
Britannia Way		
Anstruther St. G32	L21	38
Antonine Gdns., Clyde.	C 7	5
Antonine Rd., Bear.	C10	6
Anworth St. G32	M22	54
Appin Rd. G31	K19	37
Appin Way, Udd.	Q28	69
Bracken Ter.		
Appleby St. G22	H16	21
Applecross Gdns., Chr.	D27	15
Applecross St. G22	H16	21
Appledore Cres., Udd.	Q28	69
Apsley La. G11	J13	34
Apsley St. G11	J13	34
Aray St. G20	G14	20
Arbroath Av. G52	M10	48
Arcadia St. G40	L18	36
Drake St.		
Arcadia St. G40	L18	36
Arcan Cres. G15	E10	6
Arch St. G31	L19	37
Archerfield Av. G32	N22	54
Archerfield Cres. G32	N22	54
Archerfield Dr. G32	N22	54
Archerfield Gro. G32	N22	54
Archerfield Av.		
Archerhill Av. G13	F 9	18
Archerhill Cotts. G13	F10	18
Archerhill Rd.		
Archerhill Cres. G13	F10	18
Archerhill Gdns. G13	F10	18
Archerhill Rd.		
Archerhill Rd. G13	F10	18
Archerhill Sq. G13	F10	18
Kelso St.		
Archerhill St. G13	F10	18
Archerhill Rd.		
Archerhill Ter. G13	F10	18
Archerhill Rd.		
Ard Pl. G42	O18	52
Ard Rd., Renf.	H 7	17
Ard St. G32	M22	54
Ardargie Dr. G32	O23	55
River Rd.		
Ardargie Pl. G32	O23	55
River Rd.		
Ardbeg Av. G73	Q21	66
Ardbeg Av., Bish.	E20	11
Ardbeg St. G42	N16	51
Ardconnel St. G46	Q12	61
Arden Av. G46	R12	61
Arden Dr., Giff.	R13	62
Arden Pl. G46	R12	61
Stewarton Rd.		
Ardencraig Cres. G44	R17	64
Ardencraig Dr. G45	R18	64
Ardencraig La. G45	R17	64
Ardencraig Rd.		
Ardencraig Quad. G45	R18	64
Ardencraig Rd. G45	R17	64
Ardencraig St. G45	R19	65
Ardencraig Ter. G45	R18	64
Ardenlea Rd., Udd.	O27	57
Ardenlea St. G40	M19	53
Ardery St. G11	J13	34
Apsley St.		
Ardessie Pl. G20	G14	20
Ardessie St. G23	E14	8
Torrin Rd.		
Ardfern St. G32	M22	54
Ardgay Pl. G32	M22	54
Ardgay St. G32	M22	54
Ardgay Way G73	Q19	65
Ardgour Dr., Linw.	L 1	28
Ardgowan Av., Pais.	M 6	46
Ardgowan Dr., Udd.	O27	57
Ardgowan St., Pais.	N 6	46
Ardholm St. G32	L22	38
Ardhu Pl. G15	D 9	6
Ardlamont Sq., Linw.	L 2	28
Ardlaw St. G51	L12	33
Ardle Rd. G43	P15	63
Ardlui St. G32	M21	54
Ardmaleish Cres. G45	R18	64
Ardmaleish Rd. G45	R17	64
Ardmaleish St. G45	R18	64
Ardmaleish Ter. G45	R18	64
Ardmay Cres. G44	O17	52
Ardmillan St. G33	K21	38
Ardmore Oval, Pais.	L 4	29
Ardmore St. G31	K19	37
Ardmory Av. G42	O17	52
Ardmory La. G42	O18	52
Ardnacross Dr. G33	J23	39
Ardnahoe Av. G42	O17	52
Ardnahoe Pl. G42	O17	52
Ardneil Rd. G51	L12	33
Ardnish St. G51	K12	33
Ardo Gdns. G51	L13	34
Ardoch Gro. G72	P21	66
Ardoch Rd., Bear.	C13	8
Ardoch St. G22	H17	22
Ardoch Way, Chr.	E27	15
Braeside Av.		
Ardshiel Rd. G51	K12	33
Ardsloy La. G14	H10	18
Ardsloy Pl.		
Ardsloy Pl. G14	H10	18
Ardtoe Cres. G33	G24	25
Ardtoe Pl. G33	G24	25
Arduthie Rd. G51	K12	33
Ardwell Rd. G52	M12	49
Argosy Way, Renf.	J 8	31
Britannia Way		
Argyle St. G3	J14	34
Argyle St. G3	K15	35
Argyle St., Pais.	M 5	46
Argyll Arc. G2	K16	35
Argyll Av., Renf.	H 7	17
Argyll Av., Bear.	B12	7
Argyll Rd., Clyde.	E 8	5
Arisaig Dr. G52	M12	49
Arisaig Dr., Bear.	D13	8
Arisaig Pl. G52	M12	49
Ark La. G31	K18	36
Arkle Ter. G72	Q21	66
Arkleston Cres., Pais.	K 7	31
Arkleston Rd., Pais.	K 7	31
Arklet Rd. G51	L12	33
Arklie Av., Bear.	B12	7
Tweedsmuir Cres.		
Arlington St. G3	J15	35
Armadale Ct. G31	K19	37
Armadale Path G31	K19	37
Armadale Pl. G31	K19	37
Armadale St. G31	K19	37

Name	Grid	Page
Armour St. G31	L18	36
Armour St., John.	M 1	44
Arngask Rd. G51	K12	33
Arnhall Pl. G52	M12	49
Arnholm Pl. G52	M12	49
Arnisdale Pl. G34	K25	40
Arnisdale Rd. G34	K25	40
Arnisdale Way G73	Q19	65
Shieldaig Dr.		
Arniston St. G32	K21	38
Arnol Pl. G33	K24	39
Arnold Av., Bish.	E19	11
Arnold St. G20	G16	21
Arnott Way G72	P22	66
Arnprior Gdns., Chr.	E27	15
Braeside Av.		
Arnprior Quad. G45	Q17	64
Arnprior Rd. G45	Q17	64
Arnprior St. G45	Q17	64
Arnside Av., Giff.	Q14	62
Arnthern St. G72	P23	67
Arnwood Dr. G12	G13	20
Aron Ter. G72	Q21	66
Aros Dr. G52	N12	49
Arran Dr. G52	M12	49
Arran Dr., Cumb.	D 1	70
Arran Dr., Giff.	R13	62
Arran Dr., John.	N08	43
Arran Dr., Pais.	O 6	46
Arran La., Chr.	E28	15
Burnbrae Av.		
Arran Pl., Clyde.	E 8	5
Arran Pl., Linw.	L 1	28
Arran Rd., Renf.	J 8	31
Arran Ter. G73	P18	64
Arranthrue Cres., Renf.	H 8	17
Arranthrue Dr., Renf.	H 8	17
Arriochmill Rd. G20	H14	20
Kelvin Dr.		
Arrochar Ct. G23	F15	21
Sunningdale Rd.		
Arrochar Dr. G23	E14	8
Arrochar St. G23	F14	20
Arrol Pl. G40	M19	53
Arrol St. G52	K 9	32
Arrowchar Ct. G23	F15	21
Arrowchar St.		
Arrowchar St. G23	F14	20
Arrowsmith Av. G13	F11	19
Arthur Av., Barr.	R 7	59
Arthur Rd., Pais.	O 6	46
Arthur St. G3	J14	34
Arthur St., Pais.	L 5	30
Arthurlie Av., Barr.	R 8	59
Arthurlie Dr., Giff.	R14	62
Arthurlie St. G51	K12	33
Arthurlie St., Barr.	R 8	59
Arundel Dr. G42	O16	51
Arundel Dr., Bish.	D19	11
Asbury Ct., Linw.	L 2	28
Ascaig Cres. G52	N12	49
Ascog Rd., Bear.	E12	7
Ascog St. G42	N16	51
Ascot Av. G12	G12	19
Ascot Ct. G12	G13	20
Ash Gro., Bish.	E19	11
Ash Gro., Lenz.	C22	12
Ash Gro., Udd.	O28	57
Douglas Cres.		
Ash Pl., John.	N 1	44
Ash Rd., Bail.	M25	56
Ash Rd., Cumb.	A 4	71
Ash Rd., Dalm.	C 6	4
Ash Wk. G73	Q20	65
Ashburton Rd. G12	G13	20
Ashby Cres. G13	E12	7
Ashcroft Dr. G44	P18	64
Ashdale Dr. G52	M12	49
Ashdene Rd. G22	F16	21
Ashfield St. G22	H17	22
Ashfield, Bish.	D19	11
Ashgill Pl. G22	G17	22
Ashgill Rd. G22	G16	21
Ashgrove St. G40	N19	53
Ashgrove, Bail.	L27	41
Ashkirk Dr. G52	M12	49
Ashlea Dr., Giff.	Q14	62
Ashley La. G3	J15	35
Woodlands Rd.		
Ashley St. G3	J15	35
Ashmore Rd. G43	P15	63
Ashton Gdns. G12	J14	34
Ashton Rd.		
Ashton La. G12	J14	34
University Av.		
Ashton Pl. G12	H14	20
Byres Rd.		
Ashton Rd. G12	J14	34
University Av.		
Ashton Rd. G73	N19	53
Ashton Ter. G12	J14	34
Ashton Rd.		
Ashton Way G78	O 3	45
Ashtree Rd. G43	O14	50
Ashvale Cres. G21	H18	22
Ashvale Row E. G21	H18	22
Ashvale Row		
Ashvale Row W. G21	H18	22
Ashvale Row		
Aspen Pl., John.	N 1	44
Athelstane Dr., Cumb.	D 1	70
Athelstane Rd. G13	F11	19
Athena Way, Udd.	O28	57
Athol Av. G52	K 9	32
Athol Gdns., Bear.	B12	7
Athol Ter., Udd.	N27	57
Lomond Rd.		
Athole Gdns. G12	H14	20
Athole La. G12	H14	20
Saltoun St.		
Atholl Cres., Pais.	L 9	32
Atholl Dr., Giff.	S14	62
Atholl Gdns. G73	Q21	66
Atholl Gdns., Bish.	D19	11
Atholl Gdns., Chr.	E28	15
Atholl La., Chr.	E28	15
Atholl Pl., Linw.	L 1	28
Atlas Pl. G21	H18	22
Atlas Rd. G21	H18	22
Atlas St., Clyde.	F 7	17
Attlee Av., Clyde.	E 8	5
Attlee Pl., Clyde.	E 8	5
Attlee Av.		
Attow Rd. G43	P13	62
Auburn Dr., Barr.	R 8	59
Auburn Pl. G78	L20	37
Auchans Rd., Linw.	J 1	28
Auchencrow St. G34	K26	40
Auchendale, Lenz.	C24	13
Auchengeich Rd., Chr.	D26	14
Auchengill Path G34	J26	40
Auchengill Rd.		
Auchengill Pl. G34	J26	40
Auchengill Rd. G34	J26	40
Auchenglen Dr., Chr.	E27	15
Auchenlodment Rd., John.	N 1	44
Auchentorlie Quad., Pais.	M 7	47
Auchentorlie St. G11	J12	33
Auchentoshan Av., Clyde.	C 6	4
Auchentoshan Ter. G21	J18	36
Auchentoshen Cotts., Old K.	C 5	4
Auchinairn Rd., Bish.	F18	22
Auchinbee Loop Rd., Cumb.	B 1	70
Auchinlea Rd. G34	J24	39
Auchinleck Av. G33	G21	24
Auchinleck Cres. G33	G21	24
Auchinleck Dr. G33	G21	24
Auchinleck Gdns. G33	G21	24
Auchinleck Rd. G33	F21	24
Auchinleck Rd., Clyde.	B 7	5
Auchinleck Ter., Clyde.	B 7	5
Auchinleck Rd.		
Auchinloch Rd., Lenz.	D23	13
Auchinloch St. G21	H18	22
Auchmannoch Av., Pais.	L 9	32
Auckengreoch Av., John.	O08	43
Auckengreoch Rd., John.	O08	43
Auckland Pl., Dalm.	D 5	4
Auckland St. G22	H16	21
Auld Kirk Rd. G72	Q23	67
Auld Rd., The, Cumb.	B 3	71
Auld St., Dalm.	D 6	4
Auldbar Rd. G52	M12	49
Auldbar Ter., Pais.	N 7	47
Auldburn Rd. G43	P13	62
Auldearn Rd. G21	F20	23
Auldgirth Rd. G52	M12	49
Auldhouse Av. G42	P13	62
Harriet St.		
Auldhouse Rd. G43	P13	62
Auldhouse Ter. G43	P14	62
Auldhouse Rd.		
Aultbea St. G22	F16	21
Aultmore Rd. G33	K24	39
Aurs Cres., Barr.	R 8	59
Aurs Dr., Barr.	R 8	59
Aurs Pl., Barr.	R 8	59
Aurs Rd., Barr.	Q 8	59
Aursbridge Dr., Barr.	R 8	59
Austen La. G13	G12	19
Woodend Dr.		
Austen La. G13	G12	19
Skaterig La.		
Austen Rd. G13	G12	19
Avenel Rd. G13	E12	7
Avenue End Rd. G33	H22	24
Avenue St. G40	L19	37
Avenue St. G73	N19	53
Avenue, The, Kilb.	N07	42
Low Barholm		
Avenuehead Rd., Chr.	D27	15
Avenuehead Rd., Gart.	F28	27
Avenuepark St. G20	H15	21
Aviemore Gdns., Bear.	C13	8
Aviemore Rd. G52	N12	49
Avoch Dr. G46	Q12	61
Avoch St. G34	J25	40
Avon Av., Bear.	D13	8
Avon Dr. G64	F19	23
Avon Dr., Linw.	L 1	28
Avon Rd., Bish.	F19	23
Avon Rd., Giff.	R13	62
Avon St. G5	L15	35
Avonbank Rd. G73	O18	52
Avondale Dr., Pais.	L 7	31
Avondale St. G33	J22	38
Avonhead Av. G67	D 1	70
Avonhead Rd.		
Avonhead Gdns. G67	D 1	70
Avonhead Rd.		
Avonhead Pl. G67	D 1	70
Avonhead Rd.		
Avonhead Rd. G67	D 1	70
Avonspark St. G21	H19	23
Aylmer Rd. G43	P15	63
Ayr Rd., Giff.	R13	62
Ayr St. G21	H18	22
Aytoun Rd. G41	M14	50
Back Causeway G31	L20	37
Back Sneddon St., Pais.	L 6	30
Backmuir Rd. G15	D10	6
Bagnell St. G21	G18	22
Bailie Dr., Bear.	C12	7
Baillieston Rd. G32	M23	55
Baillieston Rd., Udd.	N25	56
Bain Sq. G40	L18	36
Bain St.		
Bain St. G40	L18	36
Bainsford St. G32	L21	38
Baird Av. G52	K 9	32
Baird Dr., Bear.	C11	7
Baird St. G4	J17	36
Bairdsbrae G4	H16	21
Possil Rd.		
Baker Pl. G41	N15	51
Baker St.		
Baker St. G41	N15	51
Bakewell Rd., Bail.	L25	40
Balaclava St. G2	L16	35
McAlpine St.		
Balado Rd. G33	K24	39
Balbeg St. G51	L12	33
Balbeggie Pl. G32	M23	55
Balbeggie St. G32	M23	55
Balblair Rd. G52	N12	49
Balcaldine Av., Chr.	E25	14
Balcarres Av. G12	G14	20
Balcomie St. G33	J22	38
Baldinnie Rd. G34	K25	40
Baldorran Cres., Cumb.	B 1	70
Baldovan Cres. G33	K24	39
Baldovie Rd. G52	M11	49
Baldragon Rd. G34	J25	40
Baldric Rd. G13	G11	19
Baldwin Av. G13	E11	7
Balerno Dr. G52	M12	49
Balfluig St. G34	J24	39

Name	Grid	Pg
Balfour St. G20	G14	20
Balfron Rd. G51	K12	33
Balfron Rd., Pais.	L 8	31
Balgair Dr., Pais.	L 7	31
Balgair St. G22	G16	21
Balgair Ter. G32	L22	38
Balglass St. G22	H16	21
Balgonie Av. G78	N 4	45
Balgonie Av., Pais.	N 4	46
Balgonie Dr., Pais.	N 5	46
Balgonie Rd. G52	M12	49
Balgonie Woods, Pais.	N 5	46
Balgownie Cres., Thorn.	R13	62
Balgray Cres., Barr.	R 9	60
Balgraybank St. G21	H19	23
Balgrayhill Rd. G21	G18	22
Balintore St. G32	L22	38
Baliol La. G3	J15	35
Woodlands Rd.		
Baliol St. G3	J15	35
Ballaig Av., Bear.	C11	7
Ballaig Cres. G33	G23	25
Ballantay Quad. G45	Q19	65
Ballantay Rd. G45	Q19	65
Ballantay Ter. G45	Q19	65
Ballantyne Rd. G52	K10	32
Ballater Dr., Bear.	E12	7
Ballater Dr., Pais.	N 7	47
Ballater Dr., Renf.	Γ 5	16
Ballater St. G5	L17	36
Ballayne Dr., Chr.	E28	15
Ballindalloch Dr. G31	K19	37
Balloch Gdns. G52	M12	49
Balloch Vw., Cumb.	C 2	70
Ballochmill Rd. G73	O20	53
Ballogie Rd. G44	O16	51
Balmarino Pl. G64	E20	11
Balmartin Rd. G23	E14	8
Balmeg Av., Giff.	S14	62
Balmerino Pl., Bish.	F20	23
Angus Av.		
Balmoral Cres. G42	N16	51
Queens Dr.		
Balmoral Cres., Renf.	G 6	16
Balmoral Dr. G32	O22	54
Balmoral Dr., Bear.	E13	8
Balmoral Dr., G72	P21	66
Balmoral Gdns., Blan.	R26	68
Balmoral Gdns., Udd.	N27	57
Kilmuir Rd.		
Balmoral Rd., John.	N 1	44
Balmoral St. G14	H10	18
Balmore Pl.	G16	21
Balmore Rd.		
Balmore Rd. G23	C15	9
Balmore Sq. G22	G16	21
Balmuildy Rd., Bish.	D16	9
G23		
Balornock Rd. G21	G19	23
Balruddery Pl. G64	F20	23
Balshagray Av. G11	H12	19
Balshagray Cres. G11	J12	19
Balshagray Pl. G11	H12	19
Balshagray Dr.		
Baltic Ct. G40	M19	53
Baltic St.		
Baltic La. G40	M19	53
Baltic Pl. G40	M18	52
Baltic St. G40	M19	53
Balure St. G31	K20	37
Balvaird Cres. G73	O19	53
Balvaird Dr. G73	O19	53
Balveny St. G33	J23	39
Balvicar Dr. G42	N15	51
Balvicar St. G42	N15	51
Balvie Av. G15	E10	6
Balvie Av., Giff.	R14	62
Banavie Rd. G11	H13	20
Banchory Av. G43	P13	62
Banchory Av., Renf.	F 5	16
Banchory Cres., Bear.	E13	8
Banff St. G33	J22	38
Bangorshill St. G46	Q12	61
Bank Rd. G32	O23	55
Bank St. G12	J15	35
Bank St. G72	P22	66
Bank St., Barr.	R 8	59
Bank St., Pais.	M 6	30
Bankbrae Av. G53	P10	60
Bankend St. G33	J22	38
Bankfoot Dr. G52	M10	48
Bankfoot Rd. G52	M10	48
Bankfoot Rd., Pais.	L 4	29
Bankglen Rd. G15	D10	6
Bankhall St. G42	N16	51
Bankhead Av. G13	G10	18
Bankhead Dr. G73	O19	53
Bankhead Rd. G73	P18	64
Bankhead Rd.,	B25	14
Waterside		
Bankier St. G40	L18	36
Banknock St. G32	L21	38
Bankside Av., John.	M09	43
Banling Green Rd. G44	P16	63
Clarkston Rd.		
Bannatyne Av. G31	K19	37
Banner Dr. G13	E11	7
Banner Rd. G13	E11	7
Bannercross Av., Bail.	L25	40
Bannercross Dr., Bail.	L23	40
Bannercross Gdns., Bail.	L25	40
Bannercross Dr.		
Bannerman Pl., Clyde.	E 8	5
Bannerman St., Clyde.	E 7	5
Bantaskin St. G20	F14	20
Banton Pl. G33	K25	40
Barassie Ct., Both.	R27	69
Barbae Pl., Udd.	Q28	69
Hume Dr.		
Barbreck Rd. G42	N15	51
Pollokshaws Rd.		
Barcaple St. G21	H18	22
Barclay Av., John.	N 1	44
Barclay Sq., Renf.	J 7	31
Barclay St. G21	G18	22
Balgrayhill Rd.		
Barcraigs Dr., Pais.	O 6	46
Bard Av. G13	F10	18
Bardowie St. G22	H16	21
Bardrain Av., John.	N 2	44
Bardrain Rd., Pais.	O 5	46
Bardrill Dr., Bish.	E18	10
Bardykes Rd., Blan.	R26	68
Barfillan Dr. G52	L12	33
Barfillan Rd. G52	L12	33
Bargaran Rd. G53	M10	48
Bargarron Dr., Pais.	K 7	31
Bargeddie St. G33	J20	37
Barhill Cres., Kilb.	N07	42
Barholm Sq. G33	J23	39
Barke Rd., Cumb.	B 3	71
Barlanark Av. G32	K23	39
Barlanark Pl. G32	L23	39
Hallhill Rd.		
Barlanark Pl. G33	K24	39
Barlanark Rd. G33	K23	39
Barlia Dr. G45	Q18	64
Barlia St. G45	Q18	64
Barlia Ter. G45	Q18	64
Barloch St. G22	H17	22
Barlogan Av. G52	L12	33
Barlogan Quad. G52	L12	33
Barmill Rd. G43	P13	62
Barmulloch Rd. G21	H19	23
Barn Grn. G78	M07	42
Barnard Gdns., Bish.	D19	11
Barnard Ter. G40	M19	53
Barnbeth Rd. G53	N10	48
Barnes Rd. G20	G16	21
Barnes St., Barr.	R 7	59
Barnflat St. G73	N19	53
Barnkirk Av. G15	D10	6
Barns St., Clyde.	E 8	5
Barnsford Av., Renf.	H 4	16
Barnsford Rd., Pais.	J 4	29
Barnton St. G32	K21	38
Barnwell Ter. G51	K12	33
Barochan Rd. G53	M10	48
Baron Rd., Pais.	L 7	31
Baron St., Renf.	J 8	31
Baronald Dr. G12	G13	20
Baronald Gate G12	G13	20
Baronald St. G73	N19	53
Baronhill, Cumb.	A 3	71
Barons Court Rd., John.	M 3	45
Barr Cres., Clyde.	C 7	5
Barr Pl., Pais.	M 5	46
Barr St. G20	H16	21
Barra Av., Renf.	J 8	31
Barra St. G20	F14	20
Barrachnie Cres., Bail.	L24	39
Barrachnie Rd., Bail.	L24	39
Barrack St. G4	L18	36
Barrhead Rd. G43	O 9	48
Barrhead Rd., Pais.	M 7	47
Barrie Quad., Clyde.	D 7	5
Barrie Rd. G52	K10	32
Barrington Dr. G4	J15	35
Barrisdale Rd. G20	F14	20
Barrisdale Way G73	Q19	65
Barrland Dr., Giff.	Q14	62
Barrland St. G41	M16	51
Barrochan Cres., Pais.	M 4	45
Barrochan Rd., John.	M09	43
Barrowfield St. G40	L19	37
Barrwood St. G33	J21	38
Barshaw Dr., Pais.	L 7	31
Barshaw Pl., Pais.	L 8	31
Barshaw Rd. G52	L 9	32
Barterholm Rd., Pais.	N 6	46
Bartholomew St. G40	M19	53
Bartiebeith Rd. G33	K24	39
Basset Av. G13	F10	18
Basset Cres. G13	F10	18
Bath La. G2	K16	35
Blythswood St.		
Bath La. W. G3	K15	35
North St.		
Bath St. G2	K16	35
Bathgate St. G31	L19	37
Bathgo Av., Pais.	M 9	48
Batson St. G42	N16	51
Battle Pl. G41	O15	51
Battleburn St. G32	M22	54
Battlefield Av. G42	O16	51
Battlefield Cres. G42	O16	51
Battlefield Gdns.		
Battlefield Gdns. G42	O16	51
Battlefield Rd. G42	O16	51
Bavelaw St. G33	J23	39
Bayfield Av. G15	D10	6
Bayfield Ter. G15	D10	6
Beaconsfield Rd. G12	G13	20
Beafort Av. G43	P14	62
Beard Cres., Gart.	G27	27
Beardmore Cotts., Renf.	G 6	16
Beardmore St., Dalm.	D 5	4
Beardmore Way, Dalm.	D 5	4
Bearford Dr. G52	L10	32
Bearsden Rd., Bear.	E12	7
& G13		
Beaton Rd. G41	N15	51
Beattock St. G31	L20	37
Beatty St., Dalm.	D 4	4
Beaufort Gdns., Bish.	E18	10
Beauly Dr., Pais.	N 3	45
Beauly Pl. G20	G14	20
Beauly Pl., Bish.	E20	11
Beauly Pl., Chr.	E26	14
Beauly Rd., Bail.	M25	56
Beaumont Gate G12	J14	34
Bedale Rd., Bail.	M24	55
Bedford Av., Clyde.	E 8	5
Onslow Rd.		
Bedford La. G5	L16	35
Bedford Row G5	L16	35
Dunmore St.		
Bedford St. G5	L16	35
Bedlay Ct., Chr.	D28	15
Bedlay St. G21	H18	22
Petershill Rd.		
Bedlay St. G21	H18	22
Linsburn St.		
Bedlay Wk., Chr.	D28	15
Beech Av. G41	M13	50
Beech Av. G72	P21	66
Beech Av. G73	Q20	65
Beech Av., Bail.	L25	40
Beech Av., Bear.	C13	8
Beech Av., John.	N 2	44
Beech Av., Pais.	N 7	47
Beech Av. North Av.	P21	66
G72		
Beech Dr., Dalm.	C 7	5
Beech Gdns., Bail.	L25	40
Beech Gro., Barr.	R 8	59
Arthurlie Av.		
Beech Pl., Bish.	F19	23
Beech Rd., Bish.	F19	23
Beech Rd., John.	N08	43
Beech Rd., Lenz.	C23	13
Beechcroft Pl., Blan.	R27	69
Beeches Av., Clyde.	C 6	4
Beeches Rd., Clyde.	C 6	4
Beeches Ter., Clyde.	C 7	4
Beechgrove St. G40	N19	53

Beechlands Av., Giff.	R15	63
Beechmount Cotts. G14	G 9	18
Dumbarton Rd,		
Beechmount Rd., Lenz.	D23	13
Beechwood Av. G11	H12	19
Beechwood Dr.		
Beechwood Av. G73	P20	65
Beechwood Ct., Bear.	D12	7
Beechwood Dr. G11	H12	19
Beechwood Dr., Renf.	J 7	31
Beechwood La., Bear.	D12	7
Beechwood Ct.		
Beechwood Pl. G11	H12	19
Beechwood Dr.		
Beechwood Rd., Cumb.	C 2	70
Beil Dr. G13	F 9	18
Beith Rd., John.	O07	42
Beith St. G11	J13	34
Belgrave La. G12	H15	21
Belgrave Ter.		
Belgrave Ter. G12	H15	21
Belhaven Cres. La. G12	H14	20
Lorraine Rd.		
Belhaven Ter. G12	H14	20
Belhaven Ter. W. G12	H14	20
Bell St. G1	L17	36
Bell St., Clyde.	F 8	17
Bell St., Renf.	H 8	17
Bellahouston Dr. G52	M12	49
Bellahouston La. G52	M12	49
Bellairs Pl., Blan.	R26	68
Belleisle Av., Udd.	O27	57
Belleisle St. G42	N16	51
Bellevue Pl. G21	J18	36
Bellfield Cres., Barr.	Q 7	59
Bellfield St. G31	L19	37
Bellfield St., Barr.	Q 7	59
Bellgrove St. G31	L18	36
Bellrock Cres. G33	K22	38
Bellrock St. G33	K22	38
Bellscroft Av. G73	O18	52
Bellshaugh La. G12	G14	20
Bellshaugh Pl. G12	G14	20
Bellshaugh Rd. G12	G14	20
Bellshill Rd., Both.	R28	69
Bellshill Rd., Udd.	P27	69
Belltrees Cres., Pais.	M 4	45
Bellwood St. G41	O15	51
Belmar Ct., Linw.	L 2	28
Belmont Av., Udd.	O27	57
Belmont Cres. G12	H15	21
Belmont Dr. G73	O19	53
Belmont Dr., Barr.	R 8	59
Belmont Dr., Giff.	Q13	62
Belmont La. G12	H14	20
Great Western Rd.		
Belmont Rd. G21	G18	22
Belmont Rd. G72	Q21	66
Belmont Rd., Pais.	L 7	31
Belmont St. G12	H15	21
Belmont St., Clyde.	F 7	17
Belses Dr. G52	L11	33
Belstane Pl., Udd.	Q28	69
Appledore Cres.		
Belsyde Av. G15	E10	6
Beltane St. G3	K15	35
Beltrees Av. G53	N10	48
Beltrees Cres. G53	N10	48
Beltrees Rd. G53	N10	48
Belvidere Cres., Bish.	D19	11
Belvoir Pl., Bish.	S26	68
Bemersyde Av. G43	P13	62
Bemersyde Rd. G78	O 3	45
Bemersyde, Bish.	E20	11
Ben Alder Dr., Pais.	N 8	47
Ben Buie Way, Pais.	N 8	47
Ben Ledi Av., Pais.	N 8	47
Ben Nevis Rd., Pais.	N 8	47
Ben Venue Way, Pais.	N 8	47
Benalder St. G11	J14	34
Benarty Gdns., Bish.	E19	11
Bencroft Dr. G44	P18	64
Bengairn St. G31	K20	37
Bengal Pl. G43	O14	50
Christian St.		
Bengal St. G43	O14	50
Benhar Pl. G33	K21	38
Benholme St. G32	M21	54
Benhope Av., Pais.	N 8	47
Benlawers Dr., Pais.	N 8	47
Benloyal Av., Pais.	N 8	47
Benlut Dr., Pais.	N 8	47
Benmore Dr., Pais.	N 8	47
Benmore St. G21	G18	22
Bennan Sq. G42	N17	52
Benston Pl., John.	N09	43
Benston Rd., John.	N09	43
Bentall St. G5	M17	52
Bentinck St. G3	J15	35
Bents Rd., Bail.	L25	40
Benvane Av., Pais.	N 8	47
Benvie Gdns., Bish.	E19	11
Benview St. G20	H15	21
Benview Ter., Pais.	N 7	47
Benwyvis Dr., Pais.	N 8	47
Berelands Cres. G73	O18	52
Berelands Pl.		
Berelands Pl. G73	O18	52
Beresford Av. G14	H12	19
Berkeley St. G3	K15	35
Berkeley Terrace La. G3	J15	35
Elderslie St.		
Berkley Dr., Blan.	R26	68
Bernard Path G40	M19	53
Bernard St. G40	M19	53
Bernard Ter. G40	M19	53
Berneray St. G22	F17	22
Berridale Av. G44	P16	63
Berriedale Av., Bail.	M25	56
Berryburn Rd. G21	H20	23
Berryhill Dr., Giff.	R13	62
Berryhill Rd., Cumb.	C 2	70
Berryhill Rd., Giff.	R13	62
Berryknowes Av. G52	L11	33
Berryknowes La. G52	L11	33
Berryknowes Rd. G52	M11	49
Berryknowes Rd., Chr.	F26	26
Bertram St. G41	N15	51
Bertrohill Ter. G33	K23	39
Stepps Rd.		
Bervie St. G51	L12	33
Berwick Cres., Linw.	K 1	28
Berwick Dr. G52	M10	48
Berwick Dr. G73	O20	53
Betula Dr., Dalm.	C 7	5
Bevan Gro., John.	O08	43
Beverley Rd. G43	P14	62
Bevin.Av., Clyde.	E 8	5
Bideford Cres. G32	M23	55
Biggar Pl. G31	L19	37
Biggar St. G31	L19	37
Bigton St. G33	J22	38
Bilbao St. G45	M17	52
Bilsland Dr. G20	G15	21
Binend Rd. G53	O11	49
Binnie Pl. G40	L18	36
Binniehill Rd., Cumb.	B 1	70
Binns Rd. G33	J23	39
Birch Cres., John.	N 1	44
Birch Dr., Lenz.	C23	13
Birch Gro., Udd.	O28	57
Burnhead St.		
Birch Knowle, Bish.	F19	23
Birch Rd., Dalm.	C 7	5
Birchfield Dr. G14	H10	18
Birchlea Dr., Giff.	Q14	62
Birchwood Av. G32	M24	55
Birchwood Dr., Pais.	N 4	45
Birchwood Pl. G32	M24	55
Birdston Rd. G21	G20	23
Birgidale Av. G45	R17	64
Birgidale Rd. G45	R17	64
Birgidale Ter. G45	R17	64
Birkdale Ct., Both.	R27	69
Birken Rd., Lenz.	D24	13
Birkenshaw St. G31	K19	37
Birkenshaw Way, Pais.	K 6	30
Abbotsburn Way		
Birkhall Av. G52	M 9	48
Birkhall Av., Renf.	F 5	16
Birkhall Dr., Bear.	E12	7
Birkhill Av., Bish.	D19	11
Birkhill Gdns., Bish.	D20	11
Birkmyre Rd. G51	L12	33
Birks Rd., Renf.	J 7	31
Tower Dr.		
Birkwood St. G40	N19	53
Birmingham Rd., Renf.	J 7	31
Birnam Av., Bish.	D19	11
Birnam Cres., Bear.	C13	8
Birnam Gdns., Bish.	E19	11
Birnam Rd. G31	M20	53
Birness St. G43	O14	50
Tracy St.		
Birnie Ct. G21	H20	23
Birnie Rd. G21	H20	23
Birnock Av., Renf.	J 9	32
Birsay Rd. G22	F16	21
Bishop Gdns., Bish.	E18	10
Bishopmill Pl. G21	H20	23
Bishopmill Rd. G21	H20	23
Bisset Cres., Clyde.	C 6	4
Black St. G4	J17	36
Blackburn Sq., Barr.	R 8	59
Blackburn St. G51	L14	34
Blackburn St. G51	L15	35
Blackbyres Rd., Barr.	P 8	59
Blackcraig Av. G15	D10	6
Blackcroft Gdns. G32	M23	55
Blackcroft Rd. G32	M23	55
Blackfaulds Rd. G73	O18	52
Blackford Cres. G32	M23	55
Blackford Pl. G32	M23	55
Blackford Rd., Pais.	M 7	47
Blackfriars St. G1	K17	36
Blackhall La., Pais.	M 6	46
Blackhall St., Pais.	M 6	46
Blackhill Cotts. G23	E16	9
Blackhill Pl. G33	J20	37
Blackhill Rd. G23	E14	8
Blackie St. G3	J14	34
Blacklands Pl., Lenz.	D24	13
Blacklaw La., Pais.	L 6	30
Blackstone Av. G53	O11	49
Blackstone Cres. G53	N11	49
Blackstone Rd., Candren	K 3	29
Blackstoun Av., Linw.	L 1	28
Blackstoun Oval, Pais.	L 4	29
Blackstoun Rd., Pais.	L 4	29
Blackthorn Av., Lenz.	C22	12
Blackthorn Gro., Lenz.	C22	12
Blackthorn Rd., Cumb.	B 4	71
Blackthorn St. G22	G18	22
Blackwood Av., Linw.	L 1	28
Blackwood St. G13	F12	19
Blackwood St., Barr.	R 7	59
Blackwoods Cres., Chr.	E27	15
Blacurvie Rd. G34	J25	40
Bladda La., Pais.	M 6	46
Blades Ct., Gart.	G28	27
Bladnoch Dr. G15	E11	7
Moraine Av.		
Blaeloch Av. G45	R17	64
Blaeloch Dr. G45	R17	64
Blaeloch Ter. G45	R17	64
Blair Cres., Bail.	M25	56
Blair Rd., Pais.	L 9	32
Blair St. G32	L21	38
Blairatholl Av. G11	H13	20
Blairatholl Gdns. G11	H13	20
Blairbeth Dr. G44	O16	51
Blairbeth Rd. G73	P19	65
Blairbeth Ter. G73	Q19	65
Blairdardie Rd. G15	E10	6
Blairdenan Av., Chr.	D28	15
Blairgowrie Rd. G52	M11	49
Blairhall Av. G41	O15	51
Blairhill Av., Chr. &	C25	14
Waterside		
Blairlogie St. G33	J22	38
Blairston Av., Both.	R28	69
Blairston Gdns., Both.	R28	69
Blairston Av.		
Blairtum Dr. G73	P19	65
Blairtummock Rd. G32	K23	39
Blake Rd., Cumb.	C 3	71
Blane St. G4	J17	36
Blantyre Cres., Clyde.	B 6	4
Blantyre Farm Rd.,	R26	68
Blan. & Udd.		
Blantyre Mill Rd., Both.	R27	69
Blantyre Rd., Both.	R28	69
Blantyre St. G3	J14	34
Blaven Ct., Bail.	M26	56
Bracadale Rd.		
Blawarthill St. G14	G 9	18
Blesdale Ct., Clyde.	E 7	5
Blenheim Av. G33	G23	25
Blenheim Ct. G33	G24	25
Blenheim Av.		
Blenheim La. G33	G24	25
Blochairn Rd. G21	J19	37
Bluevale St. G31	L19	37
Blyth Pl. G32	L23	39
Blyth Rd., G33	L24	39
Blythswood Av., Renf.	H 8	17

Blythswood Dr., Pais.	L 6	30
Blythswood Rd., Renf.	G 8	17
Blythswood Sq. G2	K16	35
Blythswood St. G2	K16	35
Boclair Av., Bear.	D12	7
Boclair Cres., Bear.	D13	8
Boclair Cres., Bish.	E19	11
Boclair Rd., Bear.	D13	8
Boclair Rd., Bish.	E19	11
Boclair St. G13	F12	19
Boden St. G40	M19	53
Bodmin Gdns., Chr.	D27	15
Gartferry Rd.		
Bogany Ter. G45	R18	64
Bogbain Rd. G34	K25	40
Boghall Pl., Udd.	N25	56
Boghall Rd., Udd.	N25	56
Boghall St. G33	J22	38
Boghead Rd. G21	H19	23
Boghead Rd., Lenz.	D22	12
Bogleshole Rd. G72	O21	54
Bogmoor Rd. G51	K11	33
Bogside Pl., Bail.	K26	40
Whamflet Av.		
Bogside Rd. G33	G22	24
Bogside St. G40	M19	53
Bogton Av. G44	Q15	63
Bogton Avenue La.	Q15	63
G44		
Bogton Av.		
Boleyn Rd. G41	N15	51
Bolivar Ter. G42	O17	52
Bolton Dr. G42	O16	51
Bon Accord St., Clyde.	F 7	17
Bonawe St. G20	H15	21
Kirkland St.		
Boness St. G40	M19	53
Bonhill St. G22	H16	21
Bonmore Gdns., Udd.	O27	57
Bonnar St. G40	M19	53
Bonnaughton Rd., Bear.	C10	6
Bonnyholm Av. G53	M10	48
Bonnyrigg Dr. G43	P13	62
Bonyton Av. G13	G 9	18
Boon Dr. G15	E10	6
Boquhanran Pl., Clyde.	D 7	5
Albert Rd.		
Boquhanran Rd., Clyde	E 6	4
Borden La. G13	G12	19
Borden Rd.		
Borden Rd. G13	G12	19
Boreland Dr. G13	F10	18
Boreland Pl. G13	G10	18
Borgie Cres. G72	P22	66
Borland Rd., Bear.	D13	8
Borron St. G4	H17	22
Borthwick St. G33	J22	38
Boswell Sq. G52	K 9	32
Botanic Cres. G20	H14	20
Bothlyn Cres., Gart.	F27	27
Bothlynn Dr. G33	G23	25
Bothlynn Rd., Chr.	F26	26
Bothwell La. G2	K16	35
West Campbell St.		
Bothwell Park Rd. G71	R28	69
Bothwell Rd., Udd. &	P27	69
Both.		
Bothwell St. G2	K16	35
Bothwell St. G72	P21	66
Bothwell Ter. G12	J15	35
Bank St.		
Bothwick Way, Pais.	O 3	45
Crosbie Dr.		
Boundary Rd. G73	N18	52
Bourne Cres., Renf.	F 5	16
Bourne Ct., Renf.	F 5	16
Bourtree Dr. G73	Q20	65
Bouverie St. G14	G 9	18
Bouverie St. G73	O18	52
Bowden Dr. G52	L10	32
Bower St. G12	H15	21
Bowerwalls St., Barr.	Q 9	60
Bowes Cres., Bail.	M24	55
Bowfield Av. G52	L 9	32
Bowfield Cres.		
Bowfield Cres. G52	L 9	32
Bowfield Dr. G52	L 9	32
Bowfield Pl. G52	L 9	32
Gleddoch Rd.		
Bowfield Ter. G52	L 9	32
Bowfield Cres.		
Bowhouse Way G73	Q19	65
Bowling Green La. G14	H11	19
Westland Dr.		
Bowling Green Rd. G14	H11	19
Bowling Green Rd. G32	M23	55
Bowman St. G42	N16	51
Bowmont Gdns. G12	H14	20
Bowmont Hill, Bish.	D19	11
Bowmont Ter. G12	H14	20
Bowmore Gdns. G73	Q21	66
Bowmore Rd. G52	L12	33
Boyd St. G42	N16	51
Boydstone Pl. G46	P12	61
Boydstone Rd. G43	P12	61
Boyle St., Clyde.	F 8	17
Boyleston Rd., Barr.	Q 7	59
Boyndie Path G34	K25	40
Boyndie St. G34	K25	40
Brabloch Cres., Pais.	L 6	30
Bracadale Dr., Bail.	M26	56
Bracadale Gdns., Bail.	M26	56
Bracadale Rd., Bail.	M26	56
Bracken Rd., Barr.	P 7	59
Bracken St. G22	G16	21
Bracken Ter., Udd.	Q28	69
Brackenbrae Av., Bish.	E18	10
Brackenbrae Rd., Bish.	E18	10
Brackenrig Rd. G46	R12	61
Bracla Av. G13	F 9	18
Bracora Pl. G20	G14	20
Glenfinnan Dr.		
Bradan Av. G13	F 9	18
Bradda Av. G73	Q20	65
Bradfield Av. G12	G14	20
Brae Av., Clyde.	B 7	5
Brae Cres., Clyde.	B 7	5
Braeface Rd., Cumb.	C 2	70
Braefield Dr., Thorn.	Q13	62
Braefoot Cres., Pais.	O 6	46
Braehead Rd., Clyde.	B 7	5
Braehead Rd., Cumb.	B 3	71
Braehead Rd., Pais.	P 5	58
Braehead St. G5	M17	52
Braemar Av., Dalm.	D 6	4
Braemar Cres., Bear.	E12	7
Braemar Dr., John.	N 1	44
Braemar Rd. G73	Q21	66
Braemar Rd., Renf.	G 5	16
Braemar St., G42	O15	51
Braemar Vw., Dalm.	C 6	4
Braemount Av., Pais.	P 5	58
Braes Av., Clyde.	F 8	17
Braeside Av. G73	O20	53
Braeside Av., Chr.	E27	15
Braeside Cres., Bail.	L27	41
Braeside Cres., Barr.	R 9	60
Braeside Dr., Barr.	R 8	59
Braeside Pl. G72	Q22	66
Braeside St. G20	H15	21
Braid Sq. G4	J16	35
Braid St. G4	J16	35
Braidbar Farm Rd., Giff.	Q14	62
Braidbar Rd., Giff.	Q14	62
Braidcraft Rd. G53	N11	49
Braidfauld Gdns. G32	M21	54
Braidfauld Pl. G32	N21	54
Braidfauld St. G32	N21	54
Braidfield Rd., Clyde.	C 7	5
Braidholm Cres., Giff.	Q14	62
Braidholm Rd., Giff.	Q14	62
Braids Rd., Pais.	N 6	46
Bramley Pl., Lenz.	D24	13
Branchock Av. G72	Q23	67
Brand St. G51	L14	34
Brandon Gdns. G72	P21	66
Brandon St. G31	L18	36
Branscroft G78	M07	42
Brassey St. G20	G15	21
Breadalbane Gdns. G73	Q20	65
Breadalbane St. G3	K15	35
Brech Av., Bail.	L27	41
Brechin Rd., Bish.	E20	11
Brechin St. G3	K15	35
Breck Av. G78	O 2	44
Brediland Rd., Linw.	L 1	28
Brediland Rd., Pais.	N 3	45
Bredisholm Dr., Bail.	M26	56
Bredisholm Rd., Bail.	M27	57
Bredisholm Ter., Bail.	M26	56
Brenfield Av. G44	Q15	63
Brenfield Dr. G44	Q15	63
Brentwood Av. G53	Q10	60
Brentwood Dr. G53	Q10	60
Brentwood Sq. G53	Q10	60
Brentwood Dr.		
Brentwood Sq. G53	Q10	60
Brereton St. G42	N17	52
Bressey Rd. G33	L24	39
Breval Cres., Clyde.	B 7	5
Brewery St., John.	M09	43
Brewster Av., Pais.	K 7	31
Briar Dr., Clyde.	D 7	5
Briar Neuk, Bish.	F19	23
Briar Rd. G43	P14	62
Briarlea Dr., Giff.	Q14	62
Brick La., Pais.	L 6	30
Bridge of Weir Rd.	L08	43
Kilb. & Linw.		
Bridge St., Dalm.	D 6	4
Bridge St., G72	P22	66
Bridge St., Linw.	L 2	28
Bridge St., Pais.	M 6	46
Bridgebar St., Barr.	Q 9	60
Bridgeburn Dr., Chr.	E27	15
Bridgegate G1	L17	36
Bridgend Rd. G53	O11	49
Bridgeton Cross G40	L18	36
Brigham Pl. G23	F15	21
Broughton Rd.		
Brighton Pl. G51	L13	34
Brighton St. G51	L13	34
Brightside Av., Udd.	P28	69
Brisbane St. G42	O16	51
Brisbane St., Dalm.	D 5	4
Britannia Way, Clyde.	E 7	5
Britannia Way, Renf.	J 8	31
Briton St. G51	L13	34
Broad Pl. G40	L18	36
Broad St.		
Broad St. G40	L18	36
Broadford St. G4	J17	36
Harvey St.		
Broadholm St. G22	G16	21
Broadleys Av., Bish.	D18	10
Broadlie Dr. G13	G10	18
Broadloan, Renf.	J 8	31
Broadwood Dr. G44	P16	63
Brock Oval G53	P11	61
Brock Pl. G53	O11	49
Brock Rd. G53	O11	49
Brock Ter. G53	P11	61
Brock Way G67	C 3	71
North Carbrain Rd.		
Brockburn Rd. G53	N10	48
Brockburn Ter. G53	O11	49
Brockville St. G32	L21	38
Brodick Sq. G64	F19	23
Brodick St. G21	J19	37
Brodie Park Av., Pais.	N 6	46
Brodie Pl., Renf.	J 7	31
Brodie Rd. G21	F20	23
Brogknowe, Udd.	O26	56
Glasgow Rd.		
Brook St. G40	L18	36
Brooklands Av., Udd.	O27	57
Brooklea Dr., Giff.	P14	62
Brookside St. G40	L19	37
Broom Cres., Barr.	P 7	59
Broom Dr., Clyde.	D 7	5
Broom Gdns., Lenz.	C22	12
Broom Rd. G43	P14	62
Broom Rd. G67	A 4	71
Broom Ter., John.	N 1	44
Broomdyke Way, Pais.	K 5	30
Broomfield Av. G21	H19	23
Broomfield Rd.		
Broomfield Av. G72	O20	53
Broomfield Pl. G21	G18	22
Broomfield Rd.		
Broomfield Rd. G21	G18	22
Broomfield Ter., Udd.	N27	57
Broomhill Av. G32	O22	54
Broomhill Cres. G11	H12	19
Broomhill Dr. G11	H12	19
Broomhill Dr. G73	P19	65
Broomhill Gdns. G11	H12	19
Broomhill La. G11	H12	19
Broomhill Path G11	J12	33
Broomhill Pl. G11	H12	19
Broomhill Dr.		
Broomhill Rd. G11	J12	33
Broomhill Ter. G11	J12	33
Broomieknowe Dr. G73	P19	65
Broomieknowe Rd. G73	P19	65
Broomielaw G1	L16	35

Name	Grid	Pg
Broomknowe Pl. G66	D24	13
Broomknowe, Cumb.	B 1	70
Logan Dr.		
Broomknowes Rd. G21	H19	23
Broomlands Rd., Cumb.	D 3	71
Broomlands St., Pais.	M 5	46
Broomlea Cres., Renf.	F 5	16
Broomley Dr. G46	R14	62
Broomley La., Giff.	R14	62
Broomloan Ct. G51	L13	34
Broomloan Pl. G51	L13	34
Broomloan Rd. G51	L13	34
Broompark Circus G31	K18	36
Broompark Dr. G31	K18	36
Broompark Dr., Renf.	F 5	16
Broompark St. G31	K18	36
Broomton Rd. G21	F20	23
Broomward Dr., John.	M 1	44
Brora Dr., Bear.	D13	8
Brora Dr., Giff.	R14	62
Brora Dr., Renf.	H 9	18
Brora Gdns., Bish.	E19	11
Brora La. G31	J20	37
Brora St.		
Brora Rd., Bish.	E19	11
Brora St. G33	J20	37
Broughton Dr. G23	F15	21
Broughton Rd. G23	F15	21
Brown Av., Clyde.	F 8	17
Brown Rd., Cumb.	C 2	70
Brown St. G2	K16	35
Brown St., Pais.	L 5	30
Brown St., Renf.	J 7	31
Brownhill Rd. G43	Q13	62
Brownlie St. G42	O16	51
Browns La., Pais.	M 6	46
Brownsdale Rd. G73	O18	52
Brownside Av. G72	P21	66
Brownside Av., Barr.	P 7	59
Brownside Av., Pais.	O 5	46
Brownside Cres., Barr.	P 7	59
Brownside Dr. G13	G 9	18
Brownside Dr., Barr.	P 7	59
Brownside Gro., Barr.	P 7	59
Brownside Rd. G72	P20	65
& G73		
Bruce Av., John.	O09	43
Bruce Av., Pais.	K 7	31
Bruce Rd. G41	M15	51
Bruce Rd., Pais.	L 7	31
Bruce Rd., Renf.	J 7	31
Bruce St., Clyde.	E 7	5
Bruce Ter., Blan.	R27	69
Brucefield Pl. G34	K26	40
Brunstance Rd. G34	J25	40
Brunswick Ho., Dalm.	C 5	4
Perth Cres.		
Brunswick St. G1	K17	36
Brunton St. G44	P16	63
Brunton Ter. G44	Q15	63
Bruntsfield Av. G53	Q10	48
Bruntsfield Gdns. G53	Q10	60
Brydson Pl., Linw.	L 1	28
Fulwood Av.		
Buccleuch Av. G52	K 9	32
Buccleuch La. G3	J16	35
Scott St.		
Buccleuch St. G3	J16	35
Buchan St. G5	L16	35
Norfolk St.		
Buchan Ter., G72	Q21	66
Buchanan Cres. G64	F20	23
Buchanan Dr. G64	F20	23
Buchanan Dr. G72	P21	66
Buchanan Dr. G73	P19	65
Buchanan Dr., Bear.	D13	8
Buchanan Dr., Bish.	F20	23
Buchanan Dr., Lenz.	D23	13
Buchanan St. G1	K16	35
Buchanan St., Bail.	M25	56
Buchanan St., John.	N09	43
Buchlyvie Path G34	K25	40
Buchlyvie Rd., Pais.	L 9	32
Buchlyvie St. G34	K25	40
Buckingham Bldgs. G12	H14	20
Great Western Rd.		
Buckingham Dr. G32	O22	54
Buckingham Dr. G73	O20	53
Buckingham St. G12	H14	20
Buckingham Ter. G12	H14	20
Great Western Rd.		
Bucklaw Gdns. G52	M11	49
Bucklaw Pl. G52	M11	49
Bucklaw Ter. G52	M11	49
Buckley St. G22	G17	22
Bucksburn Rd. G21	H20	23
Buddon St. G40	M20	53
Budhill Av. G32	L22	38
Bulldale St. G14	G 9	18
Bullionslaw Dr. G73	P20	65
Bulloch Av., Giff.	R14	62
Bullwood Av. G53	N 9	48
Bullwood Ct. G53	N 9	48
Bullwood Dr. G53	N 9	48
Bullwood Gdns. G53	N 9	48
Bullwood Pl. G53	N 9	48
Bunessan St. G52	L12	33
Bunhouse Rd. G3	J14	34
Burgh Hall La. G11	J13	34
Fortrose St.		
Burgh Hall St. G11	J13	34
Burgh La. G12	H14	20
Vinicombe St.		
Burghead Dr. G51	K12	33
Burgher St. G31	L20	37
Burleigh Rd., Udd.	Q28	69
Burleigh St. G51	K13	34
Burlington Av. G12	G13	20
Burmola St. G22	H16	21
Burn Gdns., Blan.	R26	68
Burn Ter. G72	O21	54
Burn Vw., Cumb.	B 4	71
Burnacre Gdns., Udd.	O27	57
Burnbank Dr., Barr.	R 8	59
Burnbank Gdns. G20	J15	35
Burnbank Pl. G4	K18	36
Drygate		
Burnbank Ter. G20	J15	35
Burnbrae Av., Bear.	B13	8
Burnbrae Av., Chr.	E28	15
Burnbrae Av., Linw.	L 2	28
Bridge St.		
Burnbrae Dr., Lenz.	D23	13
Auchinloch Rd.		
Burnbrae Dr. G73	P20	65
East Kilbride Rd.		
Burnbrae Rd., John.	M 2	44
Burnbrae Rd., Lenz.	E24	13
Burnbrae St. G21	H19	23
Burnbrae, Clyde.	C 7	5
Burncleuch Av., G72	Q22	66
Burncrooks Ct., Clyde.	C 6	4
Burndyke G51	K14	34
Burndyke St. G51	K13	34
Burnett Rd. G33	K24	39
Burnfield Av., Giff.	Q13	62
Burnfield Cotts., Giff.	Q13	62
Burnfield Dr. G43	Q13	62
Burnfield Gdns., Giff.	Q14	62
Burnfield Rd.		
Burnfield Rd., Giff.	P13	62
Burnfoot Cres. G73	P20	65
Burnfoot Cres., Pais.	O 5	46
Burnfoot Dr. G52	L10	32
Burngreen Ter.,	A 3	71
Cumb.		
Burnham Rd. G14	H10	18
Burnham Ter. G14	H10	18
Burnham Rd.		
Burnhead Rd. G43	P15	63
Burnhead Rd., Cumb.	C 1	70
Burnhead St., Udd.	O28	57
Burnhill Quadrant G73	O18	52
Burnhill St. G73	O18	52
Burnhouse St. G20	G14	20
Burnmouth Ct. G33	L24	39
Burnmouth Rd.		
Burnmouth Rd. G33	L24	39
Burnpark Av., Udd.	O26	56
Burns Dr., John.	O09	43
Burns Gro., Thorn.	R13	62
Burns Rd., Cumb.	C 3	71
Burns St. G4	J16	35
Burns St., Dalm.	D 6	4
Burnside Av., Barr.	Q 7	59
Burnside Av., Dalm.	D 6	4
Scott St.		
Burnside Gate G73	P20	65
Burnside Gdns., Kilb.	N 7	42
Burnside Rd. G73	P20	65
Burnside Rd., John.	N 2	44
Burnside Ter. G72	Q24	67
Burntbroom Dr., Bail.	M24	55
Burntbroom Gdns., Bail.	M24	55
Burntbroom Rd.,	M24	55
Udd. & Bail.		
Burntbroom St. G33	K23	39
Burntshields Rd., Kilb.	N06	42
Burr Gdns., Bish.	E20	11
Solway Rd.		
Burrells La. G4	K18	36
High St.		
Burrelton Rd. G43	P15	63
Burton La. G43	N16	51
Langside Rd.		
Bushes Av., Pais.	N 5	46
Busheyhill St. G72	P22	66
Bute Av., Renf.	J 8	31
Bute Cres., Bear.	E12	7
Bute Cres., Pais.	O 5	46
Bute Dr., John.	N08	43
Bute Gdns. G12	J14	34
Bute Gdns. G44	Q16	53
Bute Ter. G73	P19	65
Bute Ter., Udd.	O28	57
Butterbiggins Rd. G42	M16	51
Butterfield Pl. G41	N15	51
Pollokshaws Rd.		
Byrebush Rd. G53	N11	49
Byres Av., Pais.	L 7	31
Byres Cres.		
Byres Cres., Pais.	L 7	31
Byres Rd. G11	J14	34
Byres Rd., John.	N 2	44
Byron Ct., Udd.	R28	69
Shelly Dr.		
Byron La. G11	J12	33
Sandeman St.		
Byron St. G11	J12	33
Byron St., Clyde.	D 6	4
Byshot St. G22	H17	22
Cable Depot Rd., Dalm.	E 6	4
Cadder Ct., Bish.	C19	11
Cadder Gro. G20	F15	21
Cadder Rd.		
Cadder Pl. G20	F15	21
Cadder Rd. G20	F15	21
Cadder Rd., Bish.	C19	11
Cadder Way, Bish.	C19	11
Cadoc St., G72	P22	66
Cadogan St. G2	K16	35
Cadzow Av., Giff.	S13	62
Cadzow Dr., G72	P21	66
Caird Dr. G11	J13	34
Cairn Av., Renf.	J 9	32
Cairn Dr., Linw.	L 1	28
Cairn La., Pais.	K 5	30
Mosslands Rd.		
Cairn St. G21	G18	22
Cairnban St. G51	L11	33
Cairnbrook Rd. G34	K26	40
Cairncraig St. G31	M20	53
Cairndow Av. G44	Q15	63
Cairngorm Cres., Barr.	R 8	59
Cairngorm Cres., Bear.	C10	6
Cairngorm Cres., Pais.	N 6	46
Cairngorm Rd. G43	P14	62
Cairnhill Circus G52	M 9	48
Cairnhill Dr. G52	M 9	48
Cairnhill Pl. G52	M 9	48
Cairnhill Circus		
Cairnhill Rd. G61	E12	7
Cairnlea Dr. G51	L13	34
Cairnmuir Rd. G72	R21	66
Cairns Av. G72	P22	66
Cairns Rd. G72	Q22	66
Cairnsmore Pl. G15	E 9	6
Cairnsmore Rd. G15	E 9	6
Cairnswell Av. G72	Q23	67
Cairnswell Pl. G72	Q23	67
Cairntoul Dr. G14	G10	18
Cairntoul Pl. G14	G10	18
Calcots Path G34	J26	40
Auchengill Rd.		
Calcots Pl. G34	J26	40
Caldarvan St. G22	H16	21
Calder Av., Barr.	R 8	59
Calder Dr. G72	P22	66
Calder Gate, Bish.	D18	10
Calder Pl., Bail.	M25	56
Calder Rd., Pais.	L 4	29
Calder Rd., Udd.	P26	68
Calder St. G42	N16	51
Calderbank Vw., Bail.	M26	56
Calderbraes Av., Udd.	O27	57

Castle Chimmins Rd. Q23 67
G72
Castle Cres. North Court K17 36
Royal Exchange Sq.
Castle Gdns., Chr. E27 15
Castle Pl., Udd. P27 69
Ferry Rd.
Castle Rd. G78 M 2 44
Main Rd.
Castle Rd., John. M 2 44
Castle Sq., Dalm. D 6 4
Castle St. G4 K18 36
Castle St. G73 O19 53
Castle St., Bail. M25 56
Castle St., Dalm. D 6 4
Castle St., Pais. M 5 46
Castle Vw., Clyde. D 7 5
Granville St.
Castle Way, Cumb. B 4 71
Castlebank Cres., G11 J13 34
Meadowside St.
Castlebank Ct. G13 G12 19
Munro Pl.
Castlebank Gdns. G13 G12 19
Munro Pl.
Castlebank St. G11 J12 33
Castlebank Vill. G13 G12 19
Munro Pl.
Castlebay Dr. G22 E17 10
Castlebay Pl. G22 F17 22
Castlebay St. G22 F17 22
Castlecroft Gdns., Udd. P27 69
Castlefern Rd. G73 Q19 65
Castlehill Cres., Renf. H 8 17
Ferry Rd.
Castlehill Rd., Bear. C10 6
Castlelaw Gdns. G32 L22 38
Castlelaw Pl. G32 L22 38
Castlelaw St. G32 L22 38
Castlemilk Cres. G44 P18 64
Castlemilk Dr. G45 P18 64
Castlemilk Mews G44 P18 64
Castlemilk Rd.
Castlemilk Rd. G44 O18 52
Castleton Av. G21 F18 22
Colston Rd.
Castleton Ct. G42 R18 64
Cathay St. G22 F17 22
Cathcart Cres., Pais. M 7 47
Cathcart Rd. G42 O18 52
Cathcart Rd. G42 O16 51
Cathcart Rd. G73 O18 52
Cathedral Ct. G4 K17 36
Rottenrow East
Cathedral La. G4 K17 36
Cathedral St.
Cathedral Sq. G4 K18 36
Cathedral St. G1 K17 36
Cathedral St. G4 K18 36
Catherine Pl. G3 K15 35
Hydepark St.
Cathkin Av. G72 P21 66
Cathkin Av. G73 O20 53
Cathkin By-pass G73 Q20 65
Cathkin Ct. G42 R18 64
Cathkin Gdns., Udd. N27 57
Cathkin Pl., G72 P21 66
Cathkin Rd. G42 O15 51
Cathkin Rd., E.K. R19 65
Cathkin Rd., Udd. N27 57
Cathkin Vw. G32 O22 54
Cathkinview Rd. G42 O16 51
Catrine Av., Clyde. D 8 5
Causewayside St. N22 54
G32
Causeyside St., Pais. M 6 46
Cavendish Pl. G5 M16 51
Cavendish St. G5 M16 51
Cavin Dr. G45 O18 64
Cavin Rd. G45 O18 64
Caxton St. G13 G12 19
Cayton Gdns., Bail. M24 55
Cecil Pl. G11 L15 35
Paisley Rd. W.
Cecil St. G12 H14 20
Cedar Av. G78 O 1 44
Cedar Av., Dalm. D 5 4
Cedar Ct. G20 J16 35
Cedar Ct. G78 M07 42
Cedar Dr., Lenz. C23 13
Cedar Gdns. G73 Q20 65
Cedar Pl., Barr. R 8 59

Cedar Pl., Blan. R26 68
Cedar Rd., Bish. F19 23
Cedar Rd., Cumb. B 4 71
Cedar St. G20 J16 35
Cedar Wk., Bish. F19 23
Cedric Pl. G13 F11 19
Cedric Rd.
Cedric Rd. G13 F11 19
Celtic Pl. G20 F14 20
Maryhill Rd.
Cemetery Rd. G32 L23 39
Cemetery Rd. G52 M11 49
Paisley Rd. W.
Cemetery Rd., John. N 1 44
Central Av. G11 J12 33
Broomhill Ter.
Central Av. G32 M23 55
Central Av. G72 P21 66
Central Av., Udd. P29 69
Central Chambers G2 K16 35
Hope St.
Central Way, Cumb. D 2 70
Central Way, Pais. L 6 30
Centre St. G5 L16 35
Centre, The, Barr. R 7 59
Ceres Gdns. G64 E20 11
Cessnock Rd. G33 G22 24
Cessnock St. G51 L14 34
Cessnock St., Clyde. D 8 5
Chachan Dr. G51 K12 33
Skipness Dr.
Chalmers Ct. G40 L18 36
Chalmers Gate G40 L18 36
Chalmers Pl. G40 L18 36
Claythorn St.
Chalmers St. G40 L18 36
Chalmers St., Clyde. E 7 5
Chamberlain La. G13 G12 19
Chamberlain Rd. G13 G12 19
Chancellor St. G11 J13 34
Chapel Rd., Clyde. C 7 5
Chapel St. G20 G15 21
Chapel St. G73 O18 52
Chapelhill Rd., Pais. N 7 47
Chapelton Av., Bear. D12 7
Chapelton Gdns., Bear. D12 7
Chapelton St., G22 G16 21
Chaplet Av., G13 F11 19
Chapman St. G42 N16 51
Allison St.
Chappel St., Barr. Q 7 59
Charing Cross G2 J15 35
Charing Cross La. G3 K15 35
Granville St.
Charles Av., Renf. H 8 17
Charles Cres., Lenz. D23 13
Charles St. G21 J18 36
Charlotte La. G1 L17 36
London Rd.
Charlotte La. S. G1 L17 36
Charlotte St.
Charlotte Pl., Pais. N 6 46
Charlotte St., G1 L17 36
Chatelherault Av. G72 P21 66
Chatton St. G23 E14 8
Cheapside St. G3 K15 35
Chelmsford Dr. G12 G13 20
Cherry Bank, Lenz. C22 12
Cherry Cres., Clyde. D 7 5
Cherry Pl., Bish. F19 23
Cherry Pl., John. N 1 44
Cherrybank Rd. G43 P15 63
Chester St. G32 L22 38
Chesterfield Av. G12 G13 20
Chesters Pl. G73 O19 53
Chesters Rd., Bear. D11 7
Chestnut Dr., Dalm. C 7 5
Chestnut Dr., Lenz. C22 12
Chestnut Pl., John. O 1 44
Chestnut St. G22 G17 22
Cheviot Av., Barr. R 8 59
Cheviot Rd. G43 P14 62
Cheviot Rd., Pais. O 6 46
Chirnside Pl. G52 L10 32
Chirnside Rd. G52 L10 32
Chisholm St. G1 L17 36
Christian St. G43 O14 50
Christie La., Pais. L 6 30
New Sneddon St.
Christie Pl. G72 P22 66
Christie St., Pais. L 6 30
Christopher St. G21 J19 37

Chryston Rd., C25 14
Waterside & Chr.
Chryston Rd., Chr. F26 26
Church Av. G33 G23 25
Church Av. G73 P20 65
Church Dr., Lenz. C23 13
Church Hill, Pais. L 6 30
Church La. G42 N16 51
Victoria Rd.
Church Rd., Chr. F26 26
Church Rd., Giff. R14 62
Church St. G11 J14 34
Church St., Bail. M26 56
Church St., Clyde. D 7 5
Church St., John. M09 43
Church St., Kilb. M07 42
Church St., Udd. P27 69
Churchill Av., John. O08 43
Churchill Cres., Udd. Q28 69
Churchill Dr. G11 H12 19
Churchill Pl., Kilb. M07 42
Churchill Way, Bish. E18 10
Kirkintilloch Rd.
Churchill Way, Bish. E18 10
Kirkintilloch Rd.
Circus Dr. G31 K18 36
Circus Pl. G31 K18 36
Circus Place La. G31 K18 36
Circus Pl.
Civic Way, Lenz. B23 13
Kirkintilloch Rd.
Clachan Dr. G51 K12 33
Skipness Dr.
Claddens Pl., Lenz. D24 13
Claddens Quad. G22 G17 22
Claddens St. G22 G16 21
Claddens Wynd G66 D24 13
Claddon Vw., Clyde. D 8 5
Kirkoswald Dr.
Clair Rd., Bish. E20 11
Clairmont Gdns. G3 J15 35
Clare St. G21 J19 37
Claremont Av., Giff. R14 62
Claremont Pl. G3 J15 35
Claremont Ter.
Claremont St. G3 K15 35
Claremont Ter. G3 J15 35
Claremont Terrace La. J15 35
G3
Clifton St.
Clarence Dr. G11 H13 20
Clarence Gdns. G11 H13 20
Clarence St., Clyde. D 8 5
Clarence St., Pais. L 7 31
Clarendon La., G20 J16 35
Clarendon St.
Clarendon Pl. G20 J16 35
Clarendon St. G20 J16 35
Clarion Cres. G13 F10 18
Clarion Rd. G13 F10 18
Clark St. G41 L15 35
Tower St.
Clark St., Dalm. D 6 4
Clark St., John. M09 43
Clark St., Pais. L 5 30
Clark St., Renf. H 7 17
Clarkston Av. G44 Q15 63
Clarkston Rd. G44 R15 63
Clathic Av., Bear. D13 8
Claude Av. G72 Q24 67
Claude Rd., Pais. L 7 31
Claudhall Av., Gart. F27 27
Clavens Rd. G52 L 9 32
Claverhouse Pl., Pais. M 7 47
Claverhouse Rd. G52 K 9 32
Clavering St. E., Pais. L 5 30
Well St.
Clavering St. W., Pais. L 5 30
King St.
Clayhouse Rd. G33 G24 25
Claypotts Pl. G33 J22 38
Claypotts Rd. G33 J22 38
Clayslaps Rd. G3 J14 34
Argyle St.
Claython Av. G40 L18 36
Claythorn Circus G40 L18 36
Claythorn Av.
Claythorn Ct. G40 L18 36
Claythorn Pk.
Claythorn Pk. G40 L18 36
Claythorn Ter. G40 L18 36
Claythorn Pk.

Clayton Ter. G31	K18	36
Cleddans Cres., Clyde.	C 8	5
Cleddans Ct., Bish.	E10	11
Cleddans Rd., Clyde.	C 8	5
Cleeves Pl. G53	P10	60
Cleeves Quadrant G53	P10	60
Cleeves Rd. G53	P10	60
Cleghorn St. G22	H16	21
Cleland La. G5	L17	36
Cleland St.		
Cleland St. G5	L17	36
Clelland Av., Bish.	F19	23
Clerwood St. G32	L20	37
Cleveden Cres. G12	G13	20
Cleveden Cres. La. G12	G13	20
Cleveden Dr.		
Cleveden Dr. G12	G13	20
Cleveden Dr. G73	P20	65
Cleveden Gdns. G12	G14	20
Cleveden Pl. G12	G13	20
Cleveden Rd. G12	G13	20
Cleveland St. G3	K15	35
Cliff Rd. G3	J15	35
Clifford Gdns. G51	L13	34
Clifford La. G51	L14	34
Gower St.		
Clifford Pl. G51	L14	34
Clifford St.		
Clifford St. G51	L13	34
Clifton Pl. G3	J15	35
Clifton St.		
Clifton Rd., Giff.	Q13	62
Clifton St. G3	J15	35
Clifton Ter. G72	Q21	66
Clifton Ter., John.	N 1	44
Clincart Rd. G42	O16	51
Clincarthill Rd. G73	O19	53
Clinton Av., Udd.	P27	69
Clippens Rd., Linw.	L 1	28
Cloan Av. G15	E10	6
Cloan Cres., Bish.	D19	11
Cloberhill Rd. G13	E11	7
Cloch St. G33	K22	38
Clochoderick Av., Kilb.	N07	42
Mackenzie Dr.		
Clonbeith St. G33	J24	39
Closeburn St. G22	G17	22
Cloth St., Barr.	R 8	59
Clouden Rd., Cumb.	C 3	71
Cloudhowe Ter., Blan.	R26	68
Clouston Ter. G20	H15	21
Clouston La. G20	H14	20
Clouston St.		
Clouston St. G20	H14	20
Clova Pl., Udd.	P27	69
Clova St. G46	Q12	61
Clover Av., Bish.	E18	10
Cloverbank St. G21	J19	37
Clunie Rd. G52	M12	49
Cluny Av., Bear.	E13	8
Cluny Dr., Bear.	E13	8
Cluny Dr., Pais.	L 7	31
Cluny Gdns. G14	H12	19
Cluny Gdns., Bail.	M25	56
Cluny Vill. G14	H11	19
Westland Dr.		
Clutha St. G51	L15	35
Paisley Rd. W.		
Clyde Av., Barr.	R 8	59
Clyde Av., Both.	R27	69
Clyde Cres., Blan.	S26	68
Clyde Ct., Dalm.	D 6	4
Little Holm		
Clyde Pl. G5	L16	35
Clyde Pl. G72	Q23	67
Clyde Pl., John.	O08	43
Clyde Rd., Pais.	K 7	31
Clyde St. G1	L16	35
Clyde St., Clyde.	F 8	17
Clyde St., Renf.	G 8	17
Clyde Ter., Both.	R28	69
Clyde Vale G71	R28	69
Clyde Vw. G71	R28	69
Clyde Vw., Pais.	N 7	47
Clydebrae Dr. G71	R28	69
Clydebrae St. G51	K13	34
Clydeford Dr. G32	M21	54
Clydeford Dr., Udd.	O26	56
Clydeford Rd. G72	O22	54
Clydeham Ter., Clyde.	F 8	17
Clydeholm Rd. G14	J12	33
Clydeneuk Dr., Udd.	O26	56

Clydesdale Av.,	J 7	31
Pais. & Renf.		
Clydeside Expressway	H11	19
G14		
Clydeside Rd. G73	N18	52
Clydesmill Dr. G32	O22	54
Clydesmill Gro. G32	O22	54
Clydesmill Pl. G32	O22	54
Clydesmill Rd. G32	O22	54
Clydeview G11	J13	34
Dumbarton Rd.		
Clydeview La. G11	J12	33
Broomhill Ter.		
Clydeview Ter. G32	O23	55
Clydeview Ter. G40	M18	52
Newhall St.		
Clynder St. G51	L13	34
Clyth Dr., Giff.	R14	62
Coalhill St. G31	L19	37
Coatbridge Rd., Bail.	L27	41
Coatbridge Rd., Gart.	H27	27
Coates Cres. G53	O11	49
Coats Cres., Bail.	L25	40
Coatshill Av., Blan.	R26	68
Cobbleriggs Way, Udd.	P27	69
Cobinshaw St. G32	L22	38
Cobinton Pl. G38	J22	38
Coburg St. G5	L16	35
Bedford St.		
Coburg St. G5	L16	35
Cochno Rd., Clyde.	B 7	5
Cochno St., Clyde.	F 8	17
Cochran St., Pais.	M 6	46
Cochrane St. G1	K17	36
Cochrane St., Barr.	R 7	59
Cochranemill Rd., John.	N08	43
Cockels Loan, Renf.	J 7	31
Cockenzie St. G32	L22	38
Cockmuir St. G21	H19	23
Cogan Rd. G43	P14	62
Cogan St. G43	O14	50
Cogan St., Barr.	R 7	59
Colbert St. G40	M18	52
Colbreggan Ct., Clyde.	C 8	5
St. Helena Cres.		
Colbreggan Gdns.,	C 8	5
Clyde.		
Colchester Dr. G12	G13	20
Coldingham Av. G14	G 9	18
Coldstream Dr. G73	P20	65
Coldstream Dr., Pais.	N 4	45
Coldstream Pl. G21	H17	22
Keppochhill Rd.		
Coldstream Rd., Clyde.	E 7	5
Colebrook St. G72	P22	66
Colebrook Ter. G12	H15	21
Colebrooke St.		
Colebrooke La. G12	H15	21
Colebrooke St.		
Colebrooke Pl. G12	H15	21
Belmont St.		
Colebrooke St. G12	H15	21
Coleridge, Udd.	Q28	69
Colfin St. G34	J26	40
Colgrain St. G20	G16	21
Colinbar Circle, Barr.	R 7	59
Colinslee Av., Pais.	N 6	46
Colinslee Cres., Pais.	N 6	46
Colinslee Dr., Pais.	N 6	46
Colinslie Rd. G53	O11	49
Colinton Pl. G32	K22	38
Colintraive Av. G33	H21	24
Mossbank Dr.		
Coll Av., Renf.	J 8	31
Coll Pl. G21	J19	37
Coll St. G21	J19	37
Colla Gdns., Bish.	E20	11
College La. G1	L17	36
High St.		
College St. G1	K17	36
Collessie Dr. G33	J23	39
Collier St., John.	M09	43
Collina St. G20	G14	20
Collins St. G4	K18	36
Collins St., Clyde.	C 8	5
Collylin Rd., Bear.	D12	7
Colmonell Av. G13	F 9	18
Colonsay Av., Renf.	J 8	31
Colonsay Rd. G52	L12	33
Colonsay Rd., Pais.	O 5	46
Colquhoun Av. G52	K10	32
Colquhoun Dr., Bear.	C11	7

Colston Av., Bish.	F18	22
Colston Dr., Bish.	F18	22
Colston Gdns., Bish.	F18	22
Colston Path, Bish.	F18	22
Colston Gdns.		
Colston Pl., Bish.	F18	22
Colston Rd., Bish.	F18	22
Coltmuir St. G22	G16	21
Coltness La. G33	K23	39
Coltness St. G33	K23	39
Coltpark Av., Bish.	F18	22
Coltpark La., Bish.	F18	22
Columba Path , Clyde.	E 8	5
Onslow Rd.		
Columba St. G51	K13	34
Colvend Dr. G73	Q19	65
Colvend St. G40	M18	52
Colville Dr. G73	P20	65
Colwood Av. G53	Q10	60
Colwood Gdns. G53	Q10	60
Colwood Av.		
Colwood Path G53	Q10	60
Parkhouse Rd.		
Colwood Pl. G53	Q10	60
Colwood Sq. G53	Q10	60
Colwood Av.		
Comedie Rd. G33	H24	25
Comely Park St. G31	L19	37
Comley Pl. G31	L19	37
Gallowgate		
Commerce St. G5	L16	35
Commercial Ct. G5	L17	36
Commercial Rd. G5	M17	52
Commercial Rd., Barr.	Q 8	59
Commonhead Rd. G34	K26	40
Commonhead Rd., Bail.	K27	41
Commore Av., Barr.	R 8	59
Commore Dr. G13	F10	18
Comrie Rd. G33	G23	25
Comrie St. G32	M22	54
Cona St. G46	Q12	61
Conan Ct. G72	P23	67
Condorrat Ring Rd.,	D 1	70
Cumb.		
Congleton St. G53	P 9	60
Nitshill Rd.		
Conifer Pl., Lenz.	C22	12
Conisborough Path G34	J24	39
Balfluig St.		
Conisborough Rd. G34	J24	39
Connal St. G40	M19	53
Conniston St. G32	K21	38
Conon Av., Bear.	D11	7
Consett La. G33	K23	39
Consett St. G33	K23	39
Consett La.		
Contin Pl. G12	G14	20
Convair Way, Renf.	J 8	31
Lismore Av.		
Conval Way, Pais.	K 5	30
Abbotsburn Way		
Cook St. G5	L16	35
Coopers Well La. G11	J14	34
Dumbarton Rd.		
Coopers Well St. G11	J14	34
Dumbarton Rd.		
Copland Pl. G51	L13	34
Copland Quad. G51	L13	34
Copland Rd. G51	L13	34
Coplaw St. G42	M16	51
Copperfield La., Udd.	O28	57
Hamilton Vw.		
Corbett St. G32	M22	54
Corbiston Way, Cumb.	C 3	71
Cordiner St. G44	O16	51
Corkerhill Gdns. G52	M12	49
Corkerhill Pl. G52	N11	49
Corkerhill Rd. G52	N11	49
Corlaich Av. G42	O18	52
Corlaich Dr. G42	O18	52
Corn St. G4	J16	35
Cornaig Rd. G53	O10	48
Cornalee Gdns. G53	O10	48
Cornalee Pl. G53	O10	48
Cornalee Rd. G53	O10	48
Cornhill St. G21	G19	23
Cornoch St. G23	E14	8
Torrin Rd.		
Cornock Cres., Clyde.	D 7	5
Cornock St., Clyde.	D 7	5
Cornwall Av. G73	P20	65
Cornwall St. G41	L14	34

Coronation Pl., Gart.	F27	27	
Coronation Way, Bear.	E13	8	
Corpach Pl. G34	J26	40	
Corran St. G33	K21	38	
Corrie Dr., Pais.	M 9	48	
Corrie Gro. G44	Q15	63	
Corrie Pl., Lenz.	D24	13	
Corrour Rd. G43	O14	50	
Corse Ford Av., John.	O08	43	
Corse Rd. G52	L 9	32	
Corsebar Av., Pais.	N 5	46	
Corsebar Cres, Pais.	N 5	46	
Corsebar Dr., Pais.	N 5	46	
Corsebar La. G78	N 4	45	
Balgonie Av.			
Corsebar Rd., Pais.	N 5	46	
Corsehill Pl. G34	K26	40	
Corsehill St. G34	K26	40	
Corselet Rd. G53	Q10	60	
Corsewall Av. G32	M24	55	
Corsford Dr. G53	P11	61	
Corsock St. G31	K20	37	
Corston St. G33	K20	37	
Cortachy Pl., Bish.	E20	11	
Coruisk Way	O 3	45	
Spencer Dr.			
Coruisk Way, Pais.	O 3	45	
Spencer Dr.			
Corunna St. G3	K15	35	
Coshneuk Rd. G33	G22	24	
Cottar St. G20	F15	21	
Cotton Av., Linw.	L 1	28	
Cotton St. G40	N19	53	
Cotton St., Pais.	M 6	46	
Coulters La. G40	L18	36	
Countess Wk., Bail.	L28	41	
County Av. G72	O20	53	
County Pl., Pais.	L 6	30	
Moss St.			
County Sq., Pais.	L 6	30	
Couper St. G4	J17	36	
Courthill Av. G44	P16	63	
Coustonhill St. G43	O14	50	
Pleasance St.			
Coustonholm Rd. G43	O14	50	
Coventry Dr. G31	K19	37	
Cowal Dr., Linw.	L 1	28	
Cowal St. G20	F14	20	
Cowan Clo., Barr.	Q 8	59	
Cowan Cres.	R 8	59	
Cowan La. G12	J15	35	
Cowan St.			
Cowan Rd., Cumb.	A 1	70	
Cowan St. G12	J15	35	
Cowan Wilson Av.,	S26	68	
Blan.			
Cowcaddens Rd. G2	J16	35	
Cowden Dr., Bish.	D19	11	
Cowden St. G51	K11	33	
Cowdenhill Circus G13	F11	19	
Cowdenhill Pl. G13	F11	19	
Cowdenhill Rd. G13	F11	19	
Cowdie St., Pais.	K 5	30	
Cowdray Cres., Renf.	H 8	17	
Cowell Vw., Clyde.	D 7	5	
Granville St.			
Cowglen Pl. G53	O11	49	
Cowglen Rd.			
Cowglen Rd. G53	O11	49	
Cowglen Ter. G53	O11	49	
Cowie St. G41	L15	35	
Cowlairs Rd. G21	H18	22	
Coxhill St. G21	H17	22	
Coxton Pl. G33	J23	39	
Coylton Rd. G43	P15	63	
Craggan Dr. G14	G 9	18	
Cragielea St. G31	K19	37	
Crags Av., Pais.	N 6	46	
Crags Cres., Pais.	N 6	46	
Crags Rd., Pais.	N 6	46	
Craig Rd. G44	P16	63	
Craig Rd., Linw.	K 1	28	
Craigallian Av. G72	Q23	67	
Craiganour La. G43	P14	62	
Craiganour Pl. G43	P14	62	
Craigard Pl. G73	Q21	66	
Inverclyde Gdns.			
Craigbank Dr. G53	P10	60	
Craigbank St. G22	H17	22	
Craigbarnet Cres. G33	H22	24	
Craigbo Av. G23	E14	8	
Craigbo Ct. G23	F14	20	
Craigbo Dr. G23	F14	20	
Craigbo Pl. G23	F14	20	
Craigbo Rd. G23	F14	20	
Craigbo St. G23	E14	8	
Craigbog Av., John.	N08	43	
Craigellan Rd. G43	P14	62	
Craigenbay Cres., Lenz.	C23	13	
Craigenbay Rd., Lenz.	D23	13	
Craigenbay St. G21	H19	23	
Craigencart Ct., Clyde.	C 6	4	
Gentle Row			
Craigend Dr., Coat.	M29	57	
Craigend Pl. G13	G12	19	
Craigend St. G13	G12	19	
Craigendmuir Rd. G33	H24	25	
Craigendmuir St. G33	J20	37	
Craigendon Oval, Pais.	P 5	58	
Craigendon Rd., Pais.	P 5	58	
Craigends Dr., Kilb.	M07	42	
High Barholm			
Craigenfeoch Av., John.	N08	43	
Craigfaulds Av., Pais.	N04	45	
Craigflower Gdns. G53	Q10	60	
Craigflower Rd. G53	Q10	60	
Craighalbert Rd. G68	B 1	70	
Craighall Rd. G4	J16	35	
Craighead Av. G33	H20	23	
Craigheads St., Barr.	R 7	59	
Craighouse St. G33	J22	38	
Craigie Pk. G66	C24	13	
Craigie St. G42	N16	51	
Craigiebar Dr., Pais.	O 5	46	
Craigieburn Gdns. G20	F13	20	
Craigieburn Rd., Cumb.	C 2	70	
Craigiehall Pl. G51	L14	34	
Craigielea Dr., Pais.	L 5	30	
Craigielea Rd. G81	B 6	4	
Craigielea Rd., Renf.	H 8	17	
Craigielinn Av., Pais.	P 5	58	
Craigievar St. G33	J24	39	
Craigleith St. G32	L21	38	
Craiglockhart St. G33	J23	39	
Craigmaddie Ter. La. G3	K15	35	
Derby St.			
Craigmillar Rd. G42	O16	51	
Craigmont Dr. G20	G15	21	
Craigmont St. G20	G15	21	
Craigmore Rd., Bear.	B10	6	
Craigmore St. G31	L20	37	
Craigmount Av., Pais.	P 5	58	
Craigmuir Cres. G52	L 9	32	
Craigmuir Pl. G52	L 9	32	
Craigmuir Rd.			
Craigmuir Rd. G52	L 9	32	
Craigneil St. G33	J24	39	
Craignestock St. G40	L18	36	
Craignethan Gdns. G11	J13	34	
Lawrie St.			
Craignure Rd. G73	Q19	65	
Craigpark Dr. G31	K19	37	
Craigpark G31	K19	37	
Craigpark Ter. G31	K19	37	
Craigpark			
Craigpark Way, Udd.	O28	57	
Newton Dr.			
Craigs Av., Clyde.	C 8	5	
Craigston Pl., John.	N09	43	
Craigston Rd., John.	N09	43	
Craigton Av., Barr.	R 9	60	
Craigton Dr. G51	L12	33	
Craigton Dr., Barr.	R 9	60	
Craigton Pl. G51	L12	33	
Craigton Dr.			
Craigton Pl., Blan.	R26	68	
Craigton Rd. G51	L12	33	
Craigvicar Gdns. G32	L23	39	
Hailes Av.			
Craigview Av., John.	O08	43	
Craigwell Av. G73	P20	65	
Crail St. G31	L20	37	
Cramond Av., Renf.	J 9	32	
Cramond St. G5	N17	52	
Cramond Ter. G32	L22	38	
Cranborne Rd. G12	G13	20	
Cranhill St. G33	J20	37	
Cranston St. G3	K15	35	
Cranworth La. G12	H14	20	
Great George St.			
Cranworth St. G12	H14	20	
Crarae Av., Bear.	E12	7	
Crathie Dr. G11	J13	34	
Crathie La. G11	J13	34	
Exeter Dr.			
Craw Rd., Pais.	M 5	46	
Crawford Av., Lenz.	D23	13	
Crawford Cres., Blan.	R26	68	
Crawford Cres., Udd.	O27	57	
Crawford Ct., Giff.	R13	62	
Milverton Rd.			
Crawford Dr. G15	E 9	6	
Crawford St. G11	J13	34	
Crawford Dr., Pais.	L 4	29	
Crawfurd Gdns. G73	Q19	65	
Crawfurd Rd. G73	Q19	65	
Crawriggs Av., Lenz.	C23	13	
Crebar Dr., Barr.	R 8	59	
Crebar St. G46	Q12	61	
Credon Gdns. G73	Q20	65	
Cree Av., Bish.	E20	11	
Cree Gdns. G32	L21	38	
Kilmany Dr.			
Creran St. G40	L18	36	
Tobago St.			
Crescent Ct., Dalm.	D 6	4	
Swindon St.			
Crescent Rd. G13	G10	18	
Cresswell La. G12	H14	20	
Great George St.			
Cresswell St. G12	H14	20	
Cressy St. G11	K12	33	
Crest Av. G13	F10	18	
Crestlea Av., Pais.	O 6	46	
Creswell Ter., Udd.	O27	57	
Kylepark Dr.			
Crichton Ct. G42	R18	64	
Crichton St. G21	H18	22	
Crieff Ct. G3	K15	35	
North St.			
Criffell Gdns. G32	M23	55	
Criffell Rd. G32	M23	55	
Crimea St. G2	K16	35	
Crinan Gdns., Bish.	E19	11	
Crinan Rd., Bish.	E19	11	
Crinan St. G31	K19	37	
Cripps Av., Clyde.	E 8	5	
Croft Rd. G73	P22	66	
Croft St. G31	L19	37	
Croft Wynd, Udd.	P28	69	
Croftbank Av. G71	R28	69	
Croftbank Cres., Both.	R28	69	
Croftbank Cres., Udd.	P27	69	
Croftbank St. G21	H18	22	
Croftbank St., Udd.	P27	69	
Croftburn Dr. G44	Q17	64	
Croftcroighn Rd. G33	J22	38	
Croftend Av. G44	P18	64	
Croftfoor Dr. G44	Q17	64	
Croftfoot Cotts., Gart.	G28	27	
Croftfoot Cres. G45	Q19	65	
Croftfoot Dr. G45	Q18	64	
Croftfoot Quad. G45	Q18	64	
Croftfoot Rd. G45	Q17	64	
Croftfoot St. G45	Q19	65	
Croftfoot Ter. G45	Q18	64	
Crofthead St., Udd.	P27	69	
Crofthill Av., Udd.	P27	69	
Crofthill Rd. G44	P17	64	
Crofthouse Dr. G44	Q18	64	
Croftmont Av. G44	Q18	64	
Croftmoraig Av., Chr.	D28	15	
Crofton Av. G44	Q17	64	
Croftpark Av. G44	Q17	64	
Croftpark Rd., Clyde.	B 7	5	
Croftside Av. G44	Q18	64	
Croftspar Av. G32	L23	39	
Croftspar Dr. G32	L23	39	
Croftspar Pl. G32	L23	39	
Croftwood Av. G44	Q17	64	
Croftwood, Bish.	D19	11	
Cromart Pl., Chr.	E26	14	
Cromarty Av. G43	P15	63	
Cromarty Av., Bish.	E20	11	
Cromarty Gdns., Clark.	R16	63	
Crombie Gdns., Bail.	M25	56	
Cromdale St. G51	L12	33	
Cromer La., Pais.	K 5	30	
Abbotsburn Way			
Cromer St. G20	G15	21	
Cromer Way, Pais.	K 5	30	
Mosslands Rd.			
Crompton Av. G44	P16	63	
Cromwell La. G20	J16	35	
Cromwell St.			

Darvel Cres., Pais. M 8 47
Darvel St. G53 P 9 60
Darwin Pl., Dalm. D 5 4
Dava St. G51 K13 34
Davaar Rd., Pais. O 6 46
Davaar St. G40 M19 53
Daventry Dr. G12 G13 20
David Pl., Bail. M24 55
David Pl., Pais. K 7 31
Killarn Way
David St. G40 L19 37
David Way, Pais. K 7 31
Killarn Way
Davidson Gdns. G14 H11 19
Westland Dr.
Davidson Quad., Clyde. B 6 4
Davidson St. G40 N19 53
Davidson St., Clyde. F 9 18
Davidston Pl., Lenz. D24 13
Davieland Rd., Giff. R13 62
Daviot St. G51 L11 33
Dawes La. N. G14 H11 19
Upland Dr.
Dawson Pl. G4 H16 21
Dawson Dr.
Dawson Rd. G4 H16 21
Dealston Rd., Barr. Q 7 59
Dean Park Dr. G72 Q23 67
Dean Park Rd., Renf. J 9 32
Dean St., Clyde. E 8 5
Deanbrae St., Udd. P27 69
Deanfield Quad. G52 L 9 32
Deanpark Av., Udd. Q28 69
Deans Av. G72 Q23 67
Deanside La. G4 K17 36
Rotton Row
Deanside Rd., Renf. K10 32
Deanston Dr. G41 O15 51
Deanwood Av. G44 Q15 63
Deanwood Rd. G44 Q15 63
Debdale Cotts. G13 G12 19
Whittingehame Dr.
Dechmont Av. G72 Q23 67
Dechmont Gdns., Blan. R26 68
Dechmont Gdns., Udd. N27 57
Dechmont Pl. G72 Q23 67
Dechmont Rd., Udd. N27 57
Dechmont St. G31 M20 53
Dechmont Vw., Udd. O28 57
Hamilton Vw.
Dee Av. G78 N 3 45
Dee Av., Renf. H 9 18
Dee Dr., Pais. N 3 45
Dee Pl., John. O08 43
Dee St. G33 J20 37
Deepdene Rd., Bear. E11 7
Deepdene Rd., Chr. E28 15
Delburn St. G31 M20 53
Delhi Av., Dalm. D 5 4
Delhmont Vw., Udd. O28 57
Hamilton Vw.
Delny Pl. G33 K24 39
Delvin Rd., G44 P16 63
Denbeck St. G32 L21 38
Denbrae St. G32 L21 38
Dene Wk., Bish. F20 23
Denewood Av., Pais. O 5 46
Denham St. G22 H16 21
Denholme Dr., Giff. R14 62
Denkenny Sq. G15 D 9 6
Denmark St. G22 H17 22
Denmilne Path G34 K26 40
Denmilne Pl. G34 K26 40
Denmilne St. G34 K26 40
Derby St. G3 K15 35
Derby Terrace La. G3 K15 35
Derby St.
Dervaig St. G31 L20 37
Derwent St. G22 H16 21
Despard Av. G32 M24 55
Despard Gdns. G32 M24 55
Deveron Av., Giff. R14 62
Deveron Rd., Bear. E11 7
Deveron St. G33 J20 37
Devol Cres. G53 O10 48
Devon Gdns. G12 H13 20
Hyndland Rd.
Devon, Bish. D18 10
Devon Pl. G42 M16 51
Devon St. G5 M16 51
Devondale Av., Blan. R26 68
Devonshire Gdns. G12 H13 20

Devonshire Gdns. La. H13 20
G12
Hyndland Rd.
Devonshire Ter. G12 H13 20
Devonshire Ter. La. G12 H13 20
Hughenden Rd.
Diana Av. G13 F10 18
Dick St. G20 H15 21
Henderson St.
Dickens Av., Clyde. D 6 4
Dilwara Av. G14 J12 33
Dimity St., John. N09 43
Dinard Dr., Giff. Q14 62
Dinart St. G33 J20 37
Dinduff St. G34 J26 40
Dingwall St. G3 K14 34
Kelvinhaugh St.
Dinmont Pl. G41 N15 51
Norham St.
Dinmont Rd. G41 N14 50
Dinwiddie St. G21 J20 37
Dipple Pl. G15 E10 6
Dirleton Av. G41 O15 51
Dirleton Dr., Pais. N 4 45
Dirleton Gate, Bear. E11 7
Divernia Way, Barr. S 8 59
Dixon Av. G42 N16 51
Dixon Rd. G42 N17 52
Dixon St. G1 L16 35
Dixon St., Pais. M 6 46
Dobbies Loan G4 J16 35
Dobbies Loan Pl. G4 K17 36
Dochart Av., Renf. J 9 32
Dochart St. G33 J21 38
Dock St., Clyde. F 8 17
Dodhill Pl. G13 G10 18
Dodside Gdns. G32 M23 55
Dodside Pl. G32 M23 55
Dodside St. G32 M23 55
Dolan St., Bail. L25 40
Dollar Ter. G20 F14 20
Crosbie St.
Dolphin Rd. G41 N14 50
Don Av., Renf. J 9 32
Don Dr., Pais. N 3 45
Don Pl., John. O08 43
Don St. G33 K20 37
Donald Way, Udd. O28 57
Donaldson Dr., Renf. H 8 17
Ferguson St.
Donaldswood Rd., Pais. O 5 46
Doncaster St. G20 H16 21
Doon Cres., Bear. D11 7
Doon Side, Cumb. C 3 71
Doon St., Clyde. D 8 5
Doonfoot Rd. G43 P14 62
Dora St. G40 M19 53
Dorchester Av., G12 G13 20
Dorchester Ct. G12 G13 20
Dorchester Av.
Dorchester Pl. G12 G13 20
Dorian Dr., Clark. S14 62
Dorlin Rd. G33 G24 25
Dormanside Rd. G53 M10 48
Dornal Av. G13 F 9 18
Dornford Av. G32 N23 55
Dornford Rd. G32 N23 55
Dornie Dr. G46 Q12 61
Dornoch Av., Giff. R14 62
Dornoch Pl., Bish. E20 11
Dornoch Pl., Chr. E26 14
Dornoch Rd., Bear. E11 7
Dornoch St. G40 L18 36
Dorset Sq. G3 K15 35
Dorset St.
Dorset St. G3 K15 35
Dosk Av. G13 F 9 18
Dosk Pl. G13 F 9 18
Douglas Av. G32 N22 54
Douglas Av. G73 P20 65
Douglas Av., Giff. R14 62
Douglas Av., John. N 1 44
Douglas Av., Lenz. C23 13
Douglas Ct., Lenz. C23 13
Douglas Dr. G15 E 9 6
Douglas Dr. G72 P21 66
Douglas Dr., Bail. L24 39
Douglas Dr., Both. R28 69
Douglas Gdns., Bear. D12 7
Douglas Gdns., Giff. R14 62
Douglas Gdns., Lenz. C23 13
Douglas Gdns., Udd. P27 69

Douglas La. G2 K16 35
West George St.
Douglas Park Cres., C13 8
Bear.
Douglas Pl., Bear. C12 7
Douglas Pl., Lenz. C23 13
Douglas Rd., K 7 31
Pais. & Renf.
Douglas St. G2 K16 35
Douglas St., Pais. L 5 30
Douglas St., Udd. O28 57
Douglas Ter. G41 M15 51
Shields Rd.
Douglas Ter., Pais. J 6 30
Douglaston Rd. G23 E15 9
Dougrie Dr. G45 Q17 64
Dougrie Pl. G45 Q18 64
Dougrie Rd. G45 R17 64
Dougrie St. G45 Q18 64
Dougrie Ter. G45 Q17 64
Doune Cres., Bish. D19 11
Doune Gdns. G20 H15 21
Doune Quad. G20 H15 21
Dove St. G53 P10 60
Dovecot G43 O14 50
Shawhill Rd.
Dovecothall St., Barr. Q 8 59
Dowanfield Rd., Cumb. C 2 70
Dowanhill Pl. G11 J14 34
Old Dumbarton Rd.
Dowanhill St. G11 J14 34
Dowanside La. G12 H14 20
Byres Rd.
Dowanside Rd. G12 H14 20
Dowanvale Ter. G11 J13 34
White St.
Down St. G21 H18 22
Downcraig Dr. G45 R17 64
Downcraig Rd. G45 R17 64
Downcraig Ter. G45 R17 64
Downfield Gdns., Both. R27 69
Downfield St. G32 M21 54
Downiebrae Rd. G73 N19 53
Dowrie Cres. G53 N10 48
Dows Pl. G4 H16 21
Possil Rd.
Drainie St. G34 K25 40
Westerhouse Rd.
Drake St. G40 L18 36
Drakemire Av. G45 Q17 64
Drakemire Dr. G45 Q17 64
Dreghorn St. G31 K20 37
Drem Pl. G11 J13 34
Merkland St.
Drimnin Rd. G33 G24 25
Drive Gdns., John. M 3 45
Drive Rd. G51 K12 33
Drochil St. G34 J25 40
Drumbeg Dr. G53 P10 60
Drumbeg Pl. G53 P10 60
Drumbottie Rd. G21 G19 23
Drumby Cres., Clark. S14 62
Drumby Dr., Clark. S14 62
Drumcavel Rd., F26 26
Chr. & Gart.
Drumchapel Gdns. G15 E10 6
Drumchapel Pl. G15 E10 6
Drumchapel Rd. G15 E10 6
Drumclog Gdns. G33 G21 24
Auchinleck Av.
Drumclutha Dr., Both. R28 69
Drumcross Rd. G53 N11 49
Drumilaw Rd. G73 P19 65
Drumilaw Way G73 P19 65
Drumlaken Av. G23 E14 8
Drumlaken Ct. G23 E14 8
Drumlaken St. G23 E14 8
Drumlanrig Av. G34 J26 40
Drumlanrig Pl. G34 J26 40
Drumlanrig Quad. G34 J26 40
Drumlochy Rd. G33 J22 38
Drummond Av. G73 O18 52
Drummond Dr., Pais. M 8 47
Drummond Gdns. G13 G12 19
Crow Rd.
Drummore Rd. G15 D10 6
Drummyne Pl. G51 L12 33
Drumoyne Rd.
Drumover Dr. G31 M21 54
Drumoyne Av. G51 K12 33
Drumoyne Circus G51 L12 33
Drumoyne Dr. G51 K12 33

Drumoyne Quad. G51	L12	33
Drumoyne Rd. G51	L12	33
Drumoyne Sq. G51	K12	33
Drumpark St. G46	Q12	61
Drumpark St., Coat.	M28	57
Dunnachie Dr.		
Drumpeller Rd., Bail.	M25	56
Drumpellier Av., Bail.	M25	56
Drumpellier Pl., Bail.	M25	56
Drumpellier St. G33	J20	37
Drumreoch Dr. G42	O18	52
Drumreoch Pl. G42	O18	52
Drumry Pl. G15	E9	6
Drumry Rd. E. G15	E9	6
Drumry Rd., Clyde.	D7	5
Drums Av., Pais.	L5	30
Drums Cres., Pais.	L5	30
Drums Rd. G53	M10	48
Drumsabgard Rd. G73	P20	65
Drumsack Av., Chr.	F26	26
Drumshaw Dr. G32	O23	55
Drumvale Dr., Chr.	E27	15
Drury St. G2	K16	35
Dryad St. G46	P12	61
Dryborough Av., John.	N4	45
Dryburgh Av. G73	O19	53
Dryburgh Gdns. G20	H15	21
Dryburgh Rd., Bear.	C11	7
Dryburn Av. G52	L10	32
Drygate G4	K18	36
Drygrange Rd. G33	J23	39
Drymen Pl., Lenz.	D23	13
Drymen Rd., Bear.	C11	7
Drymen St. G52	L12	33
Morven St.		
Drymen Wynd, Bear.	D12	7
Drynoch Pl. G22	F16	21
Duart Dr., John.	N1	44
Duart St. G20	F14	20
Dubs Rd., Barr.	Q9	60
Dubton St. G34	J25	40
Duchall Pl. G14	H10	18
Duchess Pl. G73	O20	53
Duchess Rd. G73	N20	53
Duchray Dr., Pais.	M9	48
Duchray La. G31	J20	37
Duchray St.		
Duchray St. G33	J20	37
Ducraig St. G32	L22	38
Dudhope St. G33	J23	39
Dudley Dr. G12	H13	20
Duffus Pl. G32	O23	55
Duffus St. G34	J25	40
Duffus Ter. G32	O23	55
Duisdale Rd. G32	O23	55
Duke St., G4	K18	36
Duke St., Linw.	L2	28
Duke St., Pais.	N6	46
Dukes Rd. G72 & G73	P20	65
Dukes Rd., Bail.	L28	41
Dulsie Rd. G21	G20	23
Dumbarton Rd. G11	G9	18
Dumbarton Rd., Clyde.	C6	4
Dumbarton Rd., Old.K.	D5	4
Dalm. & Clyde.		
Dumbreck Av. G41	M13	50
Dumbreck Ct. G41	M13	50
Dumbreck Pl., Lenz.	D24	13
Dumbreck Rd. G41	M13	50
Dumbreck Sq. G41	M13	50
Dumbreck Av.		
Dunagoil Rd. G45	R17	64
Dunagoil St. G45	R18	64
Dunagoil Ter. G45	R18	64
Dunalastair Dr. G33	G22	24
Dunalistair Av. G33	G22	24
Dunan Pl. G33	K24	39
Dunard Rd. G73	O19	53
Dunard St. G20	H15	21
Dunard Way, Pais.	K5	30
Mosslands Rd.		
Dunaskin St. G11	J14	34
Dunbar Av. G73	O20	53
Dunbar Av., John.	O09	43
Dunbar Rd., Pais.	N4	45
Dunbar St. G31	L20	37
Dunbeith Pl. G20	G14	20
Dunblane St. G4	J16	35
Dunbrach Rd., Cumb.	B1	70
Duncan Av. G14	H11	19
Duncan La. G14	H11	19
Duncan Av.		

Duncan La. N. G14	H11	19
Ormiston Av.		
Duncan St., Clyde.	D7	5
Duncansby Rd. G33	L23	39
Dunchatt St. G31	K18	36
Dunchattan Pl. G31	K18	36
Duke St.		
Dunchurch Rd., Pais.	L8	31
Dunclutha Dr., Both.	R28	69
Dunclutha St. G40	N19	53
Duncombe St. G20	F14	20
Duncombe Vw., Clyde.	D8	5
Kirkoswald Dr.		
Duncraig Cres., John.	O08	43
Duncrub Dr., Bish.	E18	10
Duncruin St. G20	F14	20
Duncryne Av. G32	M23	55
Duncryne Gdns. G32	M24	55
Duncryne Pl., Bish.	F18	22
Dundas La. G1	K17	36
Dundas St. G1	K17	36
Dundasvale Ct. G4	J16	35
Maitland St.		
Dundasvale Rd. G4	J16	35
Maitland St.		
Dundee Dr. G52	M10	48
Dundonald Av., John.	N08	43
Dundonald Rd. G12	H14	20
Dundonald Rd., Pais.	K7	31
Dundrennan Rd. G42	O15	51
Dunearn Pl., Pais.	M7	47
Dunearn St. G4	J15	35
Dunegoin St. G51	K13	34
Sharp St.		
Dunellan Dr., Clyde.	B7	5
Dunellan St. G52	L12	33
Dunera Av. G14	J11	33
Dungeonhill Rd. G34	K26	40
Dunglass Av. G14	H11	19
Dunglass La. N. G14	H11	19
Verona Av.		
Dungoil Av., Cumb.	B1	70
Dungoil Rd., Lenz.	D24	13
Dungoyne St. G20	F14	20
Dunira St. G32	M21	54
Dunivaig St. G33	K24	39
Dunkeld Av. G73	O19	53
Dunkeld Dr., Bear.	D13	8
Dunkeld Gdns., Bish.	E19	11
Dunkeld La., Chr.	E28	15
Burnbrae Av.		
Dunkeld St. G31	M20	53
Dunkenny Pl. G15	D9	6
Dunkenny Rd. G15	D9	6
Dunlop Cres., Both.	R28	69
Dunlop Cres., Renf.	H8	17
Hairst St.		
Dunlop St. G1	L17	36
Dunlop St. G72	P24	67
Dunlop St., Linw.	L2	28
Dunlop St., Renf.	H8	17
Hairst St.		
Dunmore La. G5	L16	35
Norfolk St.		
Dunmore St. G5	L16	35
Dunmore St., Clyde.	F8	17
Dunn St. G40	M19	53
Dunn St., Clyde.	C6	4
Dunn St., Dalm.	D6	4
Dunn St., Pais.	M7	47
Dunnachie Dr., Coat.	M28	57
Dunnichen Pl., Bish.	E20	11
Dunning St. G31	M20	53
Dunolly St. G21	J19	37
Dunottar St. G33	J22	38
Dunottar St., Bish.	E20	11
Dunphail Dr. G34	K26	40
Dunphail Rd. G34	K26	40
Dunragit St. G31	K20	37
Dunroamin Av.,	N1	44
John.		
Dunrobin St. G31	L19	37
Dunrod St. G32	M22	54
Dunside Dr. G53	P10	60
Dunskaith Pl. G34	K26	40
Dunskaith St. G34	K26	40
Dunsmuir St. G51	K13	34
Dunster Gdns., Bish.	D19	11
Dunswin Av., Dalm.	D6	4
Dunswin Ct., Dalm.	D6	4
Dunswin Av.		
Dunsyre Pl. G23	E15	9

Dunsyre Pl. G23	F15	21
Broughton Rd.		
Dunsyre St. G33	K21	38
Duntarvie Cres. G34	K26	40
Duntarvie Pl. G34	K25	40
Duntarvie Quad. G34	K26	40
Duntarvie Rd. G34	K25	40
Dunterle Ct., Barr.	Q8	59
Dunterlie Av. G13	G10	18
Duntiglennan Rd., Clyde.	C7	5
Duntocher Rd.,	D6	4
Dalm. & Clyde.		
Duntocher Rd., Bear.	C10	6
Duntocher Rd., Clyde.	C7	5
Duntocher St. G21	H18	22
Northcroft Rd.		
Duntreath Av. G13	F9	18
Duntroon St. G31	K19	37
Dunure Dr. G73	P18	64
Dunure St. G20	F14	20
Dunvegan Av., John.	N2	44
Dunvegan Ct. G13	G10	18
Kintillo Dr.		
Dunvegan Dr., Bish.	D19	11
Dunvegan Quad., Renf.	H7	17
Kirklandneuk Rd.		
Dunvegan St. G51	K13	34
Sharp St.		
Dunwan Av. G13	F9	18
Dunwan Pl. G13	F9	18
Durban Av., Dalm.	D5	4
Durness Av., Bear.	C13	8
Durno Path G33	K24	39
Duror St. G32	L22	38
Durris Gdns. G32	M23	55
Durrockstock Rd., Pais.	O3	45
Durward G41	N14	50
Durward Cres., Pais.	N3	45
Duthil St. G51	L11	33
Dyce La. G11	J13	34
Dyers La. G1	L17	36
Turnbull St.		
Dyers Wynd, Pais.	L6	30
Gilmour St.		
Dyke Pl. G13	F10	18
Dyke Rd. G13	G9	18
Dyke St., Bail.	L26	40
Dykebar Av. G13	G10	18
Dykebar Cres., Pais.	N7	47
Dykefoot Dr. G53	O11	49
Dykehead La. G33	K23	39
Dykehead Rd., Bail.	L27	41
Dykehead St. G33	K23	39
Dykemuir Pl. G21	H19	23
Dykemuir Quadrant G21	H19	23
Dykemuir St.		
Dykemuir St. G21	H19	23
Eagle Cres., Bear.	C10	6
Eagle St. G4	J17	36
Eaglesham Ct. G51	L15	35
Blackburn St.		
Eaglesham Pl. G51	L15	35
Earl Haig Rd. G52	K9	32
Earl Pl. G14	H11	19
Earl St. G14	H10	18
Earlbank Av. G14	H11	19
Earlbank La. N. G14	H11	19
Vancouver Rd.		
Earlbank La. S. G14	H11	19
Verona Av.		
Earls Ct., Chr.	E27	15
Longdale Rd.		
Earls Gate, Both.	Q27	69
Earls Hill G68	B1	70
Earlsburn Rd., Lenz.	D24	13
Earlspark Av. G43	O15	51
Earn Av., Bear.	D13	8
Earn Av., Renf.	J9	32
Almond Av.		
Earn St. G33	J21	38
Earnock St. G33	H20	23
Earnside St. G32	L22	38
Easdale Dr. G32	M22	54
East Av., Renf.	H8	17
East Av., Udd.	P29	69
East Barns St., Clyde.	F8	17
East Bath La. G2	K16	35
Sauchiehall St.		
East Buchanan St., Pais.	L6	30

Street	Ref	Pg
Evanton Dr. G46	R12	61
Evanton Pl. G46	Q12	61
Evanton Dr.		
Everard Dr. G21	F18	22
Everard Rd. G21	F18	22
Everard Quad. G21	F18	22
Everglades, The, Chr.	F25	26
Eversley St. G32	M22	54
Everton Rd. G53	N11	49
Ewart Pl. G3	K14	34
Kelvinhaugh St.		
Ewing Pl. G31	L20	37
Ewing St. G73	O19	53
Ewing St., Kilb.	M07	42
Exchange Pl. G1	K17	36
Buchanan St.		
Exeter Dr. G11	J13	34
Exeter La. G11	J13	34
Exeter Dr.		
Eynort St. G22	F16	21
Fagan Ct., Blan.	R27	69
Faifley Rd., Clyde.	C 7	5
Fairbairn Cres., Thorn.	R13	62
Fairbairn Path G40	M19	53
Ruby St.		
Fairbairn St. G32	M19	53
Dalmarnock Rd.		
Fairburn St. G32	M21	54
Fairfax Av. G44	P17	64
Fairfield Gdns. G51	K12	33
Fairfield Pl. G51	K12	33
Fairfield Pl. G71	R28	69
Fairfield St. G51	K12	33
Fairhaven Dr. G23	F14	20
Fairhill Av. G53	O11	49
Fairholm St. G32	M21	54
Fairley St. G51	L13	34
Fairlie Park Dr. G11	J13	34
Fairway Av., Pais.	O 5	46
Fairways, Bear.	C10	6
Fairyknowe Gdns. G71	R28	69
Falcon Cres., Pais.	L 4	29
Falcon Rd., John.	O08	43
Falcon Ter. G20	F14	20
Falfield St. G5	M16	51
Falkland Cres., Bish.	F20	23
Falkland Mansions G12	H13	20
Clarence Dr.		
Falkland St. G12	H13	20
Falloch Rd., Bear.	E11	7
Fallside Rd., Both.	R28	69
Fallside Av., Pais.	N 6	46
Falside Rd. G32	M22	54
Falside Rd., Pais.	N 5	46
Fara St. G23	F15	21
Farie St. G73	O19	53
Farm Ct., Both.	Q28	69
Fallside Rd.		
Farm La., Udd.	P28	69
Myers Cres.		
Farm Pk., Lenz.	D23	13
Farm Rd. G41	M13	50
Farm Rd., Blan.	R26	68
Farm Rd., Clyde.	C 7	5
Farm Rd., Dalm.	D 5	4
Farme Cross G73	N19	53
Farmeloan Rd. G73	O19	53
Farmington Av. G32	L23	39
Farmington Gate G32	L23	39
Farmington Gdns. G32	L23	39
Farmington Gro. G32	L23	39
Farne Dr. G44	Q16	63
Farnell St. G4	J16	35
Farrier Ct., John.	M09	43
Faskally Av., Bish.	D18	10
Faskin Cres. G53	O 9	48
Faskin Pl. G53	O 9	48
Faskin Rd. G53	O 9	48
Fasque Pl. G15	D 9	6
Fastnet St. G33	K22	38
Faulbswood Cres., Pais.	N 4	45
Fauldhouse St. G5	M17	52
Faulds Gdns., Bail.	L26	40
Faulds, Bail.	L26	40
Fauldshead Rd., Renf.	H 8	17
Fauldspark Cres., Bail.	L26	40
Fauldswood Cres., Pais.	N 4	45
Fauldswood Dr., Pais.	N 4	45
Fearnmore Rd. G20	F14	20
Fendoch St. G32	M22	54
Fenella St. G32	L22	38
Fennsbank Av. G73	Q20	65
Fenwick Dr., Barr.	R 8	59
Fenwick Pl., Giff.	R13	62
Fenwick Rd., Giff.	R14	62
Fereneze Av., Barr.	Q 7	59
Fereneze Av., Pais.	K 7	31
Ferenze Cres. G13	F10	18
Ferenze Dr., Pais.	O 5	46
Fergus Ct. G20	H15	21
Fergus Dr. G20	H15	21
Ferguslie Park Av., Pais.	L 4	29
Ferguslie Park Cres., Pais.	M 4	45
Ferguslie Pk.	L 3	29
Ferguslie Wk., Pais.	M 4	45
Ferguslie, Pais.	M 4	45
Ferguson Av., Renf.	H 8	17
Ferguson St., John.	M09	43
Ferguson St., Renf.	H 8	17
Fergusson Rd., Cumb.	C 2	70
Ferguston Rd., Bear.	D12	7
Fern Av., Bish.	F19	23
Fern Av., Lenz.	C23	13
Fern Dr., Barr.	Q 7	59
Fern Hill Grange G71	R28	69
Fernan St. G32	L21	38
Fernbank Av. G72	Q23	67
Fernbank St. G22	G18	22
Fernbrae Rd. G46	Q20	65
Fernbrae Way G73	Q19	65
Ferncroft Dr. G44	P17	64
Ferndale Ct. G23	F14	20
Rothes Dr.		
Ferndale Dr. G23	F14	20
Ferndale Gdns. G23	F14	20
Ferndale Pl. G23	F14	20
Rothes Drive		
Ferness Oval G21	F20	23
Ferness Pl. G21	F20	23
Ferness Rd. G21	G20	23
Ferngrove Av. G12	G13	20
Fernhill Rd. G73	Q19	65
Fernleigh Pl., Chr.	E27	15
Fernleigh Rd. G43	P14	62
Fernslea Av. G72	S26	68
Ferry Rd. G3	K13	34
Ferry Rd., Both.	R28	69
Ferry Rd., Renf.	H 8	17
Ferry Rd., Udd.	P26	68
Ferryden St. G14	J12	33
Fersit St. G43	P14	62
Fetlar Dr. G44	P17	64
Fettercairn Av. G15	D 9	6
Fettercairn Gdns., Bish.	E20	11
Fettes St. G33	K21	38
Fidra St. G33	K21	38
Fielden Pl. G40	L19	37
Fielden St. G40	L19	37
Fieldhead Dr. G43	P13	62
Fieldhead Sq. G43	P13	62
Fife Av. G52	M10	48
Fife Cres., Both.	R28	69
Fifeway, Bish.	F20	23
Fifth Av. G12	G12	19
Fifth Av. G33	G22	24
Fifth Av., Lenz.	E23	13
Fifth Av., Renf.	J 8	31
Finart Dr., Pais.	N 7	47
Finch Pl., John.	O08	43
Findhorn Av., Renf.	H 9	18
Findhorn Cres., Pais.	N 3	45
Findhorn St. G33	K20	37
Findochty St. G33	J23	39
Fingal La. G20	F14	20
Fingal St.		
Fingal St. G20	F14	20
Fingask St. G32	M23	55
Finglas Av., Pais.	N 7	47
Fingleton Av., Barr.	R 8	59
Finhaven St. G32	M21	54
Finlarig St. G34	K26	40
Finlas St. G22	H17	22
Finlay Dr. G31	K19	37
Finlay Dr., Linw.	L 1	28
Finnart Sq. G40	M18	52
Finnart St. G40	M18	52
Finnieston Pl. G3	K15	35
Finnieston St.		
Finnieston St. G3	K15	35
Finsbay St. G51	L12	33
Fintry Av., Pais.	O 6	46
Fintry Cres., Barr.	R 8	59
Fintry Cres., Bish.	E20	11
Fintry Dr. G44	O17	52
Fir Pl. G72	P23	67
Caledonian Circuit		
Fir Pl., Bail.	M25	56
Fir Pl., John.	N 1	44
Firbank Ter., Barr.	R 9	60
Firdon Cres. G15	E10	6
Firhill Rd. G20	H16	21
Firhill St. G20	H16	21
Firpark Pl. G31	K18	36
Firpark St.		
Firpark Rd., Bish.	F19	23
Firpark St. G31	K18	36
Firpark Ter. G31	K18	36
Ark La.		
First Av. G33	H22	24
First Av. G44	R15	63
First Av., Bear.	D13	8
First Av., Lenz.	E23	13
First Av., Renf.	J 8	31
First Av., Udd.	O27	57
First Gdns. G41	M13	50
First St., Udd.	O27	57
First Ter., Clyde.	D 7	5
Firwood Dr. G44	P17	64
Fishcoates Gdns. G73	P20	65
Fishcoates Av.		
Fisher Cres., Clyde.	C 7	5
Fisher Ct. G31	K18	36
Fishers Rd., Renf.	G 8	17
Fishescoates Av. G73	Q20	65
Fitzalan Dr., Pais.	L 7	31
Fitzalan Rd., Renf.	J 7	31
Fitzroy La. G3	K15	35
Claremont St.		
Fitzroy Pl. G3	K15	35
Claremont St.		
Fitzroy Pl. G3	K15	35
Sauchiehall St.		
Flax Rd., Udd.	P28	69
Fleet Av., Renf.	J 9	32
Fleet St. G32	M22	54
Fleming Av., Chr.	F26	26
Fleming Av., Clyde.	F 8	17
Fleming Rd., Cumb.	C 2	70
Fleming St. G31	L19	37
Fleming St., Pais.	K 6	30
Flemington Rd. G72	R24	67
Flemington St. G21	H18	22
Fleurs Av. G41	M13	50
Fleurs Rd. G41	M13	50
Floors St., John.	N09	43
Floorsburn Cres., John.	N09	43
Flora Gdns., Bish.	E20	11
Florence Dr., Giff.	R14	62
Florence Gdns. G73	Q20	65
Florence St. G5	L17	36
Florence St. G73	M17	52
Florentine Pl. G12	J15	35
Gibson St.		
Florentine Ter. G12	J15	35
Southpark Av.		
Florida Av. G42	O16	51
Florida Cres. G42	O16	51
Florida Dr. G42	O16	51
Florida Gdns., Bail.	L25	40
Florida Sq. G42	O16	51
Florida St. G42	O16	51
Fochabers Dr. G52	L11	33
Fogo Pl. G20	G14	20
Forbes Dr. G40	L18	36
Forbes Pl., Pais.	M 6	46
Forbes St. G40	L18	36
Ford Rd. G12	H14	20
Fordneuk St. G40	L19	37
Fordoun St. G34	K26	40
Fordyce St. G11	J13	34
Fore St. G14	H11	19
Forehouse Rd., Kilb.	MO6	42
Forest Dr., Udd.	Q28	69
Forest Gdns., Lenz.	D22	12
Forest Pl., Lenz.	D22	12
Forest Pl., Pais.	N 6	46
Brodie Park Av.		
Forest Rd., Cumb.	C 4	71
Forest Vw., Cumb.	B 4	71
Forfar Av. G52	M10	48
Forfar Cres., Bish.	F20	23
Forgan Gdns., Bish.	F20	23
Forge St. G21	J19	37

Forglen St. G34 — J25 40
Formby Dr. G23 — E14 8
Forres Av. G46 — Q14 62
Forres Gate, Giff. — R14 62
Forres Av.
Forres St. G23 — E15 9
Tolsta St.
Forrest St. G40 — L19 37
Forrestfield St. G21 — J19 37
Fortevoit Av., Bail. — L26 40
Fortevoit Pl., Bail. — L26 40
Forth Av., Renf. — J 8 31
Third Av.
Forth Ave., Pais. — N 3 45
Forth Pl., John. — O08 43
Forth Rd. G61 — C11 7
Forth Rd., Bear. — E11 7
Forth St. G41 — M15 51
Fortingall Av. G12 — G14 20
Grantully Dr.
Fortingall Pl. G12 — G14 20
Fortrose St. G11 — J13 34
Foswell Pl. G15 — C 9 6
Fotheringay La. G41 — N15 51
Beaton Rd.
Fotheringay Rd. G41 — N14 50
Foulis La. G13 — G12 19
Foulis St. G13 — G12 19
Foundry La., Barr. — R 7 59
Main St.
Foundry Open G31 — L19 37
Fountain St. G31 — L18 36
Fountainwell Av. G.21 — J17 36
Fountainwell Dr. G21 — J17 36
Fountainwell Pl. G21 — J17 36
Fountainwell Rd. G21 — J17 36
Fountainwell Sq. G21 — J18 36
Fountainwell Ter. G21 — J18 36
Fourth Av., G33 — G22 24
Fourth Av., Lenz. — E23 13
Fourth Av., Renf. — J 8 31
Third Av.
Fourth Gdns. G41 — M13 50
Fourth St., Udd. — N27 57
Fox La. G1 — L17 36
Fox St. G1 — L16 35
Foxbar Cres., Pais. — O 3 45
Foxbar Dr. G13. — G10 18
Foxbar Dr. G78 — O 3 45
Foxbar Rd., Pais. — O 3 45
Foxes Gro. G66 — C24 13
Foxhills Pl. G23 — E15 9
Foxley St. G.32 — N23 55
Foyers Ct. G13 — G10 18
Kirkton Av.
Foyers Ter. G21 — H19 23
Francis St. G5 — M16 51
Frankfield Rd. G33 — G24 25
Frankfield St. G33 — J20 37
Frankfort St. G41 — N15 51
Franklin St. G40 — M18 52
Fraser Av. G73 — O20 53
Fraser Av., John. — N 1 44
Fraser St. G40 — L19 37
Fraser St. G72 — P21 66
Fraserbank St. G21 — H17 22
Keppochill Rd.
Frazer St. G31 — L20 37
Frederick Path G1 — K17 36
Freeland Dr. G53 — P10 60
Freeland Dr., Renf. — G 5 16
Freelands Cres., Old K — C 5 4
Freelands Ct., Old K. — C 5 4
Freelands Pl., Old K. — D 5 4
Freelands Rd., Old K. — C 5 4
French St. G40 — M18 52
French St., Dalm. — D 6 4
French St., Renf. — J 7 31
Freuchie St. G34 — K25 40
Friar Av., Bish. — D19 11
Friars Court Rd., Chr. — E25 14
Friars Pl. G13 — F11 19
Friarscourt Av. G13 — E11 7
Friarscourt La. G13 — F11 19
Arrowsmith Av.
Friarton Rd. G43 — P15 63
Friendship Way, Renf. — J 8 31
Fruin Pl. G22 — H17 22
Fruin Rd. G15 — E 9 6
Fruin St. G22 — H17 22
Fulbar Av., Renf. — H 8 17

Fulbar Ct., Renf. — H 8 17
Fulbar Av.
Fulbar La., Renf. — H 8 17
Fulbar Rd. G51 — K11 33
Fulbar Rd., Pais. — M 3 45
Fulbar St., Renf. — H 8 17
Fullarton Av. G32 — N22 54
Fullarton Rd. G32 — O21 54
Fullerton St., Pais — K 5 30
Fullerton Ter., Pais. — K 6 30
Fulmar Ct., Bish. — F18 22
Fulmar Pl., John. — O08 43
Fulton Cres., Kilb. — M07 42
Fulton St. G13 — F11 19
Fulwood Av. G13 — F 9 18
Fulwood Av., Linw. — L 1 28
Fulwood Pl. G13 — F 9 18
Fynloch Pl., Clyde — B 6 4
Fyvie Av. G43 — P13 62
Gadie Av., Renf. — J 9 32
Gadie St. G33 — K20 37
Gadloch Av., Lenz. — E23 13
Gadloch Gdns., Lenz. — D23 13
Gadloch St. G22 — G17 22
Gadlock Vw. G66 — E23 13
Gadsburn Ct. G21 — G20 23
Wallacewell Quadrant
Gadshill St. G21 — J18 36
Gailes Pk., Both. — R27 69
Eden Pk.
Gailes St. G40 — M19 53
Gairbraid Av. G20 — G14 20
Gairbraid Ct. G20 — G14 20
Gairbraid Pl. G20 — G14 20
Gairbraid Ter., Bail. — L28 41
Gairn St. G11 — J13 34
Castlebank St.
Gala Av., Renf. — J 9 32
Gala St. G33 — J21 38
Galbraith Av. G51 — K12 33
Burghead Dr.
Galbraith Dr. G51 — K11 33
Galbraith St. G51 — K11 33
Moss Rd.
Galdenoch St. G33 — J22 38
Gallacher Av., John. — N 3 45
Gallacher Av., Pais. — N 4 45
Gallan Av. G23 — E15 9
Galloway Dr. G73 — Q19 65
Galloway St. G21 — G18 22
Gallowflat St. G73 — O19 53
Gallowgate G1 — L17 36
Gallowhill Av., Lenz. — C23 13
Gallowhill Gro., Lenz. — C23 13
Gallowhill Rd., Lenz. — C23 13
Gallowhill Rd., Pais. — L 6 30
Galston St. G53 — P 9 60
Gamrie Dr. G53 — O10 48
Gamrie Gdns. G53 — O10 48
Gamrie Rd. G53 — O10 48
Gannochy Dr., Bish. — E20 11
Gantock Cres. G33 — K22 38
Gardenside Av. G32. — O22 54
Gardenside Av., Udd. — O22 54
Gardenside Cres. G32 — O22 54
Gardenside Pl. G32 — O22 54
Gardenside St., Udd. — P27 69
Gardner La., Bail. — M26 56
Church St.
Gardner St. G11 — J13 34
Gardyne St. G34 — J25 40
Garfield St. G31 — L19 37
Garforth Rd., Bail. — M24 55
Gargrave Av., Bail. — M24 55
Garion Dr. G13 — G10 18
Talbot Dr.
Garion Dr. G13 — G10 18
Garlieston Rd. G33 — L24 39
Garmouth Ct. G51 — K12 33
Elder St.
Garmouth Gdns. G51 — K12 33
Garmouth St. G51 — K12 33
Garnet La. G3 — J16 35
Garnet St.
Garnet St. G3 — J16 35
Garnethill St. G3 — J16 35
Garngaber Av., Lenz. — C23 13
Garngaber Ct. G66 — C24 13
Woodleigh Rd.
Garnkirk La. G33 — G24 25
Garnkirk St. G21 — J18 36

Garnock St. G21 — J18 36
Garrell Way, Cumb. — C 2 70
Garrioch Cres. G20 — G14 20
Garrioch Dr. G20 — G14 20
Garrioch Gate G20 — G14 20
Garrioch Quad. G20 — G14 20
Garrioch Rd. G20 — H14 20
Garriochmill Rd. G20 — H15 21
Raeberry St.
Garriochmill Way G20 — H15 21
Woodside Rd.
Garrowhill Dr., Bail. — M24 55
Garry Av., Bear. — E13 8
Garry Dr., Pais. — N 4 45
Garry St. G44 — O16 51
Garscadden G13 — F10 18
Garscadden Rd. G15 — E10 6
Garscadden Vw., Clyde. — D 8 5
Kirkoswald Dr.
Garscube Rd. G20 — H16 21
Garscube Ter., Pais. — M 7 47
Gartcarron Hill, Cumb. — B 1 70
Dunbrach Rd.
Gartconnel Dr., Bear. — C12 7
Gartconnel Gdns., Bear. — C12 7
Gartconnel Rd., Bear. — C12 7
Gartcosh Rd., — K28 41
Bail. & Gart.
Gartcraig Rd. G33 — K21 38
Gartferry Av., Chr. — E27 15
Gartferry Rd., Chr. — E27 15
Gartferry St. G21 — H19 23
Garth St. G1 — K17 36
Garthamlock Rd. G33 — J24 39
Garthland Dr. G31 — K19 37
Garthland La., Pais. — L 6 30
Gartliston Ter., Bail. — L28 41
Gartloch Cotts., Chr. — G25 26
Gartloch Cotts., Gart. — H27 27
Gartloch Rd. G33 — J21 38
Gartly St. G44 — Q15 63
Clarkston Rd.
Gartmore Gdns., Udd. — O27 57
Gartmore La., Chr. — E28 15
Gartmore Rd., Pais. — M 8 47
Gartmore Ter. G72 — Q21 66
Gartness St. G31 — K19 37
Gartocher Rd. G32 — L23 39
Gartons Rd. G21 — H20 23
Gartshore Rd., — C27 15
Drumbreck
Garturk St. G42 — N16 51
Garvald Ct. G40 — M19 53
Baltic St.
Garvald St. G40 — M19 53
Garve Av. G44 — Q16 63
Garvel Cres. G33 — L24 39
Garvel Rd. G33 — L24 39
Garvock Dr. G43 — P13 62
Gas St., John. — M 1 44
Gask Pl. G13 — F 9 18
Gatehouse St. G32 — L22 38
Gateside Av. G72 — P23 67
Gateside Cres., Barr. — R 7 59
Gateside Pl., Kilb. — M07 42
Gateside Rd., Barr. — R 7 59
Gateside St. G31 — L19 37
Gauldry Av. G52 — M11 49
Gauze St., Pais. — L 6 30
Gavins Rd., Clyde. — C 7 5
Gavinton St. G44 — Q15 63
Gear Ter. G40 — N19 53
Geary St. G23 — E14 8
Torrin Rd.,
Geddes Rd. G21 — F20 23
Gelston St. G32 — M22 54
General Terminus Quay G51 — L15 35
Generals Gate, Udd. — P27 69
Cobbleriggs Way
Gentle Row, Clyde. — C 6 4
George Av., Clyde. — D 8 5
Robert Burns Av.
George Cres., Clyde. — D 8 5
George Gray St. G73 — O20 53
George Mann Ter. G73 — P19 65
George Pl., Pais. — M 6 46
George Reith Av. G12 — G12 19
George Sq. G2 — K17 36
George St. G1 — K17 36
George St., Bail. — M25 56

Street	Ref	Pg
Gogar Pl. G33	K21	38
Gogar St. G33	K21	38
Goldberry Av. G14	G10	18
Goldie Rd., Udd.	Q28	69
Golf Ct. G44	R15	63
Golf Dr. G15	E 9	6
Golf Dr., Pais.	M 8	47
Golf Rd. G73	Q19	65
Golf Vw., Bear.	C10	6
Golf Vw., Dalm.	D 6	4
Golfhill Dr. G31	K19	37
Golfhill La. G31	K19	37
Whitehill St.		
Golfhill Ter. G31	K18	36
Firpark St.		
Golspie St. G51	K13	34
Goosedubbs G1	L17	36
Stockwell St.		
Gopher Av., Udd.	O28	57
Myrtle Rd.		
Gorbals Cross G5	L17	36
Gorbals La. G5	L16	35
Oxford St.		
Gorbals St. G5	L16	35
Gordon Av. G44	R15	63
Gordon Av., Bail.	L24	39
Gordon Dr. G44	Q15	63
Gordon La. G1	K16	35
Gordon St.		
Gordon Rd. G44	R15	63
Gordon St. G1	K16	35
Gordon St., Pais.	M 6	46
Gordon Ter., Blan.	R26	68
Gorebridge St. G32	K21	38
Gorget Av. G13	E11	7
Gorget Pl. G13	E11	7
Gorget Quad. G15	E10	6
Gorget Av.		
Gorse Dr., Barr.	Q 7	59
Gorse Pl., Udd.	O28	57
Myrtle Rd.		
Gorsewood, Bish.	E18	10
Gorstan Pl. G20	G14	20
Wyndford Rd.		
Gorstan St. G23	F14	20
Gosford La. G14	G 9	18
Dumbarton Rd.		
Goudie St., Pais.	K 5	30
Gough St. G33	K20	37
Gourlay Path G21	H17	22
Endrick St.		
Gourlay St. G21	H17	22
Gourlay St. G21	H18	22
Millarbank St.		
Gourock Sq., Barr.	R 9	60
Gourock St. G5	M16	51
Govan Cross G51	K13	34
Govan Rd. G51	K12	33
Govanhill St. G42	N16	51
Gowanbank Gdns., John.	N09	43
Floors St.		
Gowanbrae, Lenz.	C23	13
Gallowhill Rd.		
Gowanlea Av. G15	E10	6
Gowanlea Dr., Giff.	Q14	62
Gowanlea Ter., Udd.	O28	57
Gower La. G51	L14	34
Gower St.		
Gower St. G43	M14	50
Gower Ter. G41	L14	34
Goyle Av. G15	D11	7
Grace Av., Bail.	L27	41
Grace St. G3	K15	35
Graffham Av., Giff.	Q14	62
Grafton Pl. G4	K17	36
Graham Av. G72	P23	67
Graham Av., Clyde.	D 7	5
Graham Sq. G31	L18	36
Graham St., Barr.	Q 7	59
Graham St., John.	N09	43
Graham Ter., Bish.	F19	23
Grahamston Cres., Pais.	O 8	47
Grahamston Ct., Pais.	O 8	47
Grahamston Pl., Pais.	O 8	47
Grahamston Rd.		
Grahamston Rd., Barr.	P 7	59
Graighead Av. G33	H20	23
Grainger Rd., Bish.	E20	11
Grampian Av., Pais.	O 5	46
Grampian Cres. G32	M22	54
Grampian Pl. G32	M22	54
Grampian St. G32	M22	54
Grampian Way, Barr.	R 8	59
Gran St., Clyde.	F 9	18
Granby La. G12	H14	20
Great George St.		
Granby Pl. G12	H14	20
Great George St.		
Grandtully Dr. G12	G14	20
Grange Gdns. G71	R28	69
Blairston Av.		
Grange Rd. G42	O16	51
Grange Rd., Bear.	C12	7
Grangeneuk Gdnd., Cumb.	C 1	70
Grant St. G3	J15	35
Grantlea Gro. G32	M23	55
Grantlea Ter. G32	M23	55
Grantley Gdns. G41	O14	50
Grantley St. G41	O14	50
Granton St. G5	N18	52
Granville St. G3	K15	35
Granville St., Clyde.	D 7	5
Gray Dr., Bear.	D12	7
Gray St. G3	J14	34
Great Dovehill G1	L17	36
Great George La. G12	H14	20
Great George St.		
Great George St. G12	H14	20
Great Kelvin La. G12	H15	21
Glasgow St.		
Great Western Rd. G12	H14	20
Great Western Ter. G12	H14	20
Great Western Terrace La. G12	H14	20
Westbourne Gdns. W.		
Green Av., Lenz.	B23	13
Green Farm Rd., Linw.	L 1	28
Green Lodge Ter. G40	M18	52
Greenhead St.		
Green Pk., Both.	R28	69
Green St.		
Green Rd. G73	O19	53
Green Rd., Pais.	M 4	45
Green St. G40	L18	36
Green St., Both.	R28	69
Green St., Clyde.	D 7	5
Green, The, G40	L18	36
Greenan Av. G42	O18	52
Greenbank Dr., Pais.	O 5	46
Greenbank Rd., Cumb.	C 1	70
Burnhead Rd.		
Greenbank St. G43	P13	62
Harriet St.		
Greenbank St. G73	O19	53
Greendyke St. G1	L17	36
Greenend Av., John.	N08	43
Greenend Pl. G32	K23	39
Greenfaulds Cres., Cumb.	D 3	71
Greenfaulds Rd., Cumb.	D 2	70
Greenfield Av. G32	K22	38
Greenfield Pl. G32	L22	38
Budhill Av.		
Greenfield Rd. G32	L23	39
Greenfield St. G51	K12	33
Greengairs Av. G51	K11	33
Greenhaugh St. G51	K13	34
Greenhead Rd., Bear.	D12	7
Greenhead Rd., Renf.	F 5	16
Greenhead St. G40	M18	52
Greenhill Av., Gart.	F27	27
Greenhill Av., Giff.	R13	62
Greenhill Cres., John.	N 2	44
Greenhill Cres., Linw.	L 2	28
Greenhill Ct. G73	O19	53
Greenhill Rd. G73	O19	53
Greenhill Rd., Pais.	L 5	30
Greenhill St. G73	O19	53
Greenhill, Bish.	E19	11
Greenholm Av., Udd.	O27	57
Greenholme St. G40	P16	63
Holmlea Rd.		
Greenknowe Rd. G43	P13	62
Greenlaw Av., Pais.	L 7	31
Greenlaw Dr., Pais.	L 7	31
Greenlaw Rd. G14	G 9	18
Greenlaw Ter., Pais.	L 7	31
Greenlaw Av.		
Greenlea Rd., Chr.	F25	26
Greenlea St. G13	G12	19
Greenlees Gdns. G72	Q21	66
Greenlees Pk. G72	Q22	66
Greenlees Rd. G72	P22	66
Greenloan Av. G51	K11	33
Greenloan Av. G51	K11	33
Kenneth Dr.		
Greenmount G22	F16	21
Greenock Av. G44	P16	63
Greenock Rd., Pais.	K 5	30
Greenock Rd., Renf.	G 5	16
Greenrig St. G33	H20	23
Greenrig St., Udd.	P27	69
Greenrigg Rd., Cumb.	C 3	71
Greenshields Rd., Bail.	L25	40
Greenside Cres. G33	H21	24
Greenside St. G33	H21	24
Greentree Dr., Bail.	M24	55
Greenview St. G43	O14	50
Greenways Av., Pais.	N 4	45
Greenways Ct., John.	N 4	45
Greenwell Pl. G51	K13	34
Greenwell St. G51	K13	34
Govan Rd.		
Greenwood Av. G72	P24	67
Greenwood Av., Chr.	E27	15
Greenwood Dr., Bear.	D13	8
Greenwood Quad., Clyde.	E 8	5
Greer Quad., Clyde.	D 7	5
Grenville Dr. G72	Q21	66
Greran Dr., Renf.	H 7	17
Gretna St. G40	M19	53
Greyfriars St. G32	K21	38
Greystone Av. G73	P20	65
Greywood St. G13	F12	19
Grier Path G31	L20	37
Grierson St. G33	K20	37
Grieve Rd., Cumb.	B 3	71
Griqua Ter. G71	R28	69
Grogary Rd. G15	D10	6
Springside Pl.		
Grosvenor Cres. G12	H14	20
Observatory Rd.		
Grosvenor Cres. La. G12	H14	20
Byres Rd.		
Grosvenor La. G12	H14	20
Byres Rd.		
Grosvenor Mansions G12	H14	20
Observatory Rd.		
Grosvenor Ter. G12	H14	20
Grove Pk., Lenz.	D23	13
Grove, The, Giff.	S13	62
Grove, The, Kilb.	M07	42
Groveburn Av., Thorn.	Q13	62
Grovepark Pl. G20	H16	21
Grovepark St. G20	H16	21
Groves, The, Bish.	F20	23
Woodhill Rd.		
Grudie St. G34	K25	40
Gryffe Av., Renf.	H 7	17
Gryffe Cres., Pais.	N 3	45
Gryffe St. G44	P16	63
Guildford St. G33	J23	39
Gullane St. G11	J13	34
Purdon St.		
Guthrie St. G20	G14	20
Hagg Cres., John.	M09	43
Hagg Pl., John.	M09	43
Hagg Rd., John.	N09	43
Haggs Rd. G41	N14	50
Haggs Wood Av. G41	N14	50
Haghill Rd. G31	K20	37
Haig Dr., Bail.	M24	55
Haig St. G21	H19	23
Hailes Av. G32	L23	39
Haining Rd., Renf.	H 8	17
Hairmyres St. G42	N16	51
Govanhill St.		
Hairst St., Renf.	H 8	17
Halbeath Av. G15	D 9	6
Halbert St. G41	N15	51
Haldane La. G14	H11	19
Haldane St.		
Haldane St. G14	H11	19
Halgreen Av. G15	D 9	6
Halifax Way, Renf.	J 8	31
Britannia Way		
Hall St., Clyde.	E 7	5
Hallbrae St. G33	J21	38
Halley Dr. G13	F 9	18
Halley Pl. G13	F 9	18
Halley Sq. G31	G 9	18

Name	Grid	Page
Halley St. G13	F 9	18
Halley Ter. G13	G 9	18
Hallhill Cres. G33	L24	39
Hallhill Rd. G32	L22	38
Hallhill Rd., John.	O08	43
Hallidale Cres., Renf.	J 9	32
Hallrule Dr. G52	L11	33
Hallside Av. G72	P24	67
Hallside Cres. G72	P24	67
Hallside Dr. G72	P24	67
Hallside Rd. G72	Q24	67
Hallside St. G5	M17	52
Hallydown Dr. G13	G11	19
Halton Gdns., Bail.	M24	55
Hamilton Av. G41	M13	50
Hamilton Cres. G72	Q23	67
Hamilton Cres., Bear.	B12	7
Hamilton Cres., Renf.	G 8	17
Hamilton Dr. G12	H15	21
Hamilton Dr. G72	P22	66
Hamilton Dr., Both.	R28	69
Hamilton Dr., Giff.	R14	62
Hamilton Park Av. G12	H15	21
Hamilton Rd. G32	N24	55
Hamilton Rd. G72 & Blan.	P22	66
Hamilton Rd. G73	O19	53
Hamilton Rd., Both.	R28	69
Hamilton St. G42	N17	52
Hamilton St., Clyde.	F 8	17
Hamilton St., Pais.	L 6	30
Hamilton Ter., Clyde.	F 8	17
Hamilton Vw., Udd.	O28	57
Hamiltonhill Rd. G22	H16	21
Hampden Dr. G42	O16	51
Cathcart Rd.		
Hampden La. G42	O16	51
Cathcart Rd.		
Hampden Ter. G42	O16	51
Cathcart Rd.		
Hampden Way, Renf.	J 8	31
Lewis Av.		
Hangingshaw Pl. G42	O17	52
Haning, The, Renf.	J 8	31
Hanover St. G1	K17	36
Hanson St. G31	K18	36
Hapland Av. G53	N11	49
Hapland Rd. G53	N11	49
Harbour La., Pais.	L 6	30
Harbour Rd., Pais.	K 6	30
Harburn Pl. G23	E15	9
Harcourt Dr. G31	K19	37
Hardgate Rd. G51	K11	33
Hardie Av. G73	O20	53
Hardridge Av. G52	N11	49
Hardridge Rd.		
Hardridge Pl. G52	N12	49
Hardridge Rd. G52	N11	49
Harefield Dr. G14	G10	18
Harelaw Av. G44	Q15	63
Harelaw Av., Barr.	R 8	59
Harelaw Cres., Pais.	O 5	46
Harhill St. G51	K12	33
Harland Cotts. G14	J11	33
South St.		
Harland St. G14	H11	19
Harlaw Gdns. G64	E20	11
Harley St. G51	L14	34
Harmetray St. G22	G17	22
Harmony Pl. G51	K13	34
Harmony Row G51	K13	34
Harmony Sq. G51	K13	34
Harmsworth St. G11	J12	33
Harport St. G46	Q12	61
Harriet St. G43	P13	62
Harriet St. G73	O19	53
Harrington St. G20	G15	21
Maryhill Rd.		
Harris Rd. G23	E15	9
Harrison Dr. G51	L13	34
Harrow Ct. G15	D 9	6
Linkwood Dr.		
Harrow Pl. G15	D 9	6
Hart St. G31	L21	38
Hart St., Linw.	L 1	28
Hartfield Ter., Pais.	N 7	47
Hartlaw Cres. G52	L10	32
Hartree Av. G13	F 9	18
Hartstone Pl. G53	O10	48
Hartstone Rd. G53	O10	48
Hartstone Ter. G53	O10	48
Harvey St. G4	J17	36

Name	Grid	Page
Harvey St. G4	J17	36
Harvie St. G51	L14	34
Harwood St. G32	K21	38
Hastie St. G3	J14	34
Old Dumbarton Rd.		
Hatfield Dr. G12	G12	19
Hathaway Dr., Giff.	R13	62
Hathaway St. G20	G15	21
Hathersage Av., Bail.	L25	40
Hathersage Dr., Bail.	L25	40
Hathersage Gdns., Bail.	L25	40
Hatters Row G40	M18	52
Dalmarnock Rd.		
Hatton Dr. G52	M10	48
Hatton Gdns. G52	M10	48
Haugh Rd. G3	K14	34
Haughburn Pl. G53	O10	48
Haughburn Rd. G53	O10	48
Haughburn Ter. G53	O11	49
Havelock La. G11	J14	34
Downhill St.		
Havelock St. G11	J14	34
Hawick Av. G78	N 4	45
Hawick St. G13	F 9	18
Hawkhead Av., Pais.	N 7	47
Hawkhead Rd., Pais.	M 7	47
Hawthorn Av., Bish.	F19	23
Hawthorn Av., Lenz.	C23	13
Hawthorn Dr., Barr.	S 8	59
Hawthorn Quad. G22	G17	22
Hawthorn St. G22	G17	22
Hawthorn St., Clyde.	D 7	5
Hawthorn Wk. G72	P20	65
Hawthorn Wk., Bish.	F20	23
Letham Dr.		
Hawthornden Gdns. G23	E15	9
Broughton Rd.		
Hawthorne Av., Bear.	B13	8
Hawthorne Av., John.	N 1	44
Hawthorne Ter., Udd.	O28	57
Douglas St.		
Hay Dr., John.	M 1	44
Hayburn Cres. G11	H13	20
Hayburn Ct. G11	J13	34
Rosevale St.		
Hayburn La. G12	H13	20
Queensborough Gdns.		
Hayburn St. G11	J13	34
Hayfield St. G5	M17	52
Hayhill Cotts., Gart.	G28	27
Hayle Gdns., Chr.	D27	15
Haylynn St. G14	J12	33
Haymarket St. G32	K21	38
Haystack Pl., Lenz.	D23	13
Hayston Cres. G22	G16	21
Hayston St. G22	G16	21
Haywood St. G22	G16	21
Hazel Av. G44	Q15	63
Clarkston Rd.		
Hazel Av., John.	N 1	44
Hazel Av., Lenz.	C23	13
Hazel Dene, Bish.	E19	11
Hazel Gro., Lenz.	C23	13
Hazel Rd., Cumb.	B 4	71
Hazel Ter., Udd.	O28	57
Douglas St.		
Hazelden Gdns. G44	Q15	63
Hazellea Dr., Giff.	Q14	62
Hazelwood Av. G78	O 3	45
Hazelwood Dr., Blan.	S26	68
Hazelwood Gdns. G73	Q20	65
Hazelwood Rd. G41	M14	50
Hazlitt St. G20	G16	21
Heath Av., Bish.	F19	23
Heath Av., Lenz.	D23	13
Heathcliffe Av., Blan.	R26	68
Heathcot Av. G15	E 9	6
Heathcot Pl. G15	E 9	6
Heathcot Av.		
Heather Av., Barr.	P 7	59
Heather Dr., Lenz.	D22	12
Heather Gdns., Lenz.	D22	12
Heather Pl., John.	N 1	44
Heather Pl., Lenz.	C22	12
Heather St. G41	L15	35
Scotland St.		
Heatherbrae, Bish.	E18	10
Heatheryknowe Rd., Bail.	K27	41
Heathfield Av., Chr.	E27	15
Heathfield St. G33	K23	39

Name	Grid	Page
Heathfield Ter. G21	G18	22
Broomfield Rd.		
Heathside Rd., Giff.	Q14	62
Heathwood Dr., Thorn.	Q13	62
Hecla Av. G15	D 9	6
Hecla Pl. G15	D 9	6
Hector Rd. G41	O14	50
Heggie Ter. G14	H11	19
Dumbarton Rd.		
Helen St. G52	L12	33
Helenburgh Dr. G13	G11	19
Helenslea G72	Q23	67
Helenvale Ct. G31	L20	37
Helenvale St.		
Helenvale St. G31	M20	53
Helmsdale Av., Blan.	Q26	68
Helmsdale Ct. G72	P23	67
Hemlock St. G13	F12	19
Henderland Rd., Bear.	E12	7
Henderson Av. G72	P23	67
Henderson St. G20	H15	21
Henderson St., Clyde.	F 9	18
Henderson St., Pais.	L 5	30
Henrietta St. G14	H11	19
Henry St., Barr.	Q 7	59
Hepburn Rd. G52	K10	32
Herald Av. G13	E11	7
Herald Way, Renf.	J 8	31
Viscount Av.		
Herbert St. G20	H15	21
Herbertson St. G5	L16	35
Eglinton St.		
Hercules Way, Renf.	J 8	31
Friendship Way		
Herichell St. G13	G12	19
Foulis La.		
Heriot Av., Pais.	O 3	45
Heriot Cres., Bish.	D19	11
Heriot Rd., Lenz.	D23	13
Herma St. G23	F15	21
Hermiston Av. G32	L23	39
Hermiston Pl. G32	L23	39
Hermiston Rd. G32	K22	38
Hermitage Av. G13	G11	19
Heron Ct., Clyde.	C 7	5
Heron Pl., John.	O08	43
Heron St. G40	M18	52
Heron Way, Renf.	J 8	31
Britannia Way		
Herries Rd. G41	N14	50
Herriet St. G41	M15	51
Herschell St. G13	G12	19
Foulis La.		
Hertford Av. G12	G13	20
Hexham Gdns. G41	N14	50
Heys St., Barr.	R 8	59
Hickman St. G42	N16	51
Hickory St. G22	G18	22
High Barholm, Kilb.	M07	42
High Calside, Pais.	M 5	46
High Craighall Rd. G4	J16	35
High Parksail, Renf.	F 5	16
High Rd., Pais.	M 5	46
High St. G1	L17	36
High St. G73	O19	53
High St., John.	M09	43
High St., Pais.	M 5	46
High St., Renf.	H 8	17
Highburgh Dr. G73	P19	65
Highburgh Rd. G12	J14	34
Highburgh Ter. G12	J14	34
Highburgh Rd.		
Highcraig Av., John.	N08	43
Highcroft Av. G44	P17	64
Highfield Av., Pais.	O 5	46
Highfield Cres., Pais.	O 5	46
Highfield Dr. G12	G13	20
Highfield Dr. G73	Q20	65
Highfield Pl. G12	G13	20
Highkirk Vw., John.	N09	43
Highland La. G51	K14	34
Hilary Av. G73	P20	65
Hilary Dr., Bail.	L24	39
Hilda Cres. G33	H21	24
Hill Path G52	L10	32
Hill Pl. G52	L10	32
Hill St. G3	J16	35
Hillcrest Av. G32	O22	54
Hillcrest Av. G44	Q15	63
Hillcrest Av., Clyde.	B 7	5
Hillcrest Av., Cumb.	D 2	70
North Carbrain Rd.		

Street	Grid	Page
Iain Dr., Bear.	C11	7
Iain Rd., Bear.	C11	7
Ibrox St. G51	L14	34
Ibrox Ter. G51	L13	34
Ibrox Terrace La. G51	L13	34
Ibroxholm La. G51	L14	34
Paisley Rd. W.		
Ibroxholm Oval G51	L13	34
Ibroxholm Pl. G51	L14	34
Ilay Av., Bear.	F12	19
Ilay Ct., Bear.	F13	20
Ilay Rd., Bear.	F13	20
Inchbrae Rd. G52	M11	49
Inchfad Dr. G15	D 9	6
Inchholm St. G11	J12	33
Inchinnan Rd., Pais.	K 6	30
Inchinnan Rd., Renf.	H 7	17
Inchkeith Pl. G32	K22	38
Inchlee St. G14	J12	33
Inchoch St. G33	J24	39
Inchrory Pl. G15	D 9	6
Incle St., Pais.	L 6	30
India Dr., Renf.	G 5	16
India St. G2	K16	35
India St. G73	O19	53
Inga St. G20	F15	21
Ingerbreck Av. G73	Q20	65
Ingleby Dr. G31	K19	37
Inglefield St. G42	N16	51
Ingleneuk Av. G33	G22	24
Inglestone Av., Thorn.	R13	62
Inglis St. G31	L19	37
Ingram St. G1	K17	36
Inishail Rd. G33	J23	39
Inkerman Rd. G52	L 9	32
Innerwick Dr. G52	L10	32
Inver Rd. G33	K24	39
Inverary Dr., Bish.	D19	11
Invercanny Dr. G15	D 9	6
Invercanny Pl. G15	D10	6
Inverclyde Gdns. G11	H12	19
Broomhill Dr.		
Inverclyde Gdns. G73	Q21	66
Inveresk Cres. G32	L22	38
Inveresk St. G32	L22	38
Inverewe Av. G46	Q11	61
Inverewe Dr. G46	R11	61
Inverewe Gdns. G46	R11	61
Inverewe Pl. G46	Q11	61
Invergarry Av. G46	R11	61
Invergarry Ct. G46	R11	61
Invergarry Dr. G46	R11	61
Invergarry Gdns. G46	R11	61
Invergarry Gro. G46	R11	61
Invergarry Pl. G46	R11	61
Invergarry Quad. G46	R12	61
Invergarry Vw. G46	R12	61
Inverglas Av., Renf.	J 9	32
Morriston Cres.		
Invergordon Av. G43	O15	51
Invergyle Dr. G52	L10	32
Inverkar Dr., Pais.	N 4	45
Brediland Rd.		
Inverkip St. G5	L17	36
Inverlair Av. G43	P15	63
Inverleith St. G32	L20	37
Inverlochy St. G33	J23	39
Invernairn St. G31	L20	37
Inverness St. G51	L11	33
Inveroran Dr., Bear.	D13	8
Invershiel Rd. G23	E14	8
Invershin Dr. G20	G14	20
Wyndford Rd.		
Inverurie St. G21	H17	22
Inzievar Ter. G32	N22	54
Iona Ct. G51	K13	34
Iona Dr., Pais.	O 5	46
Iona La., Chr.	E28	15
Heathfield Av.		
Iona Rd. G73	Q21	66
Iona Rd., Renf.	J 8	31
Iona St. G51	K13	34
Irongray St. G31	K20	37
Irvine Dr., Linw.	L 1	28
Irvine St. G40	M19	53
Irving Av., Clyde.	C 7	5
Stewart Dr.		
Irving Quad., Clyde.	C 7	5
Stewart Dr.		
Iser La. G41	O15	51
Island Rd., Cumb.	D 1	70
Islay Av. G73	Q21	66
Islay Cres., Pais.	O 5	46
Ivanhoe Rd. G13	F11	19
Ivanhoe Rd., Cumb.	D 2	70
Ivanhoe Rd., Pais.	N 3	45
Ivanhoe Way, Pais.	N 3	45
Ivanhoe Rd.		
Ivybank Ave. G72	Q23	67
Jacks Rd., Udd.	P28	69
Jagger Gdns., Bail.	M24	55
Jamaica St. G1	L16	35
James Dunlop Gdns., Bish.	F19	23
Graham Ter.		
James Gray St. G41	O15	51
James Morrison St. G1	L17	36
St. Andrews Sq.		
James Nisbet St. G21	K18	36
James St. G40	M18	52
James Watt La. G2	K16	35
James Watt St.		
James Watt St. G2	K16	35
Jamieson Ct., Clyde.	B 7	5
Jamieson St. G42	N16	51
Janebank Av. G72	Q23	67
Janefield Av., John.	N 9	43
Janefield St. G31	L19	37
Janes Brae, Cumb.	D 2	70
Janetta St., Clyde.	D 7	5
Jardine St. G20	H15	21
Jardine Ter., Gart.	G27	27
Jasgray St. G42	N15	51
Jean Armour Dr., Clyde.	D 8	5
Jedburgh Av. G73	O19	53
Jedburgh Dr., Pais.	N 4	45
Jedburgh Gdns. G20	H15	21
Jedworth Av. G15	D10	6
Jellicoe St. Dalm.	D 6	4
Jennys Well Rd., Pais.	N 7	47
Jerviston Rd. G33	J23	39
Jessie St. G42	N17	52
Jessiman Sq., Renf.	J 7	31
John Brown Pl., Chr.	F26	26
John Knox La. G4	K18	36
Drygate		
John Knox St. G4	K18	36
John Knox St., Clyde.	F 8	17
John Lang St., John.	M1	44
John St. G1	K17	36
John St., Barr.	Q 7	59
John St., Pais.	M 5	46
Johnshaven St. G43	O14	50
Bengal St.		
Johnston Av., Clyde.	F 8	17
Johnston Rd., Gart.	G28	27
Johnston St., Pais.	M 6	46
Gordon St.		
Johnston St., Pais.	M 6	46
Johnstone Av. G52	L10	32
Johnstone Cotts.,	B21	12
Johnstone Dr. G72	P22	66
Johnstone Dr. G73	O19	53
Joppa St. G33	K21	38
Jordan St. G14	J11	33
Jordan Vale Av. G14	J11	33
Jordanhill Cres. G13	G11	19
Jordanhill Dr.		
Jordanhill Dr. G13	G11	19
Jordanhill La. G13	G12	19
Austen Rd.		
Jowitt Av., Clyde.	E 8	5
Joycelyn Sq. G1	L17	36
Jubilee Bank, Lenz.	D23	13
Heriot Rd.		
Jubilee Path, Bear.	D12	7
Jubilee Ter. G78	N08	43
Kilbarchan Rd.		
Jubilee Ter., John.	O08	43
Julian Av. G12	H14	20
Julian La. G12	H14	20
Julian Av.		
Juniper Ct., Lenz.	C22	12
Juniper Pl. G32	M24	55
Juniper Pl., John.	O 1	44
Juniper Ter. G32	M24	55
Jura Av., Renf.	J 8	31
Jura Ct. G52	L12	33
Jura Dr., Blan.	Q26	68
Jura Rd., Pais.	O 5	46
Jura St. G52	L12	33
Kaim Dr. G53	P11	61
Kames St. G5	M16	51
Karol Path G4	J16	35
St. Peters St.		
Katewell Av. G15	D 9	6
Katrine Av., Bish.	E19	11
Katrine Dr., Pais.	N 3	45
Kay St. G21	H18	22
Kaystone Rd. G15	E10	6
Keal Av. G15	F10	18
Keal Cres. G15	F10	18
Keal Dr. G15	F10	18
Keal Pl. G15	F10	18
Kearn Av. G15	E10	6
Kearn Pl. G15	E10	6
Keats Pk., Udd.	Q28	69
Keir Dr., Bish.	E18	10
Keir St. G41	M15	51
Keirhill Rd, Cumb.	C 1	70
Woodburn Rd.		
Keirs Wk. G72	P22	66
Keith Av., Giff.	Q14	62
Keith Ct. G11	J14	34
Keith St.		
Keith St. G11	J14	34
Kelbourne St. G20	H15	21
Kelburn St., Barr.	R 7	59
Kelburne Dr., Pais.	L 7	31
Kelburne Gdns., Bail.	M25	56
Kelburne Gdns., Pais.	L 7	31
Kelburne Oval, Pais.	L 7	31
Kelhead Av. G52	L 9	32
Kelhead Dr. G52	L 9	32
Kelhead Path G52	L10	32
Kelhead Pl. G52	L 9	32
Kellas St. G51	L13	34
Kells Pl. G15	D 9	6
Kelso Av. G73	O19	53
Kelso Av., Pais.	N 4	45
Kelso St. G13	G 9	18
Kelton St. G32	M22	54
Kelty Pl. G5	L16	35
Bedford St.		
Kelty St. G5	M16	51
Eglinton St.		
Kelvin Av. G52	J 9	32
Kelvin Cres., Bear.	E12	7
Kelvin Ct. G12	G12	19
Kelvin Dr. G20	H14	20
Kelvin Dr., Barr.	R 8	59
Kelvin Dr., Bish.	E19	11
Kelvin Dr., Chr.	E27	15
Kelvin Rd., Cumb.	D 3	71
Kelvin Rd., Udd.	O27	57
Kelvin Way G3	J14	34
Kelvin Way, Udd.	Q28	69
Bracken Ter.		
Kelvindale Bldgs. G12	G14	20
Kelvindale Rd.		
Kelvindale Cotts. G12	G14	20
Kelvindale Rd.		
Kelvindale Glen G12	G14	20
Kelvindale Rd.		
Kelvindale Pl. G20	G14	20
Kelvindale Rd. G12	G14	20
Kelvingrove St. G3	K15	35
Kelvingrove Ter. G3	K15	35
Kelvingrove St.		
Kelvinhaugh Pl. G3	K14	34
Kelvinhaugh St.		
Kelvinhaugh St. G3	K14	34
Kelvinside Av. G20	H15	21
Queen Margaret Dr.		
Kelvinside Dr. G20	H15	21
Kelvinside Gdns. E. G20	H15	21
Kelvinside Gdns. G20	H15	21
Kelvinside Ter. S. G20	H15	21
Kelvinside Ter. W. G20	H15	21
Kemp Av., Renf.	J 7	31
Kemp St. G21	H18	22
Kempock St. G31	M20	53
Kempsthorn Cres. G53	N10	48
Kempsthorn Path G53	N10	48
Kempsthorn Rd. G53	N10	48
Kendal Av., Giff.	Q14	62
Kendal Dr. G12	G13	20
Kendal Ter. G12	G13	20
Kendoon Av. G15	D 9	6
Kenilworth Av. G41	O14	50
Kenilworth Cres., Bear.	C11	7
Kenilworth, Pais.	O 3	45
Kenmar Gdns., Udd.	O26	56

Name	Grid	Pg
Kenmore Gdns., Bear.	C13	8
Kenmore Rd., Cumb.	C 3	71
Kenmore St. G32	L22	38
Kenmuir Av. G32	M24	55
Kenmuir Rd. G32	O23	55
Kenmuirhill Rd. G32	N23	55
Kenmure Av., Bish.	E18	10
Kenmure Cres., Bish.	E18	10
Kenmure Dr., Bish.	E18	10
Kenmure Gdns., Bish.	E18	10
Kenmure Row G22	E16	9
Kenmure St. G41	M15	51
Kenmure Way G73	Q19	65
Kennedar Dr. G51	K12	33
Kennedy Ct., Giff.	Q14	62
Braidholm Cres.		
Kennedy St. G4	K17	36
Kennet St. G21	J19	37
Kennishead Av. G46	P12	61
Kennishead Pl. G46	P12	61
Kennishead Rd. G46	Q12	61
Kennishead Rd. G53	Q11	61
Kennisholm Av. G46	P12	61
Kennisholm Pl. G46	P12	61
Kennoway Dr. G11	J12	33
Kennoway La. G11	J12	33
Thornwood Dr.		
Kennyhill Sq. G31	K19	37
Kensington Dr., Giff.	R14	62
Kensington Gate G12	H14	20
Kensington Rd.		
Kensington Rd. G12	H14	20
Kent Dr. G73	P20	65
Kent Rd. G3	K15	35
Kent St. G40	L18	36
Kentallen Rd. G33	L24	39
Kentigern Ter., Bish.	F19	23
Keppel Dr. G44	O18	52
Keppoch St. G21	H17	22
Keppochhill Rd. G22	H17	22
Kerfield Pl. G15	D 9	6
Kerr St. G40	L18	36
Kerr St., Barr.	R 7	59
Kerr St., Blan.	S27	69
Kerr St., Pais.	L 5	30
Kerrera Pl. G33	L23	39
Kerrera Rd. G33	L23	39
Kerry Pl. G15	D 9	6
Kerrycroy Av. G42	O17	52
Kerrycroy Pl. G42	O17	52
Kerrycroy Av.		
Kerrycroy St. G42	O17	52
Kerrydale St. G40	M19	53
Kerrylamont Av. G42	O18	52
Kersland La. G12	H14	20
Kersland St.		
Kersland St. G12	H14	20
Kessington Dr., Bear.	D13	8
Kessington Rd., Bear.	D13	8
Kestral Ct., Clyde.	C 7	5
Kestrel Pl., John.	O08	43
Kestrel Rd. G13	G11	19
Kew Gdns. G12	H14	20
Ruthven St.		
Kew Gdns., Udd.	O28	57
Kew La. G12	H14	20
Saltoun St.		
Kew Ter. G12	H14	20
Keyden St. G41	L15	35
Kibbleston Rd., Kilb.	M07	42
Kidston Dr. G5	M17	52
Kilbarchan Rd., John.	N08	43
Kilbarchan St. G5	L16	35
Bedford St.		
Kilbarchan St. G5	L16	35
Bedford St.		
Kilbeg Ter. G46	Q11	61
Kilberry St. G21	J19	37
Kilbirnie St. G5	M16	51
Kilbowie Ct., Clyde.	D 7	5
Crown Av.		
Kilbowie Rd., Clyde.	C 7	5
Kilbowie Rd., Cumb.	C 3	71
Kilbrennan Rd., Linw.	L 1	28
Kilbride St. G5	N17	52
Kilbride Vw., Udd.	O28	57
Hamilton Dr.		
Kilburn Gro., Blan.	R26	68
Kilburn Pl. G13	G10	18
Kilchattan Dr. G44	O17	52
Kilchoan Rd. G33	J23	39
Kilcloy Av. G15	D10	6
Kildale St. G73	O18	52
Kildale Way G73	O18	52
Kildary Av. G44	P16	63
Kildary Rd. G44	P16	63
Kildermorie Rd. G34	K25	40
Kildonan Dr. G11	J13	34
Kildonan Ter. G51	L13	34
Copland Rd.		
Kildrostan St. G41	N15	51
Terregles Av.		
Kildrum Rd., Cumb.	B 3	71
Kilearn Rd., Pais.	K 7	31
Kilfinan St. G22	F16	21
Kilkerran Dr. G33	G21	24
Saughs Av.		
Killarn Way, Pais.	K 7	31
Killearn Dr., Pais.	M 9	48
Killearn St. G22	H16	21
Killermont Av., Bear.	E13	8
Killermont Ct., Bear.	D13	8
Killermont Rd., Bear.	D13	8
Killermont St. G1	K17	36
Killermont Vw. G20	E13	8
Killiegrew Rd. G41	N14	50
Killin Dr., Linw.	L 1	28
Killin St. G32	M22	54
Killoch Av., Pais.	L 4	29
Killoch Dr. G13	F10	18
Killoch Dr., Barr.	R 8	59
Killoch Rd., Pais.	L 4	29
Kilmailing Rd. G44	P16	63
Kilmair Pl. G20	G14	20
Wyndford Rd.		
Kilmaluag Ter. G46	Q11	61
Kilmany Dr. G32	L21	38
Kilmardinny Av., Bear.	C12	7
Kilmardinny Cres., Bear.	C12	7
Kilmardinny Dr., Bear.	C12	7
Kilmardinny Gate, Bear.	C12	7
Kilmardinny Av.		
Kilmardinny Gro., Bear.	C12	7
Kilmarnock Rd. G43	P14	62
Kilmartin Pl., Thorn.	Q12	61
Kilmaurs Dr., Giff.	Q15	63
Kilmaurs St. G51	L12	33
Kilmorie Dr. G73	O18	52
Kilmory Av., Udd.	O28	57
Spindlehow Rd.		
Kilmuir Cres. G46	Q11	61
Kilmuir Dr. G46	Q12	61
Kilmuir Rd. G46	Q12	61
Kilmuir Rd., Udd.	N27	57
Kilmun La. G20	F14	20
Kilmun St.		
Kilmun Pl. G20	F14	20
Kilmun St.		
Kilmun St. G20	F14	20
Kilnside Rd., Pais.	L 6	30
Kiloran St. G46	Q12	61
Kilpatrick Cres., Pais.	N 5	46
Kiltearn Rd. G33	K24	39
Kilvaxter Dr. G46	Q12	61
Kimberley St., Dalm.	C 5	4
Kinalty Rd. G44	P16	63
Kinarvie Cres. G53	O 9	48
Kinarvie Gdns. G53	O 9	48
Kinarvie Rd.		
Kinarvie Gdns. G53	O 9	48
Kinarvie Rd.		
Kinarvie Pl. G53	O 9	48
Kinarvie Rd. G53	O 9	48
Kinarvie Ter. G53	O 9	48
Kinbuck St. G22	H17	22
Kincardine Cres., Bish.	F19	23
Graham Ter.		
Kincardine Dr., Bish.	F19	23
Kincardine Pl., Bish.	F20	23
Kincardine Sq. G33	J23	39
Kincath Av. G73	Q20	65
Kinclaven Av. G15	D10	6
Kincraig St. G51	L11	33
Kinellan Rd., Bear.	E12	7
Kinfauns Dr. G15	D 9	6
Kinfauns Ter. G51	L13	34
Copland Rd.		
King Edward Rd. G13	G12	19
King George V Bridge G5	L16	35
King St. G1	L17	36
King St. G73	O19	53
King St., Clyde.	F 8	17
King St., Pais.	L 5	30
Kingarth St. G42	N16	51
Kinghorn Dr. G44	O17	52
Kinglas Rd., Bear.	E11	7
Kings Cres. G72	P22	66
Kings Cres., John.	M 2	44
Kings Cross G31	K18	36
Kings Dr. G40	M18	52
Kings Inch Rd., Renf.	G 8	17
Kings La. W., Renf.	H 8	17
Bell St.		
Kings Park Av. G44	P17	64
Kings Park Rd. G44	O16	51
Kings Pl. G22	F16	21
Kings Rd., John.	N 1	44
Kingsacre Rd. G44	O17	52
Kingsbarns Dr. G44	O16	51
Kingsborough Gate G12	H13	20
Prince Albert Rd.		
Kingsborough Gdns. G12	H13	20
Kingsborough Ter. G12	H13	20
Hyndland Rd.		
Kingsbrae Dr. G44	O17	52
Kingsbridge Cres. G44	P17	64
Kingsbridge Dr. G44	P17	64
Kingsburgh Dr., Pais.	L 7	31
Kingsburn Dr. G73	P19	65
Kingsburn Gro. G73	P19	65
Kingscliffe Av. G44	P17	64
Kingscourt Av. G44	P17	64
Kingsdale Av. G44	O17	52
Kingsdyke Av. G44	O17	52
Kingsford Av. G44	Q15	63
Kingshall Cotts., Gart.	H28	27
Kingsheath Av. G73	P18	64
Kingshill Dr. G44	P17	64
Kingshouse Av. G44	P17	64
Kingshurst Av. G44	O17	52
Kingsknowe Dr. G73	P18	64
Kingsland Cres. G52	L10	32
Kingsland Dr. G52	L10	32
Kingsley Av. G42	N16	51
Kingsley Ct., Udd.	O28	57
Kingslynn Dr. G44	P17	64
Kingslynn La. G44	P17	64
Kingslynn Dr.		
Kingsmuir Dr. G73	P18	64
Kingston Bri. G3	L15	34
Kingston Pl., Dalm.	D 5	4
Kingston St. G5	L16	35
Kingstone Av. G14	G10	18
Kingsway Ct. G14	G10	18
Kingsway G14	G10	18
Kingswood Dr. G44	P17	64
Kingussie Dr. G44	P17	64
Kiniver Dr. G15	E10	6
Kinloch Av. G72	Q22	66
Kinloch Av., Linw.	L 1	28
Pentland Dr.		
Kinloch Rd., Renf.	J 7	31
Kinloch St. G40	M20	53
Kinmount Av. G44	O16	51
Kinmount La. G44	O16	51
Kinmount Av.		
Kinnaird Cres., Bear.	D13	8
Kinnaird Dr., Linw.	L 1	28
Kinnaird Pl. G64	F19	23
Kinnear Rd. G40	M19	53
Kinnell Av. G52	M11	49
Kinnell Cres. G52	M11	49
Kinnell Pl. G52	N12	49
Mosspark Dr.		
Kinnell Sq. G52	M11	49
Kinnellar Dr. G14	G10	18
Kinning St. G5	L15	35
Kinnoul Pl. G12	H13	20
Crown Rd.		
Kinpurnie Rd., Pais.	L 8	31
Kinross Av. G52	M10	48
Kinsail Dr. G52	L 9	32
Kintessack Pl., Bish.	E20	11
Kintillo Dr. G13	G10	18
Kintore Rd. G43	P15	63
Kintra St. G51	L13	34
Kintyre Av., Linw.	L 1	28
Kintyre St. G21	J19	37
Kippen St. G22	G17	22
Kippford St. G32	M23	55
Kirconnell Dr. G73	P18	64
Kirk La. G43	O14	50
Riverbank St.		
Kirk Pl., Udd.	P27	69
Kirk Rd., Bear.	C12	7

Kirkaig Av., Renf.	J 9	32
Kirkbean Av. G73	Q19	65
Kirkburn Av. G72	Q22	66
Kirkcaldy Rd. G41	N14	58
Kirkconnel Av. G13	G 9	18
Kirkdale Dr. G52	M12	49
Kirkfield Rd., Udd.	Q28	69
Kirkford Rd., Chr.	E27	15
Bridgeburn Dr.		
Kirkhill Av. G72	Q22	66
Kirkhill Dr. G20	G14	20
Kirkhill Gdns. G72	Q22	66
Kirkhill Gro. G72	Q22	66
Kirkhill Pl. G20	G14	20
Kirkhill Rd., Gart.	G27	27
Kirkhill Rd., Udd.	O27	57
Kirkhill Ter. G72	Q22	66
Kirkhope Dr. G15	E10	6
Kirkinner Rd. G32	M23	55
Kirkintilloch Rd., Bish.	F18	22
Kirkintilloch Rd., Lenz.	C23	13
Kirkland St. G20	H15	21
Kirklandneuk Rd., Renf.	H 7	17
Kirklands Cres., Udd.	Q28	69
Kirklea Av., Pais.	L 4	29
Kirklee Circus G12	H14	20
Kirklee Gardens La. G12	G14	20
Bellshaugh Rd.		
Kirklee Gdns. G12	G14	20
Bellshaugh Rd.		
Kirklee Pl. G12	H14	20
Kirklee Quad. G12	H14	20
Kirklee Quad. La. G12	H14	20
Kirklee Quad.		
Kirklee Rd. G12	H14	20
Kirklee Ter. G12	H14	20
Kirklee Terrace La. G12	H14	20
Kirklee Ter.		
Kirkliston St. G32	L21	38
Kirkmuir Av., Renf.	J 7	31
Kirkmuir Dr. G73	Q19	65
Kirknewton St. G32	L22	38
Kirkoswald Dr., Clyde.	D 8	5
Kirkoswald Rd. G43	P14	62
Kirkpatrick St. G40	L19	37
Kirkriggs Av. G73	P19	65
Kirkriggs Gdns. G73	P19	65
Kirkriggs Way, Ruth.	P19	65
Kirkstall Gdns., Bish.	D19	11
Kirkstonside, Barr.	R 7	59
Kirkton Av. G13	G10	18
Kirkton Cres. G13	G10	18
Kirkton Rd. G72	P22	66
Kirkview Gdns., Udd.	O27	57
Glencroft Av.		
Kirkville Pl. G15	E10	6
Kirkwall Av., Blan.	Q26	68
Kirkwall, Cumb.	A 3	71
Kirkwell Rd. G44	P16	63
Kirkwood Av., Clyde.	E 8	5
Kirkwood Quad., Clyde.	E 8	5
Kirkwood Av.		
Kirkwood Rd., Udd.	N27	57
Newlands Rd.		
Kirkwood St. G51	L14	34
Kirkwood St. G73	O19	53
Kirn St. G20	F14	20
Kilmun St.		
Kirriemuir Av. G52	M11	49
Kirriemuir Gdns., Bish.	E20	11
Kirriemuir Rd., Bish.	E20	11
Kirtle Dr., Renf.	J 9	32
Kirton Av., Barr.	R 7	59
Kishorn Pl. G32	J23	39
Knapdale St. G22	F16	21
Knightsbridge Rd. G13	G11	19
Knightscliffe Av. G13	F11	19
Knightswood Cross G13	F11	19
Knightswood Rd. G13	E11	7
Knightswood Ter., Blan.	R27	69
Knock Way, Pais.	K 7	31
Knockburnie Rd., Udd.	Q28	69
Knockhall St. G33	J23	39
Knockhill Dr. G44	O16	51
Knockhill La. G44	O16	51
Mount Annan Dr.		
Knockhill Rd., Renf.	J 7	31
Knockside Av., Pais.	O 5	46
Knowe Rd., Chr.	F26	26
Knowe Rd., Pais.	K 7	31
Knowe Ter. G22	F16	21
Hillend Rd.		
Knowehead Dr., Udd.	P27	69
Knowehead Gdns., Udd.	P27	69
Knowetap St. G20	F15	21
Knowehead Ter. G41	M15	51
Albert Dr.		
Knox St., Pais.	M 4	45
Kyle Dr., Giff.	Q14	62
Kyle Rd., Cumb.	B 3	71
Kyle Sq. G73	P19	65
Kyle St. G4	J17	36
Kyleakin Gdns., Blan.	R25	68
Kyleakin Rd. G46	Q11	61
Kyleakin Ter. G46	Q11	61
Kylepark Av., Udd.	P26	68
Kylepark Cres., Udd.	O26	56
Kylepark Dr., Udd.	O26	56
Kylerhea Rd. G46	Q11	61
La Belle Pl. G3	J15	35
Laburnum Gdns., Lenz.	C22	12
Laburnum Gro.		
Laburnum Gro., Lenz.	C22	12
Laburnum Pl., John.	O 1	44
Laburnum Rd. G41	M14	50
Laburnum Rd., Cumb.	C 4	71
Lacrosse Ter. G12	H15	21
Lacy St., Pais.	L 7	31
Lade Ter. G52	M10	48
Ladeside Dr., John.	N08	43
Ladhope Pl. G13	F 9	18
Lady Anne St. G14	G 9	18
Lady Isle Cres., Udd.	P27	69
Lady Jane Gate, Both.	Q27	69
Lady La., Pais.	M 5	46
Ladybank Dr. G52	M12	49
Ladyburn St., Pais.	M 7	47
Ladyhill Dr., Bail.	M25	56
Ladykirk Cres. G52	L10	32
Ladykirk Cres., Pais.	M 6	46
Ladykirk Dr. G52	L10	32
Ladyloan Av. G15	D 9	6
Ladyloan Pl. G15	D 9	6
Ladymuir Cres. G53	N11	49
Ladysmith Av., Kilb.	N08	43
Ladywell St. G4	K18	36
Wishart St.		
Laggan Rd. G43	P15	63
Laggan Rd., Bish.	E19	11
Laggan Ter., Renf.	H 7	17
Laidlaw Gdns., Udd.	N27	57
Laidlaw St. G5	L16	35
Laigh Kirk La., Pais.	M 6	46
Causeyside St.		
Laigh Possil Rd. G23	F16	21
Balmore Rd.		
Laighcartside St., John.	M 1	44
Laighlands Rd. G71	R28	69
Laighmuir St., Udd.	P27	69
Laighpark Harbour, Pais.	K 6	30
Lainshaw Dr. G45	R16	63
Laird Pl. G40	M18	52
Lairds Hill, Cumb.	C 2	70
Lairg Dr., Blan.	R26	68
Lamb St. G22	G16	21
Lambhill St. G41	L14	34
Lamerton Dr. G52	L10	32
Lamerton Rd., Cumb.	C 4	71
Lamington Rd. G52	M10	48
Lamlash Cres. G33	K22	38
Lammermoor Av. G52	M11	49
Lammermoor Dr., Cumb.	D 2	70
Lammermuir Dr., Pais.	O 6	46
Lamont Rd. G21	G19	23
Lanark St. G1	L17	36
Lancaster Cres. G12	H14	20
Lancaster Cres. La. G12	G13	20
Clevedon Rd.		
Lancaster Rd., Bish.	D19	11
Lancaster Ter. G12	H14	20
Westbourne Gdns. W.		
Lancaster Ter. La. G12	H14	20
Westbourne Gdns. W.		
Lancefield Quay G3	K15	35
Lancefield St. G3	K15	35
Landemer Dr. G73	P18	64
Landressy St. G40	M18	52
Lanfine Rd., Pais.	M 7	47
Lang Av., Renf.	J 8	31
Lang St., Pais.	M 7	47
Langa St. G20	F15	21
Langbank St. G5	M16	51
Eglinton St.		
Langbar Cres. G33	K24	39
Langbar Path G33	K23	39
Langcraigs Cres., Pais.	P 5	58
Langcraigs Ter., Pais.	P 5	58
Langcroft Dr. G72	Q23	67
Langcroft Pl. G51	K11	33
Langcroft Rd. G51	K11	33
Langcroft Ter. G51	K11	33
Langdale Av. G33	H21	24
Langdale Av., Cumb.	C 1	70
Langdale St. G33	H21	24
Langfaulds Cres., Clyde.	C 8	5
Langford Av. G53	Q10	60
Langford Dr. G53	Q10	60
Langford Pl. G53	Q10	60
Langford Dr.		
Langhill Dr., Cumb.	B 1	70
Redhill Rd.		
Langholm Ct., Chr.	E28	15
Heathfield Av.		
Langholm Dr., Linw.	L 2	28
Langholm St. G14	G 9	18
Langlands Av. G51	K11	33
Langlands Dr. G51	K11	33
Langlands Path G51	K12	33
Langlands Rd. G51	K11	33
Langlands St. G51	K13	34
Langlea Av. G72	Q20	65
Langlea Gro. G72	Q21	66
Langlea Rd. G72	Q21	66
Langley Av. G13	F10	18
Langmulr Rd., Bail.	I28	41
Langmuirhead Rd., Lenz.	F22	24
Langness Rd. G33	K22	38
Langrig Rd. G21	H19	23
Langshot St. G51	L14	34
Langside Av. G41	N15	51
Langside Av., Udd.	P29	69
Langside Dr. G43	P15	63
Langside Dr. G78	N07	42
Langside La. G42	N16	51
Langside Pk. G78	N07	42
Langside Pl. G41	O15	51
Langside Rd. G42	O16	51
Langside Rd., Both.	R28	69
Langside St., Clyde.	C 9	6
Langstile Pl. G52	L 9	32
Langstile Rd. G52	L 9	32
Langton Cres. G53	N11	49
Langton Cres., Barr.	R 8	59
Langton Gdns., Bail.	M24	55
Langton Rd. G53	N11	49
Langtree Av., Giff.	R13	62
Lanrig Pl., Chr.	F26	26
Lanrig Rd., Chr.	F26	26
Lansbury Gdns., Pais.	K 5	30
Cowdie St.		
Lansdowne Cres. G20	J15	35
Lansdowne Cres. La. G12	H15	21
Great Western Rd.		
Lanton Dr. G52	L10	32
Lanton Rd. G43	P15	63
Lappin St., Clyde.	F 8	17
Larch Av., Bish.	F19	23
Larch Av., Lenz.	C23	13
Larch Cres., Lenz.	C23	13
Larch Ct., Cumb.	B 4	71
Larch Gro. G67	B 5	71
Larch Pl., John.	O 1	44
Larch Rd. G41	M13	50
Larch Rd., Cumb.	B 4	71
Larches, The, Chr.	D28	15
Larchfield Av. G14	H10	18
Larchfield Dr. G73	Q19	65
Larchfield Pl. G14	H10	18
Larchfield Rd. G69	E27	15
Larchfield Rd., Bear.	E12	7
Larchgrove Av. G32	L23	39
Larchgrove Pl. G32	K23	39
Larchgrove Rd.		
Larchgrove Rd. G32	K23	39
Larchwood Ter., Barr.	R 9	60
Largie Rd. G43	P15	63
Largo Pl. G51	K12	33
Largs St. G31	K19	37
Larkfield Rd., Lenz.	C24	13
Larkfield St. G42	N16	51
Cathcart Rd.		
Larkin Gdns., Pais.	K 5	30
Lasswade St. G14	G 9	18
Latherton Dr. G20	G14	20

Latherton Pl. G20	G14	20
Latherton Dr.		
Latimer Gdns. G52	M10	48
Lauder Dr. G73	O20	53
Lauder Dr., Linw.	L 1	28
Lauder Gdns., Blan.	R26	68
Lauder St. G5	M16	51
Eglinton St.		
Lauderdale Gdns. G12	H13	20
Laundry La. G33	G23	25
Laurel Av., Dalm.	D 5	4
Laurel Av., Lenz.	C23	13
Laurel Bank Rd., Chr.	F25	26
Laurel Pl. G11	J13	34
Laurel St. G11	J13	34
Laurel Way, Barr.	Q 7	59
Graham St.		
Laurel Wk. G73	Q20	65
Laurence Dr., Bear.	C11	7
Laurie Ct., Udd.	O28	57
Hillcrest Rd.		
Laurieston La. G51	L14	34
Paisley Rd.		
Laurieston Way G73	Q19	65
Laverock Ter., Chr.	E27	15
Laverockhall St. G21	H18	22
Law St. G40	L19	37
Lawers Rd. G43	P13	62
Lawers Rd., Bear.	C11	7
Lawers Rd., Renf.	J 8	31
Lawhill Av. G44	Q17	64
Lawmoor Av. G5	M17	52
Lawmoor La. G5	L17	36
Ballater St.		
Lawmoor Rd. G5	M17	52
Lawmoor St. G5	M17	52
Lawn St., Pais.	L 6	30
Lawrence Av., Giff.	R14	62
Lawrence St. G11	J14	34
Lawrie St. G11	J13	34
Lawside Dr. G53	O11	49
Laxford Av. G44	Q16	63
Laxton Dr., Lenz.	D24	13
Leabank Av., Pais.	O 6	46
Leadburn Rd. G21	H20	23
Rye Rd.		
Leadburn St. G32	K21	38
Leader St. G33	J20	37
Leander Cres., Renf.	J 9	32
Leckethill St. G21	H18	22
Springburn Rd.		
Leckie St. G43	O14	50
Ledaig Pl. G31	K20	37
Ledaig St. G31	K20	37
Ledard Rd. G42	O15	51
Ledcameroch Cres., Bear.	D11	7
Ledcameroch Pk., Bear.	D11	7
Ledcameroch Rd.		
Ledcameroch Rd., Bear.	D11	7
Ledgowan Pl. G20	F14	20
Ledi Dr., Bear.	B10	6
Ledi Rd. G43	P14	62
Ledmore Dr. G15	D 9	6
Lednock Rd. G33	G23	25
Lednock Rd. G52	L10	32
Lee Av. G33	J21	38
Lee Cres., Bish.	F18	22
Leebank Dr. G44	R15	63
Leefield Av. G44	R15	63
Leehill Rd. G21	F18	22
Leeside Rd. G21	F18	22
Leewood Dr. G44	R15	63
Leicester Av. G12	G13	20
Leighton St. G20	G15	21
Leitchland Rd. G78	O 2	44
Leitchs Ct. G1	L17	36
Trongate		
Leith St. G33	K20	37
Leithland Av. G53	O10	48
Leithland Rd. G53	N10	48
Lendale La., Bish.	D19	11
Lendel Pl. G51	L15	35
Paisley Rd. W.		
Lenhall Dr. G45	R18	64
Lenhall Ter. G45	R18	64
Lennox Av. G14	H11	19
Lennox Cres., Bish.	F18	22
Lennox Ct., Bear.	B12	7
Lennox Dr., Bear.	C12	7
Lennox Dr., Clyde.	B 8	5
Lennox La. W. G14	H11	19
Lennox Av.		
Lennox La. W. G14	H11	19
Lennox Av.		
Lennox Pl. G14	H11	19
Scotstoun St.		
Lennox Pl., Dalm.	D 6	4
Swindon St.		
Lennox Rd., Cumb.	C 2	70
Lennox Ter., Pais.	K 7	31
Lennox Vw., Clyde.	D 7	5
Granville St.		
Lentran St. G34	K26	40
Leny St. G20	H16	21
Lenzie Dr. G21	G18	22
Lenzie Rd. G33	G23	25
Lenzie St. G21	G18	22
Lenziemill Rd., Cumb.	D 3	71
Lerwick St. G4	J16	35
Dobbies Loan		
Leslie Rd. G41	N15	51
Leslie St. G41	M15	51
Lesmuir Dr. G14	G10	18
Lesmuir Pl. G14	G 9	18
Letham Ct. G43	P15	63
Letham Dr. G43	P15	63
Letham Dr. G64	F20	23
Lethamhill Cres. G33	J21	38
Lethamhill Pl. G33	J21	38
Lethamhill Rd. G33	J21	38
Letherby Dr. G44	O16	51
Lethington Av. G41	O15	51
Letterickhills Cres. G72	Q24	67
Lettoch St. G51	L13	34
Leven Av., Bish.	E19	11
Leven Ct., Barr.	P 7	59
Leven Dr., Bear.	D12	7
Leven Sq., Renf.	H 7	17
Leven St. G41	M15	51
Leven Vw., Clyde.	D 7	5
Radnor St.		
Leven Way, Pais.	N 3	45
Levern Cres., Barr.	R 7	59
Levern Gdns., Barr.	Q 7	59
Chappel St.		
Levernside Av., Barr.	R 7	59
Levernside Cres. G53	N10	48
Levernside Rd. G53	N10	48
Lewis Av., Renf.	J 8	31
Lewis Gdns., Bear.	C10	6
Lewiston Dr. G23	E14	8
Lewiston Rd.		
Lewiston Pl. G23	E14	8
Lewiston Rd.		
Lewiston Rd. G23	E14	8
Lexwell Av., John.	M 2	44
Lexwell Rd., Pais.	N 3	45
Leyden Ct. G20	G15	21
Leyden St.		
Leyden Gdns. G20	G15	21
Leyden St.		
Leyden St. G20	G15	21
Leys, The, Bish.	E19	11
Liberton St. G33	K20	37
Liberty Av., Bail.	L28	41
Libo Av. G53	N11	49
Liddale Way G73	O18	52
Liddel Rd., Cumb.	C 2	70
Liddell St. G32	N23	55
Liddesdale Av.	O 2	44
Liddesdale Pl. G22	F17	22
Liddesdale Sq.		
Liddesdale Rd. G22	F17	22
Liddesdale Sq. G22	F17	22
Liddesdale Ter. G22	F18	22
Liff Gdns., Bish.	F20	23
Liff Pl. G34	J26	40
Lightburn Pl. G32	K22	38
Lightburn Rd. G72	Q23	67
Lilac Av., Dalm.	D 6	4
Lilac Gdns., Bish.	F19	23
Lilac Pl., John.	N 1	44
Lily St. G40	M19	53
Lilybank Av. G72	Q23	67
Lilybank Av., Chr.	F26	26
Lilybank Gardens La. G12	H14	20
Great George St.		
Lilybank Gdns. G12	J14	34
Lilybank Ter. G12	H14	20
Great George St.		
Lilybank Terrace La. G12	H14	20
Great George St.		
Lilyburn Pl. G15	C 9	6
Lime Gro., Blan.	R26	68
Lime Gro., Lenz.	C23	13
Lime St. G14	H11	19
Limecraigs Cres., Pais.	O 5	46
Limecraigs Rd., Pais.	O 5	46
Limekiln St., Clyde.	B 8	5
Limeside Av. G73	O19	53
Limeside Gdns. G73	O20	53
Calderwood Rd.		
Limetree Av., Udd.	O28	57
Limetree Dr., Dalm.	D 7	5
Linacre Dr. G32	L23	39
Linacre Gdns. G32	L23	39
Linbank Av. G53	O11	49
Linburn Pl. G52	L10	32
Linburn Rd. G52	K 9	32
Linclive Link Rd., Linw.	L 3	29
Linclive Ter., Linw.	L 2	28
Lincoln Av. G13	G10	18
Lincoln Av., Udd.	N27	57
Lincuan Av., Giff.	S14	62
Lindams, Udd.	P27	69
Linden St. G13	F12	19
Lindores Av. G73	O19	53
Lindores St. G42	O16	51
Somerville Dr.		
Lindrick Dr. G23	E15	9
Lindsay Dr. G12	G13	20
Lindsay Pl. G12	G13	20
Lindsay Pl., Lenz.	D23	13
Lindsaybeg Rd., Lenz.& Chr.	D24	13
Linfern Rd. G12	H14	20
Links Rd. G32	M23	55
Links Rd. G44	Q17	64
Linkwood Av. G15	D 9	6
Kinfauns Dr.		
Linkwood Cres. G15	D 9	6
Linkwood Dr. G15	D 9	6
Linkwood Pl. G15	D 9	6
Kinfauns Dr.		
Linlithgow Gdns. G32	L23	39
Hailes Av.		
Linn Cres., Pais.	O 5	46
Linn Dr. G44	Q15	63
Linnet Av., John.	O08	43
Linnhe Av. G44	Q16	63
Linnhe Av., Bish.	E19	11
Linnhe Dr., Barr.	P 7	59
Linnhe Pl., Blan.	R26	68
Linnhead Dr. G53	P10	60
Linnhead Pl. G14	H10	18
Linnpark Av. G44	R15	63
Linnpark Ct. G44	R15	63
Linnpark Gdns., John.	N 1	44
Lunn Brae		
Linside Av., Pais.	M 7	47
Lintfield Loan, Udd.	P28	69
Myers Cres.		
Linthaugh Rd. G53	N10	48
Linthouse Bldgs. G51	K12	33
Lintlaw Dr. G52	L11	33
Lintlaw, Blan.	R26	68
Linton St. G33	K21	38
Linwell Cres., Pais.	O 5	46
Linwood Ct. G44	P16	63
Clarkston Rd.		
Linwood Moss Rd., Linw.	L 2	28
Linwood Rd., John.	L 2	28
Linwood Ter. G12	H15	21
Glasgow St.		
Lismore Av., Renf.	J 8	31
Lismore Dr., Pais.	O 5	46
Lismore Pl., Chr.	D28	15
Altnacreag Gdns.		
Lismore Rd. G12	H13	20
Lister Rd. G52	K10	32
Lister St. G4	J17	36
Lithgow Cres., Pais.	N 7	47
Little Dovehill G1	L17	36
Little Holm, Dalm.	D 6	4
Little St. G3	K15	35
Littlehill St. G21	H18	22
Edgefauld Rd.		
Littleton Dr. G23	E14	8
Rothes Dr.		
Littleton St. G23	E14	8
Rothes Dr.		
Livingstone Av. G52	K10	32

Name	Ref	Pg
Maclehose Rd., Cumb.	B 4	71
Maclellan St. G41	L14	34
Madison Av. G44	P16	63
Madison La. G44	P16	63
Carmunnock Rd.		
Madras Pl. G40	M18	52
Madras St.		
Madras St. G40	M18	52
Mafeking St. G51	L13	34
Magdalen Way, Pais.	O 2	44
Magnus Cres. G44	Q16	63
Mahon Ct., Chr.	E27	15
Maida St. G43	O13	50
Maidland Rd. G53	O11	49
Mailerbeg Gdns., Chr.	D27	15
Mailing Av., Bish.	E19	11
Main Rd., John.	M 2	44
Main St. G40	M18	52
Main St. G72	P22	66
Main St. G73	O19	53
Main St., Bail.	M25	56
Main St., Barr.	R 7	59
Main St., Both.	R28	69
Main St., Chr.	E26	14
Main St., Cumb.	A 3	71
Main St., Thorn.	Q12	61
Main St., Udd.	P27	69
Mainhead Ter., Cumb.	A 3	71
Roadside		
Mainhill Av., Bail.	L26	40
Mainhill Pl., Bail.	L26	40
Mainhill Rd., Bail.	L27	41
Mains Av., Giff.	R13	62
Mains Dr., Renf.	E 5	4
Mains Hill, Renf.	E 5	4
Mains Holm, Renf.	E 5	4
Mains River, Renf.	E 5	4
Mains Wood, Renf.	E 5	4
Mainscroft, Renf.	E 5	4
Mair St. G51	L15	35
Maitland Pl., Renf.	J 7	31
Maitland St. G4	J16	35
Malcolm St. G31	L20	37
Malin Pl. G33	K21	38
Mallaig Path G51	K11	33
Mallaig Pl. G51	K11	33
Mallaig Rd. G51	K11	33
Mallard Rd., Clyde.	C 7	5
Malloch Cres., John.	N 1	44
Malloch St. G20	G15	21
Malta St., Clyde.	F 8	17
Maltbarns St. G20	H16	21
Malvern Ct. G31	L19	37
Malvern Way, Pais.	K 5	30
Mambeg Dr. G51	K12	33
Mamore Pl. G43	P14	62
Mamore St. G43	P14	62
Manchester Dr. G12	G13	20
Manitoba Pl. G31	L19	37
Janefield St.		
Mannering Ct. G41	O14	50
Pollokshaws Rd.		
Mannering Rd. G31	O14	50
Mannering Rd., Pais.	O 3	45
Mannofield, Bear.	D11	7
Chesters Rd.		
Manor Rd. G14	H12	19
Manor Rd. G15	E 9	6
Manor Rd., Gart.	G27	27
Manor Rd., Pais.	N 3	45
Manor Way G73	Q19	65
Manse Av., Bear.	C12	7
Manse Brae G44	P16	63
Manse Ct., Barr.	Q 8	59
Manse Rd. G32	M23	55
Manse Rd., Bail.	L27	41
Manse Rd., Bear.	C12	7
Manse St., Renf.	H 8	17
Mansefield Av. G72	Q22	66
Mansefield Dr., Udd.	P28	69
Mansefield St. G11	J14	34
Mansel St. G21	G18	22
Mansewood Rd. G43	P13	62
Mansfield Rd. G52	K 9	32
Mansion Ct. G72	P22	66
Mansion St. G22	G17	22
Mansion St. G72	P22	66
Mansionhouse Av. G32	O23	55
Mansionhouse Dr. G32	L23	39
Mansionhouse Gdns. G41	O15	51
Mansionhouse Rd.		
Mansionhouse Rd. G32	M24	55
Mansionhouse Rd. G42	O15	51
Mansionhouse Rd., Pais.	L 7	31
Maple Ct., Barr.	S 8	59
Oakbank Dr.		
Maple Dr., Dalm.	C 6	4
Maple Dr., John.	O 1	44
Maple Dr., Lenz.	C22	12
Maple Rd. G41	M13	50
Mar Gdns. G73	Q20	65
March La. G41	N15	51
Nithsdale Dr.		
March St. G41	N15	51
Marchfield Av., Pais.	K 5	30
Marchfield, Bish.	D18	10
Marchfield, Bish.	D18	10
Westlands		
Marchglen Pl. G51	K11	33
Mallaig Rd.		
Marchmont Gdns., Bish.	D18	10
Marchmont Ter. G12	H14	20
Observatory Rd.		
Maree Dr. G52	M12	49
Maree Gdns., Bish.	E19	11
Maree Rd., Pais.	N 4	45
Marfield St. G32	L21	38
Margaret St. G41	K17	36
Martha St.		
Margarette Bldgs. G44	P16	63
Clarkston Rd.		
Marguerite Av., Lenz.	C23	13
Marguerite Dr., Lenz.	C23	13
Marguerite Gdns., Lenz.	C23	13
Marguerite Gdns., Udd.	Q28	69
Marguerite Gro., Lenz.	C23	13
Mariscat Rd. G41	N15	51
Marjory Dr., Pais.	K 7	31
Marjory Rd., Renf.	J 7	31
Market Rd., Lenz.	B25	14
Market St. G40	L18	36
Markinch St. G5	L16	35
West St.		
Marlborough Av. G11	H12	19
Marlinford Rd., Renf.	H10	18
Marlow St. G41	M15	51
Marlow Ter. G41	L15	35
Seaward St.		
Marmion Pl., Cumb.	D 2	70
Marmion Rd., Cumb.	D 2	70
Marmion Rd., Pais.	O 3	45
Marmion St. G20	H15	21
Marne St. G31	K19	37
Marnock Ter., Pais.	N 7	47
Marnock Way, Chr.	E27	15
Braeside Av.		
Marr St. G51	K13	34
Marshalls La., Pais.	M 6	46
Mart St. G1	L17	36
Martha St. G1	K17	36
Martin Cres., Bail.	L26	40
Martin St. G40	M18	52
Martlet Dr., John.	O08	43
Martyr St. G4	K18	36
Martyrs Pl. G64	F19	23
Marwick St. G31	K19	37
Marwood Av., Chr. & Waterside	C25	14
Mary St. G4	J16	35
Mary St., John.	M 1	44
Mary St., Pais.	N 6	46
Maryhill Rd., Bear.& G20	E13	8
Maryland Dr. G52	L12	33
Maryland Gdns. G52	L12	33
Marys La., Renf.	H 8	17
Maryston Pl. G33	J20	37
Maryston St. G33	J20	37
Maryview Gdns., Udd.	N26	56
Edinburgh Rd.		
Maryville Av., Giff.	R14	62
Marywood Sq. G41	N15	51
Masonfield Av., Cumb.	C 1	70
Middlerigg Rd.		
Masterton St. G21	H17	22
Mathieson La. G5	M17	52
Mathieson St.		
Mathieson Rd. G73	N20	53
Mathieson St. G5	M17	52
Mathieson St., Pais.	L 7	31
Matilda Rd. G41	M15	51
Mauchline St. G5	M16	51
Maukinfauld Ct. G31	M21	54
Maukinfauld Rd. G32	M21	54
Mauldslie St. G40	M19	53
Maule Dr. G11	J13	34
Mause Av., Both.	R28	69
Mavis Bank, Bish.	F18	22
Mavisbank Rd. G51	K13	34
Govan Rd.		
Mavisbank Ter., Pais.	M 6	46
Maxton Ter. G72	Q21	66
Maxwell Av. G41	M15	51
Maxwell Av., Bail.	M25	56
Maxwell Av., Barr.	Q 7	59
Maxwell Av., Bear.	E12	7
Maxwell Dr. G41	M14	50
Maxwell Dr., Bail.	L25	40
Maxwell Gdns. G41	M14	50
Maxwell Gro. G41	M14	50
Maxwell Oval G41	M15	51
Maxwell Pl. G41	M16	51
Maxwell Rd. G41	M15	51
Maxwell Sq. G41	M15	51
Maxwell St. G18	L17	36
Maxwell St., Bail.	M25	56
Maxwell St., Dalm.	D 6	4
Maxwell St., Pais.	L 6	30
Maxwellton Rd. G78	M 4	45
Maxwellton St., Pais.	M 5	46
Maxwelton Rd. G33	J20	37
May Rd., Pais.	O 6	46
May Ter. G42	O16	51
Prospecthill Rd.		
May Ter., Giff.	Q14	62
Maybank La. G42	N16	51
Victoria Rd.		
Maybank St. G42	N16	51
Mayberry Cres. G32	L23	39
Mayberry Gdns. G32	L23	39
Maybole St. G53	P 9	60
Mayfield St. G20	G15	21
McAlpine St. G2	L16	35
McArthur St. G43	O14	50
Pleasance St.		
McArthur St., Clyde.	G 8	17
McAslin Ct. G4	K17	36
McAslin St. G4	K18	36
McCallum Av. G73	O19	53
McClue Av., Renf.	H 7	17
McClue Rd., Renf.	H 7	17
McCracken Av., Renf.	J 7	31
McCreery St., Clyde.	F 8	17
McCulloch St. G41	M15	51
McDonald Av., John.	N09	43
McDonald Cres., Clyde.	F 8	17
McEwan St. G31	L20	37
McFarlane St. G4	L18	36
McFarlane St., Pais.	K 5	30
McGhee St., Clyde.	D 7	5
McGown St., Pais.	L 5	30
McGregor Av., Renf.	J 7	31
Porterfield Rd.		
McGregor Rd., Cumb.	C 2	70
McGregor St. G51	L12	33
McGregor St., Clyde.	F 8	17
McIntosh Ct. G31	K18	36
McIntosh St.		
McIntosh St. G31	K18	36
McIntyre Pl., Pais.	N 5	46
McIntyre St. G72	K15	35
McIntyre Ter. G72	P22	66
McIver St. G72	P23	67
McKay Cres., John.	N 1	44
McKean St., Pais.	L 5	30
McKenzie Av., Clyde.	D 7	5
McKenzie St., Pais.	L 5	30
McKerrel St., Pais.	L 7	31
McLaren Av., Renf.	J 8	31
Newmains Rd.		
McLaurin Cres., John.	N08	43
McLean Pl., Pais.	K 5	30
McLean Sq. G51	L14	34
McLean St., Clyde.	F 9	18
Wood Quad.		
McLennan St. G42	O16	51
McNair St. G32	L22	38
McNeil St. G5	M17	52
McNeil Av., Clyde.	E 9	6
McPhail St. G40	M18	52
McPhater St. G4	J16	35
Dunblane St.		
McPherson Dr., Udd.	Q28	69
Wordsworth Way		

Name	Grid	Map
McPherson St. G1	L17	36
High St.		
McTaggart Rd., Cumb.	D 2	70
Meadow La., Renf.	G 8	17
Meadow Rd. G11	J13	34
Meadow Vw., Cumb.	B 4	71
Meadowbank La., Udd.	P26	68
Meadowbank La., Udd.	P27	69
Meadowburn Av. G66	C24	13
Meadowburn, Bish.	D19	11
Meadowhead Av., Chr.	E27	15
Meadowpark St. G31	K19	37
Meadowside Av., John.	N 2	44
Meadowside St. G11	J13	34
Meadowside St., Renf.	G 8	17
Meadowwell St. G32	L22	38
Meadside Av. G78	M07	42
Meadside Rd., Kilb.	M07	42
Mears Way, Bish.	E20	11
Medlar Rd., Cumb.	C 4	71
Medwin St. G72	P24	67
Mill Rd.		
Medwyn St. G14	H11	19
Meek Pl. G72	P22	66
Meetinghouse La., Pais.	L 6	30
Moss St.		
Megan Gate G40	M18	52
Megan St.		
Megan St. G40	M18	52
Meikle Av., Renf.	J 8	31
Meikle Rd. G53	O11	49
Meiklerig Cres. G53	N11	49
Meikleriggs Dr., Pais.	N 4	45
Meiklewood Rd. G51	L11	33
Melbourne Av., Dalm.	C 5	4
Melbourne St. G31	L18	36
Meldon Pl. G51	K12	33
Meldrum Gdns. G41	N14	50
Meldrum St., Clyde.	F 9	18
Melford Av., Giff.	R14	62
Melford Way, Pais.	K 7	31
Knock Way		
Melfort Av., Clyde.	D 7	5
Melfort Av., G41	M13	50
Melfort Gdns., John.	N08	43
Milliken Park Rd.		
Melness Pl. G51	K11	33
Mallaig Rd.		
Melrose Av. G73	O19	53
Melrose Av., Bail.	L27	41
Melrose Av., Linw.	L 1	28
Melrose Av., Pais.	N 4	45
Melrose Gdns. G20	H15	21
Melrose Gdns., Udd.	N27	57
Lincoln Av.		
Melrose Pl., Blan.	R26	68
Melrose St. G4	J16	35
Queens Cres.		
Melvaig Pl. G20	G14	20
Melvick Pl. G51	K11	33
Mallaig Rd.		
Melville St. G1	K17	36
Brunswick St.		
Melville Gdns., Bish.	E19	11
Melville St. G41	M15	51
Memel St. G21	G18	22
Memus Av. G52	M11	49
Mennock Dr., Bish.	D19	11
Menock Rd. G44	P16	63
Menteith Av., Bish.	E19	11
Menteith Dr. G73	R20	65
Menteith Pl. G73	R20	65
Menzies Dr. G21	G19	23
Menzies Pl. G21	G19	23
Menzies Rd. G21	G19	23
Merchant La. G1	L17	36
Clyde St.		
Merchants Clo., Pais.	M07	42
Church St.		
Merchiston Av., Linw.	L 1	28
Merchiston St. G32	K21	38
Merkland Ct. G11	J13	34
Vine St.		
Merkland St. G11	J13	34
Merksworth Way, Pais.	K 5	30
Mosslands Rd.		
Merlewood Av. G71	Q28	69
Merlin Way, Pais.	K 7	31
Merrick Gdns. G51	L13	34
Merrick Ter., Udd.	O28	57
Merrick Way G73	Q19	65
Merryburn Av., Giff.	P14	62
Merrycrest Av., Giff.	Q14	62
Merrycroft Av., Giff.	Q14	62
Merryland Pl. G51	K14	34
Merryland St. G51	K13	34
Merrylea Cres., Giff.	P14	62
Merrylee Park Av., Giff.	Q14	62
Merrylee Park La., Giff.	Q14	62
Merrylee Park Ms., Giff.	Q14	62
Merrylee Rd. G43	P14	62
Merryton Av. G15	D10	6
Merryton Av., Giff.	Q14	62
Merryton Pl. G15	D10	6
Merryvale Av., Giff.	Q14	62
Merryvale Pl., Giff.	P14	62
Merton Dr. G52	L10	32
Meryon Gdns. G32	N23	55
Meryon Rd. G32	N23	55
Methil St. G14	H11	19
Methuen Rd., Renf.	J 7	31
Methven Av., Bear.	C13	8
Methven St. G31	M20	53
Methven St., Dalm.	D 6	4
Metropole La. G1	L16	35
Howard St.		
Michillen Rd.,	C14	8
Bear.& G23		
Mid Cotts, Gart.	H26	26
Midcroft Av. G44	P17	64
Midcroft, Bish.	D18	10
Westlands		
Midcroft, Bish.	D18	10
Middle Hard St., Clyde.	B 8	5
Middlemuir Av., Lenz.	C23	13
Middlemuir Rd., Lenz.	C23	13
Middlerigg Rd., Cumb.	C 1	70
Middlesex St. G41	L15	35
Middleton Cres., Pais.	L 5	30
Middleton Rd., Linw.	K 2	28
Middleton St. G51	L14	34
Midland St. G1	L16	35
Midlem Dr. G52	L11	33
Midlem Oval G52	L11	33
Midlock St. G51	L14	34
Midlothian Dr. G41	N14	50
Midton Cotts., Chr.	E28	15
Midton St. G21	H18	22
Midwharf St. G4	J17	36
Migvie Pl. G20	G14	20
Wyndford Rd.		
Milan St. G41	M16	51
Milford St. G33	K22	38
Mill Cres. G40	M18	52
Mill Pl., Linw.	L 1	28
Mill Rd. G72	Q23	67
Mill Rd., Barr.	Q 7	59
Mill Rd., Both.	R28	69
Mill Rd., Clyde.	F 8	17
Mill River, Lenz.	D23	13
Mill Road Gdns. G40	L18	36
Mill St. G40	M18	52
Mill St. G73	O19	53
Mill St., Pais.	M 6	46
Mill Vennel, Renf.	H 9	18
High St.		
Mill Way, Lenz.	C25	14
Millands Av., Blan.	R26	68
Millar Ter. G73	N19	53
Millarbank St. G21	H18	22
Millarston Av., Pais.	M 4	45
Millarston Dr., Pais.	M 4	45
Millbeg Cres. G33	L24	39
Millbeg Pl. G33	L24	39
Millbrae Cres. G13	F 8	17
Millbrae Cres. G42	O15	51
Millbrae Ct. G42	O15	51
Millbrae Rd.		
Millbrae Rd. G42	O15	51
Millbrix Av. G14	G10	18
Millburn Av. G73	P19	65
Millburn Av., Clyde.	F 9	18
Millburn Av., Renf.	H 9	18
Millburn Dr., Renf.	H 8	17
Millburn Rd., Renf.	H 8	17
Millburn St. G21	J19	37
Millburn Way, Renf.	H 9	18
Millcroft Rd. G73	N18	52
Millcroft Rd., Cumb.	C 3	71
Miller St. G1	K17	36
Miller St., Bail.	M25	56
Miller St., Clyde.	E 7	5
Miller St., John.	M 1	44
Millerfield Pl. G40	M19	53
Millerfield Rd. G40	M19	53
Millers Pl., Lenz.	D23	13
Millersneuk Av., Lenz.	D23	13
Millersneuk Cres. G33	G22	24
Millersneuk Dr., Lenz.	D23	13
Millerston St. G31	L19	37
Millford Dr., Linw.	L 1	28
Millgate Av., Udd.	O27	57
Millgate, Udd.	O27	57
Millholm Rd. G44	Q16	63
Milliken Dr., Kilb.	N08	43
Milliken Park Rd., Kilb.	N07	42
Millpond Dr. G40	L18	36
Millport Av. G44	O17	52
Millroad Dr. G40	L18	36
Millroad St. G40	L18	36
Millwood St. G41	O15	51
Milnbank St. G31	K19	37
Milncroft Rd. G33	J22	38
Milner Rd. G13	G12	19
Milngavie Rd., Bear.	D12	7
Milnpark St. G41	L15	35
Milovaig St. G23	E14	8
Milrig Rd. G73	O18	52
Milton Av. G72	P21	66
Milton Douglas Rd.,	C 7	5
Clyde.		
Milton Dr., Bish.	F18	22
Milton Gdns., Udd.	O27	57
Milton Mains Rd., Dalm.	C 7	5
Milton St. G4	J17	35
Milverton Av., Bear.	C11	7
Milverton Rd., Giff.	R13	62
Minard Rd. G41	N15	51
Minard Way, Udd.	O28	57
Newton Dr.		
Minerva St. G3	K15	35
Minerva Way G3	K15	35
Mingarry La. G20	H14	20
Clouston St.		
Mingary St. G20	H15	21
Minguley Cres. G22	F17	22
Mingulay Pl. G22	F18	22
Mingulay St. G22	F17	22
Minmoir Rd. G53	O 9	48
Minstrel Rd. G13	E11	7
Minto Av. G73	Q20	65
Minto Cres. G52	L12	33
Minto St. G52	L12	33
Mireton St. G22	G16	21
Mirrlees Dr. G12	H14	20
Mirrlees La. G12	H14	20
Redlands Rd.		
Mitchell Av. G72	P24	67
Mitchell Av., Renf.	J 7	31
Mitchell Dr. G73	P19	65
Mitchell La. G1	K16	35
Buchanan St.		
Mitchell Rd., Cumb.	C 3	71
Mitchell St. G1	K16	35
Mitchell St., Coat.	M28	57
Mitchellhill Rd. G42	R18	64
Mitchison Rd., Cumb.	B 3	71
Mitre Ct. G14	H11	19
Mitre Rd.		
Mitre La. G14	H12	19
Mitre La. W. G14	H12	19
Mitre La.		
Mitre Rd. G14	H12	19
Moat Av. G13	F11	19
Mochrum Rd. G43	P15	63
Moffat Pl., Blan.	R26	68
Moffat St. G5	M17	52
Mogarth Av., Pais.	O 4	45
Amochrie Rd.		
Moidart Av., Renf.	H 7	17
Moidart Cres. G52	L12	33
Moidart Rd.		
Moidart Ct., Barr.	P 8	59
Moidart Pl. G52	L12	33
Moidart Rd.		
Moidart Rd. G52	L12	33
Moir La. G1	L17	36
Moir St.		
Moir St. G1	L17	36
Molendinar St. G1	L17	36
Mollinsburn St. G21	H18	22
Monach Rd. G33	K23	39
Monachie Gdns.	E20	11
Muirhead Way		
Moncrieff Av., Lenz.	C23	13

Moncrieff Gdns., Lenz. C23 13
Moncrieff Pl. G4 J16 35
   North Woodside Rd.
Moncrieff St. G4 J16 35
   Balnain St.
Moncur St. G40 L18 36
Moness Dr. G52 M12 49
Monifieth Av. G52 M11 49
Monikie Gdns., Bish. E20 11
   Muirhead Way
Monkcastle Dr. G73 P22 66
Monkland Av., Lenz. C23 13
Monkland View Cres., L28 41
Bail.
Monkland Vw., Udd. N28 57
   Lincoln Av.
Monksbridge Av. G13 E11 7
Monkscroft Av. G11 H13 20
Monkscroft Gdns. G11 H13 20
   Monkscroft Av.
Monkscroft Gdns. G11 H13 20
   Kirkmichael Av.
Monkton Dr. G15 E10 6
Monmouth Av. G12 G13 20
Monreith Av., Bear. E11 7
Monreith Rd. E. G44 P16 63
Monreith Rd. G43 P14 62
Monroe Dr., Udd. N27 57
Monroe Pl., Udd. N27 57
Montague La. G12 H13 20
Montague St. G4 J15 35
Montague Ter. G12 H13 20
   Hyndland Rd.
Montclair Pl., Linw. L 1 28
Monteith Dr., Clark. S15 63
Monteith Gdns., Clark. S15 63
Monteith Pl. G40 L18 36
Monteith Pl., Blan. R27 69
Monteith Row G40 L18 36
Monteith Row La. G40 L18 36
   Monteith Pl.
Montford Av. G44 O17 52
Montgomerie Gdns. G14 H11 19
   Lennox Av.
Montgomery Av., Pais. K 7 31
Montgomery Dr., Giff. R14 62
Montgomery Dr., Kilb. M07 42
   Meadside Av.
Montgomery La. G42 O16 51
   Somerville Dr.
Montgomery Rd., Pais. K 7 31
Montgomery St. G42 M18 52
   London Rd.
Montgomery St. G72 P24 67
   Mill Rd.
Montrave St. G52 M11 49
Montrave St. G73 N19 53
Montreal Ho., Dalm. C 5 4
   Perth Cres.
Montron Dr. G15 E10 6
   Moraine Av.
Montrose Av. G32 N22 54
Montrose Av. G52 K 9 32
Montrose Dr., Bear. B12 7
Montrose Gdns., Blan. R26 68
Montrose Pl., Linw. L 1 28
Montrose Rd., Pais. O 3 45
Montrose St. G4 K17 36
Montrose St., Clyde. E 7 5
Montrose Ter., Bish. F20 23
Monymusk Gdns., Bish. E20 11
Monymusk Pl. G15 C 9 6
Moodies Ct. G2 K16 35
   Argyle St.
Moodiesburn St. G33 J20 37
Moorburn Av., Giff. Q13 62
Moore Dr., Bear. D12 7
Moore St. G31 L19 37
   Gallowgate
Moorehouse Av., Pais. N 4 45
Moorfoot Av. G46 Q13 62
Moorfoot Av., Pais. N 5 46
Moorfoot St. G32 L21 38
Moorfoot, Bish. E20 11
Moorhouse Av. G13 G 9 18
Moorhouse St., Barr. R 8 59
Moorpark Av. G52 L 9 32
Moorpark Av., Chr. F26 26
Moorpark Dr. G52 L10 32
Moorpark Pl. G52 L 9 32
Moorpark Sq., Renf. J 7 31
Morag Av., Blan. R26 68

Moraine Av. G15 E10 6
Moraine Circus G15 E10 6
Moraine Dr. G15 E10 6
Moraine Pl. G15 E10 6
   Moraine Dr.
Morar Cres., Bish. E18 10
Morar Ct., Cumb. DO 70
Morar Dr. G73 Q19 65
Morar Dr., Bear. D13 8
Morar Dr., Cumb. DO 70
Morar Dr., Linw. L 1 28
Morar Dr., Pais. N 4 45
Morar Pl., Renf. H 7 17
Morar Rd. G52 L12 33
Morar Ter., Udd. O28 57
Moravia Av., Both. Q28 69
Moray Gate, Both. Q27 69
Moray Gdns., Udd. O27 57
Moray Pl. G41 N15 51
Moray Pl., Bish. E20 11
Moray Pl., Linw. L 1 28
Mordaunt St. G40 M19 53
Moredun Cres. G32 K23 39
Moredun Dr., Pais. N 4 45
Moredun Rd., Pais. N 4 45
Moredun St. G32 K23 39
Morefield Rd. G51 K11 33
Morgan Ms. G42 M16 51
Morion Rd. G13 F11 19
Morley St. G42 O16 51
Morna Pl. G41 J12 33
   Victoria Park Dr. S.
Morningside St. G33 K20 37
Morrin Path G21 H18 22
   Crichton St.
Morrin Sq. G4 K18 36
   Collins St.
Morrin St. G21 H18 22
Morris Pl. G40 L18 36
Morrison Quad., Clyde. E 9 6
Morrison St. G5 L16 35
Morrison St., Clyde. C 6 4
Morrisons Ct. G2 K16 35
   Argyle St.
Morriston Cres., Renf. J 9 32
Morriston St. G72 P22 66
Mortimer St. G20 H15 21
   Hotspur St.
Morton Gdns. G41 N14 50
Morven Av., Bish. E20 11
Morven Av., Blan. R26 68
Morven Av., Pais. O 5 46
Morven Dr., Linw. L 1 28
Morven Gdns., Udd. O27 57
Morven Rd. G72 Q21 66
Morven Rd., Bear. C12 7
Morven St. G52 L12 33
Mosesfield St. G21 G18 22
Mosesfield Ter. G21 G18 22
   Balgray Hill Rd.
Moss Av., Linw. L 1 28
Moss Dr., Barr. P 7 59
Moss Heights G52 L11 33
Moss Knowe, Cumb. C 4 71
Moss Rd. G51 K11 33
Moss Rd., Chr. F26 26
Moss Rd., Cumb. B 4 71
Moss Rd., Lenz. C23 13
Moss Sq. G33 J22 38
Moss St., Pais. L 6 30
Moss-side Rd. G41 N15 51
Mossbank Dr. G33 H21 24
Mosscastle Rd. G33 J23 39
Mossend La. G33 K23 39
Mossend Rd., Pais. K 5 30
   Mosslands Rd.
Mossend St. G33 K23 39
Mossgiel Av. G73 P19 65
Mossgiel Dr., Clyde. D 8 5
Mossgiel Gdns., Udd. O27 57
Mossgiel Pl. G73 P19 65
Mossgiel Rd. G43 P14 62
Mossgiel Rd., Cumb. C 3 71
Mossgiel Ter., Blan. R26 68
Mosshead Rd., Bear. B13 8
Mossland Rd. G52 K 9 32
Mosslands Rd. G52 J 9 32
Mosslands Rd., Pais. K 5 30
Mossneuk Dr., Pais. O 5 46
Mosspark Av. G52 M12 49
Mosspark Boulevard M12 49
G52

Mosspark Dr. G52 M11 49
Mosspark La. G52 N12 49
   Mosspark Dr.
Mosspark Oval G52 M12 49
Mosspark Sq. G52 M12 49
Mossvale Cres. G33 J23 39
Mossvale La., Pais. L 5 30
Mossvale Path G33 H23 25
Mossvale Rd. G33 H22 24
Mossvale Rd. G33 J24 39
Mossvale Sq. G33 J23 39
Mossvale St., Pais. K 5 30
Mossvale Ter., Chr. D28 15
Mossvale Way G33 J23 39
Mossvale Wk. G33 J23 39
Mossview Cotts., Chr. G26 26
Mossview Quad. G52 L11 33
Mossview Rd. G33 G24 25
Mote Hill Rd., Pais. L 7 31
Moulin Circus G52 M10 48
Moulin Pl. G52 M10 48
Moulin Rd. G52 M10 48
Moulin Ter. G52 M10 48
Mount Annan Dr. G44 O16 51
Mount Harriet Av. G33 G24 25
Mount Harriet Dr. G33 G23 25
Mount St. G20 H15 21
Mount Stuart St. G41 O15 51
Mount Vernon Av. G32 M24 55
Mountainblue St. G31 L19 37
Mountblow Ho., Dalm. C 5 4
   Melbourne Av.
Mountblow Rd., Dalm. C 6 4
Mountgarrie Path G51 K11 33
   Mountgarrie Rd.
Mountgarrie Rd. G51 K11 33
Mowbray Av., Gart. G27 27
Mowcraigs Ct., Clyde. F 8 17
   Yokerburn Ter.
Moy St. G11 J14 34
   Church St.
Moyne Rd. G53 N10 48
Muckcroft Rd., Chr. D25 14
Muir Park Ter. G64 F18 22
Muir St. G21 H18 22
Muir St., Bish. E19 11
Muir St., Renf. H 8 17
Muir Ter., Pais. K 7 31
Muirbank Av. G73 O18 52
Muirbank Gdns. G73 O18 52
   Cathcart Rd.
Muirbrae Rd. G73 Q19 65
Muirbrae Way G73 Q19 65
Muirburn Av. G44 Q15 63
Muirdrum Av. G52 M11 49
Muirdykes Av. G52 L10 32
Muirdykes Cres., Pais. L 4 29
Muirdykes Rd. G52 L10 32
Muirdykes Rd., Pais. L 4 29
Muiredge Ct., Udd. P27 69
   Watson St.
Muiredge Ter., Bail. M25 56
Muirend Av. G44 Q15 63
Muirend Rd. G44 Q15 63
Muirfield Cres. G23 E15 9
Muirfield Rd., Cumb. A 3 71
Muirhead Ct., Bail. M26 56
Muirhead Dr., Linw. L 1 28
Muirhead Gdns., Bail. M26 56
Muirhead Rd., Udd. & M25 56
Bail.
Muirhead St. G11 J13 34
   Purdon St.
Muirhead Way, Bish. E20 11
Muirhill Av. G44 Q15 63
Muirhill Cres., G13 F10 18
Muirhouse St. G41 N15 51
   Pollokshaws Rd.
Muirkirk Dr. G13 F12 19
Muirpark Av., Renf. J 8 31
Muirpark Dr., Bish. F19 23
Muirpark St. G11 J13 34
Muirpark Ter., Bish. F18 22
   Crowhill Rd.
Muirshiel Av. G53 P11 61
Muirshiel Cres. G53 P11 61
Muirside Av. G32 M24 55
Muirside Rd., Bail. M25 56
Muirside St., Bail. M25 56
Muirskeith Cres. G43 P15 63
Muirskeith Pl. G43 P15 63
Muirskeith Rd. G43 P15 63

Muirton Dr., Bish. D18 10
Muirton Gdns., Bish. D18 10
Muiryfauld Dr. G31 M21 54
Mulben Cres. G53 O 9 48
Mulben Pl. G53 O 9 48
Mulben Ter. G53 O 9 48
Mulberry Rd. G43 P14 62
Mull Av., Pais. O 6 46
Mull Av., Renf. J 8 31
Mull St. G21 J19 37
Mullardoch St. G23 E14 8
  Rothes Dr.
Mungo Pl., Udd. N28 57
  Lincoln Av.
Munlochy Rd. G51 K11 33
Munro Ct., Clyde. C 6 4
  Gentle Row
Munro La. G13 G12 19
Munro Pl. G13 G12 19
Munro Pl., Udd. N28 57
  Kirkwood Rd.
Munro Rd. G13 G12 19
Munro Vw., Udd. N28 57
  Kirkwood Rd.
Murano St. G20 H15 21
Murdoch St. G21 G18 22
  Lenzie St.
Muriel St., Barr. Q 8 59
Murray Pl., Barr. Q 8 59
Murray Rd., Both. Q28 69
Murray St., Pais. L 5 30
Murray St., Renf. H 8 17
Murrayfield Dr., Bear. E12 7
Murrayfield St. G32 K21 38
Murrayfield, Bish. D19 11
  Ashfield
Murrin Av., Bish. E20 11
Murroes Rd. G51 K11 33
Muslin St. G40 M18 52
Mybster Pl. G51 K11 33
Mybster Rd. G51 K11 33
Myers Cres., Udd. P28 69
Myreside Pl. G32 L20 37
Myreside St. G32 L20 37
Myrie Gdns., Bish. E19 11
Myroch Pl. G34 J26 40
Myrtle Av., Lenz. C23 13
Myrtle Hill La. G42 O17 52
Myrtle Hill Vw. G42 O17 52
Myrtle Pk. G42 N17 52
Myrtle Pl. G42 O17 52
Myrtle Rd., Dalm. D 5 4
Myrtle Rd., Udd. O28 57
Myrtle Sq., Bish. F19 23
Myrtle St., Blan. R26 68
Myrtle Wk. G72 P21 66

Naburn St. G5 M17 52
Nairn Av., Blan. R26 68
Nairn Gdns., Bear. D11 7
Nairn Pl., Dalm. D 6 4
  Dumbarton Rd.
Nairn St. G3 J14 34
Nairn St., Dalm. D 6 4
Nairnside Rd. G21 F20 23
Naismith St. G32 O23 55
Nansen St. G20 H16 21
Napier Ct., Old.K. C 5 4
  Freelands Rd.
Napier Dr. G51 K13 34
Napier Gdns., Linw. L 2 28
Napier Gdns., Linw. L 2 28
Napier Pl. G51 K13 34
Napier Pl., Old.K. C 5 4
  Old Dalnottar Rd.
Napier Rd. G52 J 9 32
Napier Rd. G63 K13 34
Napier St. G51 K14 34
Napier St., Clyde. F 8 17
Napier St., Linw. L 2 28
Napier Ter. G51 K13 34
Napiershall La. G20 J15 35
  Napiershall St.
Napiershall Pl. G20 J15 35
  Napiershall St.
Napiershall St. G20 J15 35
Naseby Av. G11 H12 19
Nasmyth Rd. G52 K10 32
Nasmyth Rd. N. G52 K10 32
Nasmyth Rd. S. G52 K10 32
Navar Pl., Pais. N 7 47

Naver St. G33 J21 38
Neilsland Oval G53 O11 49
Neilsland Sq. G53 N11 49
Neilston Av. G53 P11 61
Neilston Rd., Barr. R 7 59
Neilston Rd., Pais. M 6 46
Neilvaig Dr. G73 Q20 65
Nelson Mandela Pl. G2 K17 36
Nelson Pl., Bail. M25 56
Nelson St. G5 L16 35
Nelson St., Bail. M25 56
Nelson Ter. G12 H15 21
  Glasgow St.
Neptune St. G51 K13 34
Nerston Av. G53 O11 49
Ness Av., John. O08 43
Ness Dr., Blan. R27 69
Ness Gdns., Bish. E19 11
Ness Rd., Renf. H 7 17
Ness St. G33 J21 38
Netham St. G51 K13 34
Nether Auldhouse Rd. P13 62
  G43
Netherburn Av. G44 R15 63
Netherby Dr. G41 M14 50
Nethercairn Rd. G43 Q14 62
Nethercliffe Av. G44 R15 63
Nethercommon Harbour, K 6 30
  Pais.
Nethercraig Cotts., Pais. P 5 58
  Glenfield Rd.
Nethercraigs Dr., Pais. O 5 46
Nethercraigs Rd., Pais. O 4 45
Netherdale Dr., Pais. M 9 48
Netherfield St. G31 L20 37
Netherhill Av. G44 R15 63
Netherhill Cres., Pais. L 7 31
Netherhill Rd., Chr. E27 15
Netherhill Rd., Pais. L 6 30
Netherhouse Av., Lenz. D24 13
Netherhouse Pl., Bail. K27 41
  Netherhouse Rd.
Netherhouse Rd., Bail. K26 40
Netherlee Rd., G44 Q15 63
Netherpark Av. G44 R15 63
Netherplace Cres. G53 O10 48
Netherplace Rd. G53 O10 48
Netherton Ct. G42 R18 64
Netherton Dr., Barr. R 9 60
Netherton Rd. G13 F12 19
Netherton St. G13 F12 19
  Crow Rd.
Nethervale Av. G44 R15 63
Netherview Rd. G44 R16 63
Netherway G44 R15 63
Nethy Way, Renf. J 9 32
  Teith Av.
Neuk Way G32 O23 55
Nevis Rd. G43 P13 62
Nevis Rd., Bear. B10 6
Nevis Rd., Renf. J 7 31
New City Rd. G4 J16 35
New Edinburgh Rd., O27 57
  Udd.
New Inchinnan Rd., Pais. K 6 30
New Kirk Pl., Bear. C12 7
  New Kirk Rd.
New Kirk Rd., Bear. C12 7
New Rd. G72 Q24 67
New Sneddon St., Pais. L 6 30
New St., Clyde. C 7 5
New St., Kilb. M07 42
New St., Pais. M 6 46
New Wynd G1 L17 36
Newark Dr. G41 M14 50
Newark Dr., Pais. O 5 46
Newbattle Ct. G32 N22 54
Newbattle Gdns. G32 N22 54
Newbattle Pl. G32 N22 54
Newbattle Rd. G32 N22 54
Newbold Av. G21 F18 22
Newburgh St. G43 O14 50
Newcastleton Dr. E15 9
Newcroft Dr. G44 P17 64
Newfield Pl. G73 O18 52
Newfield Pl., Thorn. R12 61
  Rouken Glen Rd.
Newfield Sq. G53 P10 60
Newhall St. G40 M18 52
Newhaven Rd. G33 K22 38
Newhaven St. G32 K22 38
Newhills Rd. G33 K24 39

Newington St. G32 L21 38
Newlands Gdns., John. N 2 44
  Renshaw Rd.
Newlands Rd. G43 P15 63
Newlands Rd., Udd. O27 57
Newlandsfield Rd. G43 O14 50
Newluce Dr. G32 M23 55
Newmains Rd., Renf. J 7 31
Newmill Rd. G21 G20 23
Newnham Rd., Pais. M 9 48
Newshot Ct., Clyde. F 8 17
  Clydeholm Ter.
Newshot Dr., Renf. E 5 4
Newton Av. G72 P23 67
Newton Av., Barr. R 8 59
Newton Av., John. M 3 45
Newton Av., Pais. K 7 31
Newton Brae G72 P24 67
Newton Dr., John. M 3 45
Newton Dr., Udd. O28 57
Newton Farm Rd. G72 O24 55
Newton Pl. G3 J15 35
Newton Rd., Lenz. D24 13
Newton St., Pais. M 5 46
Newton Station Rd. P24 67
  G72
Newton Ter. G3 K15 35
  Sauchiehall St.
Newton Terrace La. G3 J15 35
  Elderslie St.
Newtongrange Av. G32 N22 54
Newtongrange Gdns. N22 54
  G32
Newtyle Pl., Bish. E20 11
Newtyle Rd., Pais. M 8 47
Nicholas St. G1 K17 36
Nicholson La. G5 L16 35
  Nicholson St.
Nicholson St. G5 L16 35
Nicholson St. G5 L16 35
Niddrie Rd. G42 N15 51
Niddrie Sq. G42 N15 51
Niddry St., Pais. L 6 30
Nigel Gdns. G41 N14 50
Nigg Pl. G34 K25 40
Nightingale Pl., John. O08 43
Nimmo Dr. G51 K12 33
Nisbet St. G31 L20 37
Nith Av., Pais. N 3 45
Nith Dr., Renf. J 9 32
Nith Pl., John. O08 43
Nith St. G33 J20 37
Nithsdale Cres., Bear. C11 7
Nithsdale Dr. G41 N15 51
Nithsdale Pl. G41 M15 51
  Sheilds Rd.
Nithsdale Rd. G41 M13 50
Nithsdale St. G41 N15 51
Nitshill Rd. G53 P 9 60
Niven St. G20 G14 20
Noldrum Av. G32 O23 55
Noldrum Gdns. G32 O23 55
Norbreck Dr., Giff. Q14 62
Norby Rd. G11 H12 19
Norfield Dr. G44 O16 51
Norfolk Cres., Bish. D18 10
Norfolk Ct. G5 L16 35
Norfolk La. G5 L16 35
  Norfolk St.
Norfolk St. G5 L16 35
Norham St. G41 N15 51
Norman St. G40 M18 52
Norse La. N. G14 H11 19
  Ormiston Av.
Norse La. S. G14 H11 19
  Verona Av.
Norse La. S. G14 H11 19
  Duncan Av.
Norse Rd. G14 H11 19
North Av. G72 P21 66
North Av., Clyde. E 7 5
North Bank Pl., Clyde. F 8 17
  North Bank St.
North Bank St., Clyde. F 8 17
North Brae Pl., G13 F10 18
North British Rd., Udd. P27 69
North Canalbank St. G4 J17 36
North Carbrain Rd., D 2 70
  Cumb.
North Claremont St. G3 J15 35
North Corsebar Av., N 5 46
  Pais.

North Court La. G1   K17 36
Buchanan St.
North Croft St., Pais.   L 6 30
North Deanpark Av.,   Q28 69
Udd.
Fallside Rd.
North Douglas St.,   F 8 17
Clyde.
North Dr. G1   L17 36
North Dr., Linw.   L 1 28
North Elgin St., Clyde.   F 8 17
North Erskine Pk., Bear.   C11 7
North Gardner St. G11   H13 20
North Grange Rd., Bear.   C12 7
North Greenhill Rd.,   K 5 30
Pais.
North Hanover Pl. G4   J17 36
North Hanover St. G1   K17 36
North Iverton Park Rd.,   M 1 44
John.
North Lodge Rd., Renf.   H 8 17
North Moraine La. G15   E11 7
Moraine Av.
North Park Av., Thorn.   Q12 61
North Park St. G20   H15 21
North Pl. G3   K15 35
North St.
North Portland St. G1   K17 36
North Queen St. G2   K17 36
George Sq.
North Rd., John.   N09 43
North St. G3   K15 35
North St., Clyde.   E 7 5
Dumbarton Rd.
North St., Pais   L 6 30
North Vw., Bear.   E11 7
North Wallace St. G4   J17 36
North Way, Blan.   R26 68
North Woodside Rd.   H15 21
G20
Northampton Dr. G12   G13 20
Northampton La. G12   G13 20
Northampton Dr.
Northbank Av. G72   P23 67
Northbank St. G72   P23 67
Northcroft Rd. G21   H18 22
Northcroft Rd., Chr.   E27 15
Northgate Quad. G21   F20 23
Northgate Rd. G21   F20 23
Northinch St. G14   J11 33
Northland Dr. G14   G11 19
Northland La. G14   H11 19
Northland Dr.
Northmuir Rd. G15   D10 6
Northpark Ter. G12   H15 21
Hamilton Dr.
Northumberland St.   H15 21
G20
Norval St. G11   J13 34
Norwich Dr. G12   G13 20
Norwood Dr., Giff.   R13 62
Norwood Ter. G12   J15 35
Southpark Av.
Norwood, Bear.   D12 7
Nottingham Av. G12   G13 20
Nottingham La. G12   G13 20
Northampton Dr.
Novar Dr. G12   H13 20
Novar Gdns., Bish.   E18 10
Numrow Ct., Clyde.   C 6 4
Nuneaton St. G40   M19 53
Nurseries Rd., Bail.   L24 39
Nursery La. G41   N15 51
Nursery St. G41   N15 51
Pollokshaws Rd.
Nursery Street La. G41   N15 51
Nithsdale Dr.

Oak Cres., Bail.   M25 56
Oak Dr. G72   Q23 67
Oak Dr., Lenz.   C22 12
Oak Pl., Bish.   E19 11
Oak Rd., Dalm.   C 6 4
Oak Rd., Pais.   N 7 47
Oakbank Dr., Barr.   S 8 59
Oakbank La. G20   H16 21
Oakbank Ter. G20   H16 21
Oakdene Av., Udd.   O28 57
Oakfield Av. G12   J15 35
Oakfield Ter. G12   J15 35
Oakfield Av.
Oakhill Av., Bail.   M24 55

Oakley Dr. G44   Q15 63
Oakley Ter. G31   K18 36
Oaks, The, John.   N08 43
Oakshaw School Brae,   L 5 30
Pais.
Oakshaw St., Pais.   L 5 30
Oakshawhead, Pais.   L 5 30
Oakwood Av., Pais.   N 4 45
Oatfield St. G21   H19 23
Oban Ct. G22   H15 21
Oban Dr. G20   H15 21
Observatory La. G12   H14 20
Observatory Rd.
Observatory Rd. G12   H14 20
Ochil Dr., Barr.   R 8 59
Ochil Dr., Pais.   O 6 46
Ochil Pl. G32   M22 54
Ochil Rd., Bish.   E20 11
Ochil Rd., Renf.   J 7 31
Ochil St. G32   M22 54
Ochiltree Av. G13   F12 19
Ogilvie Pl. G31   M21 54
Ogilvie St. G31   M20 53
Old Bothwell Rd., Both.   R28 69
Old Castle Rd. G44   P16 63
Old Dalmarnock Rd.   M18 52
G40
Old Dalnottar Rd.,   C 5 4
Old K.
Old Dumbarton Rd. G3   J14 34
Old Edinburgh Rd., Udd.   N27 57
Old Gartcosh Rd., Gart.   G27 27
Old Glasgow Rd., Udd.   O26 56
Old Govan Rd., Renf.   H 9 18
Old Greenock Rd., Renf.   F 5 16
Old Manse Rd. G32   L23 39
Old Mill Rd. G72   P23 67
Old Mill Rd., Both.   R28 69
Old Mill Rd., Clyde.   C 7 5
Old Mill Rd., Udd.   P27 69
Old Rd., John.   M 2 44
Old Renfrew Rd., Renf.   J10 32
Old Roundknowe Rd.,   N26 56
Udd.
Old Rutherglen Rd. G5   M17 52
Old Shettleston Rd. G32   L21 38
Old Sneddon St., Pais.   L 6 30
Old St., Clyde.   C 6 4
Old Wood Rd., Bail.   M25 56
Old Wynd G1   L17 36
Oldhall Rd., Pais.   L 8 31
Olifard Av., Udd.   Q28 69
Oliphant Cres., Pais.   O 3 45
Olive St. G33   H20 23
Olrig Ter. G41   M15 51
Shields Rd.
Olympia St. G40   L18 36
Onslow Dr. G31   K19 37
Onslow Rd., Clyde.   E 8 5
Onslow Sq. G31   K19 37
Onslow Dr.
Oran Gate G20   H15 21
Oran Gdns. G20   G15 21
Oran Pl. G20   G15 21
Oran St. G20   G15 21
Oransay Cres., Bear.   D13 8
Orcades Dr. G44   Q16 63
Orchard Av. G17   R28 69
Orchard Ct. G32   O22 54
Orchard Ct., Thorn.   Q13 62
Orchard Dr. G73   O18 52
Orchard Dr., Giff.   Q13 62
Orchard Gro., Giff.   Q13 62
Orchard Park Av.,   Q13 62
Thorn. & Giff.
Orchard Pk., Giff.   Q14 62
Orchard Pl., Lenz.   B24 13
Orchard Sq., Pais.   M 6 46
Orchard St., Pais.   M 6 46
Orchard St., Renf.   H 8 17
Orchardfield, Lenz.   D23 13
Orchy Cres., Bear.   E11 7
Orchy Cres., Pais.   N 3 45
Orchy Ct., Clyde.   C 8 5
Orchy Dr., Clark.   R15 63
Orchy Gdns., Clark.   R15 63
Orchy St. G44   P16 63
Oregon Pl. G5   M17 52
Orkney Pl. G51   K13 34
Orkney St.
Orkney St. G51   K13 34
Orleans Av. G14   H12 19

Orleans La. G14   H12 19
Ormiston Av. G14   H11 19
Ormiston La. G14   H11 19
Ormiston Av.
Ormiston La. S. G14   H11 19
Ormiston Av.
Ormonde Av. G44   Q15 63
Ormonde Cres. G44   Q15 63
Ormonde Ct. G44   Q15 63
Ormonde Dr. G44   Q15 63
Ornsay St. G22   F17 22
Orr Pl. G40   L18 36
Orr Sq. , Pais.   L 6 30
Orr St. G40   L18 36
Orr St., Pais.   L 6 30
Orr St., Pais.   M 6 46
Orton St. G51   L13 34
Orwell St. G51   H18 22
Osborn Ter. G51   L13 34
Copland Rd.
Osborne St. G1   L17 36
Osborne St., Clyde.   D 7 5
Osborne Vill. G44   P16 63
Holmhead Rd.
Osprey Dr., Udd.   O28 57
Ossian Av., Pais.   L 9 32
Auchmannoch Av.
Ossian Rd. G43   P15 63
Oswald La. G1   L16 35
Oswald St.
Oswald St. G1   L16 35
Otago La. G12   J15 35
Otago St.
Otago La. N. G12   J15 35
Otago St.
Otago St. G12   J15 35
Ottawa Cres., Dalm.   D 5 4
Otter La. G11   J13 34
Castlebank St.
Otterburn Dr., Giff.   R14 62
Otterswick Pl. G33   J23 39
Oulnain St. G72   P24 67
Oval, The, Clark.   R15 63
Overbrae Pl. G15   C 9 6
Overdale Av. G42   O15 51
Overdale Gdns. G42   O15 51
Overdale St. G42   O15 51
Overdale Vills. G42   O15 51
Overdale St.
Overlea Av. G73   P20 65
Overnewton Pl. G3   K14 34
Kelvinhaugh St.
Overnewton Sq. G3   K14 34
Overnewton St. G3   J14 34
Overton Cres., John.   M 1 44
Overton Rd. G72   Q23 67
Overton Rd., John.   N 1 44
Overton St. G72   Q23 67
Overtoun Ct., Dalm.   D 6 4
Dunswin Av.
Overtoun Dr. G73   O19 53
Overtoun Dr., Dalm.   D 6 4
Overtoun Rd.,   D 6 4
Dalm. & Clyde.
Overtown Av. G53   P10 60
Overtown St. G31   L19 37
Overwood Dr. G44   P17 64
Oxford Dr., Linw.   L 1 28
Oxford La. G5   L16 35
Oxford Rd., Renf.   H 8 17
Oxford St. G5   L16 35
Oxgang Pl., Lenz.   B24 13
Oxton Dr. G52   L10 32

Paisley Ct., Barr.   Q 7 59
Paisley Rd.
Paisley Rd. G5   L15 35
Paisley Rd. W. G5   M10 48
Paisley Rd., Barr.   Q 7 59
Paisley Rd., Renf.   J 7 31
Palace St. G31   M20 53
Paladin Av. G13   F11 19
Palermo St. G21   H18 22
Palmer Av. G13   E11 7
Palmerston Pl. G3   K14 34
Kelvinhaugh St.
Palmerston Pl., John.   O08 43
Pandora Way, Udd.   O28 57
Hillcrest Rd.
Panmure St. G20   H16 21
Park Av. G3   J15 35
Park Av., Bar.   R 7 59

Richmond Dr., Bish. D19 11
  G64
Richmond Dr., G73 P21 66
Richmond Dr., Linw. K 1 28
Richmond Gdns., Chr. E25 14
Richmond Pl. G73 O20 53
Richmond St. G1 K17 36
Richmond St., Clyde. E 8 5
Riddell St., Clyde. D 8 5
Riddon Av. G13 F 9 18
Riddrie Cres. G33 K21 38
Riddrie Knowes G33 K21 38
Riddrie Ter. G33 H20 23
  Provamill Rd.
Riddrievale Ct. G33 J21 38
Riddrievale St. G33 J21 38
Rigby St. G32 L20 37
Rigg Pl. G33 K24 39
Rigghead Av. G67 A 3 71
  Roadside
Riggside Rd. G33 J23 39
Riggside St. G33 J23 39
Riglands Way, Renf. H 8 17
Riglaw Pl. G13 F10 18
Rigmuir Rd. G51 L11 33
Rimsdale St. G40 L19 37
Ringford St. G21 H18 22
Ripon Dr. G12 G13 20
Risk St. G40 L18 36
Risk St., Dalm. D 6 4
Ristol Rd. G13 G11 19
  Anniesland Rd.
Ritchie Cres., John. M 2 44
Ritchie St. G5 M16 51
River Rd. G32 O22 54
River Rd. Mansion- O15 51
  house Rd. G41
Riverbank St. G43 O14 50
Riverford Rd. G43 O14 50
Riverford Rd. G43 N20 53
Riversdale Cotts G14 G 9 18
  Dumbarton Rd.
Riversdale La. G14 G 9 18
  Dumbarton Rd.
Riverside Pl. G72 P24 67
Riverside Rd. G43 O15 51
Riverview Av. G5 L16 35
  West Rd.
Riverview Dr. G5 L16 35
Riverview Pl. G5 L16 35
  Riverview Dr.
Roadside, Cumb. A 3 71
Robb St. G21 H18 22
Robert Burns Av., Clyde. D 8 5
Robert St. G51 K13 34
Roberton Av. G41 N14 50
Roberts St., Dalm. D 6 4
Robertson La. G2 K16 35
  Robertson St.
Robertson St. G2 K16 35
Robertson St., Barr. Q 7 59
Robertson Ter., Bail. L26 40
  Edinburgh Rd.
Robin Way G32 O23 55
Robroyston Av. G33 H21 24
Robroyston Rd. G33 G21 24
Robslee Cres., Thorn. Q13 62
Robslee Dr., Giff. Q13 62
Robslee Rd., Thorn. R13 62
Robson Gro. G42 N16 51
Rock Dr. G78 N 7 42
Rock St. G4 H16 21
Rockall Dr. G44 Q17 64
Rockbank Pl. G40 L19 37
  Broad Rd.
Rockbank Pl., Clyde. C 7 5
  Glasgow Rd.
Rockbank St. G40 L19 37
Rockburn Dr., Clark. S14 62
Rockcliffe St. G40 M18 52
Rockfield Pl. G21 G20 23
Rockfield Rd. G21 G20 23
Rockmount Av., Pais. R 8 59
Rockmount Av., Thorn. Q13 62
Rockwell Av., Pais. O 5 46
Roden Av., Pais. O 3 45
Roden Rd., Pais. O 3 45
Rodger Dr. G73 P19 65
Rodger Pl., Ruth. P19 65
Rodil Av. G44 Q17 64
Rodney St. G4 J16 35
Roebank Dr., Barr. R 8 59

Roebank St. G31 K19 37
Roffey Park Rd., Pais. L 8 31
Rogart St. G40 L18 36
Rogerfield Rd., Bail. K26 40
Rokeby Ter. G12 H14 20
  Great Western Rd.
Roman Av. G15 E10 6
Roman Av., Bear. C12 7
Roman Ct., Bear. C12 7
Roman Dr., Bear. C12 7
Roman Gdns., Bear. C12 7
Roman Rd., Bear. C12 7
Roman Rd., Clyde. C 7 5
Romney Av. G44 P17 64
Rona Ter. G72 Q21 66
Ronaldsay Dr., Bish. E20 11
Ronaldsay Pl., Cumb. D 1 70
Ronaldsay St. G22 F17 22
Ronay St. G22 F17 22
Rooksdell Av., Pais. N 5 46
Rose Cotts. G13 G12 19
  Crow Rd.
Rose Dale, Bish. F19 23
Rose Knowe G73 N18 52
Rose St. G3 K16 35
Rosebank Av., Blan. R27 69
Rosebank Dr. G72 Q23 67
Rosebank Ter., Bail. M27 57
Roseberg Pl., Clyde. E 7 5
  Kilbowie Rd.
Rosebery Pl., Clyde. E 7 5
  Miller St.
Rosebery St. G5 N18 52
Rosedale Av. G78 O 2 44
Rosedale Dr., Bail. M25 56
Rosedale Gdns. G20 F14 20
Rosefield Gdns., Udd. O27 57
Roselea Gdns. G13 F12 19
Roselea Pl., Blan. R26 68
Rosemount Cres. G21 J19 37
Rosemount St. G21 J18 36
Rosemount Ter. G51 L15 35
  Paisley Rd. W.
Rosevale Rd., Bear. D12 7
Rosevale St. G11 J13 34
Rosewood Av., Pais. N 4 45
Rosewood St. G13 F12 19
Roslea Dr. G31 K19 37
Roslyn Dr., Bail. L27 41
Rosneath St. G51 K13 34
Ross Av., Renf. J 7 31
Ross Hall Pl., Renf. H 8 17
Ross St. G40 L17 36
Ross St., Pais. M 7 47
Ross St., Pais. M 7 47
Rossendale Rd. G43 O14 50
Rosshall Av., Pais. M 8 47
Rosshill Av. G52 L 9 32
Rosshill Rd. G52 L 9 32
Rossie Cres., Bish. F20 23
Rosslea Dr., Giff. R14 62
Rosslyn Av. G73 O19 53
Rosslyn Av., Bear. C10 6
Rosslyn Ter. G12 H14 20
  Horslethill Rd.
Rostan Rd. G43 P14 62
Rosyth Rd. G5 N18 52
Rosyth St. G5 N18 52
Rotherwick Dr., Pais. M 9 48
Rotherwood Av. G13 E11 7
Rotherwood Av., Pais. O 3 45
Rotherwood La. G13 E11 7
  Rotherwood Av.
Rotherwood Pl. G13 F11 19
Rothes Dr. G23 E14 8
Rothes Pl. G23 E14 8
Rothlinn Av., Lenz. B24 13
Rottenrow East G4 K17 36
Roual Ter., Pais. L 7 31
  Greenlaw Av.
Rouken Glen Rd., R12 61
  Thorn.& Giff.
Roukenburn St. G46 Q12 61
Roundhill Dr., John. M 3 45
Rowallan Gdns. G11 H13 20
Rowallan La. E. G11 H13 20
  Churchill Dr.
Rowallan La. G11 H13 20
  Churchill Dr.
Rowallan Rd., Thorn. R12 61
Rowallan Ter. G33 H22 24
Rowan Av., Renf. H 8 17

Rowan Cres., Lenz. C23 13
Rowan Dr., Dalm. D 6 4
Rowan Gate, Pais. N 6 46
Rowan Gdns. G41 M13 50
Rowan Gdns., Giff. Q14 62
Rowan Gdns. G71 Q28 69
Rowan Pl. G72 P22 66
  Allison Dr.
Rowan Pl. G72 P23 67
  Caledonian Circuit
Rowan Pl., Blan. S26 68
Rowan Rd. G41 M13 50
Rowan Rd., Cumb. B 4 71
Rowan Rd., Linw. K 1 28
Rowan St., Pais. N 6 46
Rowand Av. Giff. R14 62
Rowandale Av., Bail. M25 56
Rowanlea Av. G78 O 3 45
Rowanlea Dr., Giff. Q14 62
Rowanpark Dr., Barr. P 7 59
Rowans Gdns., Both. Q28 69
Rowans, The, Bish. E18 10
Rowantree Av. G73 P19 65
Rowantree Gdns. G73 P19 65
Rowantree Rd., John. N09 43
Rowchester St. G40 L19 37
Rowena Av. G13 E11 7
Roxburgh Dr., Bear. B12 7
Roxburgh La. G12 H14 20
  Saltoun St.
Roxburgh Rd., Pais O 2 44
Roxburgh St. G12 H14 20
Roy St. G21 H17 22
Royal Bank Pl. G1 K17 36
  Buchanan St.
Royal Cres. G3 J15 35
Royal Cres. G42 N16 51
Royal Exchange Bldgs. K17 36
  G1
  Royal Exchange Sq.
Royal Exchange Ct. G1 K17 36
  Queen St.
Royal Exchange Sq. G1 K17 36
Royal Inch Cres., Renf. G 8 17
  Campbell St.
Royal Ter. G3 J15 35
Royal Ter. G42 N16 51
  Queens Dr.
Royal Terrace La. G3 J15 35
  North Claremont St.
Royston Hill, G21 J18 36
Royston Rd. G21 J18 36
Royston Sq. G21 J18 36
Rozelle Av. G15 D10 6
Rubislaw Dr., Bear. D12 7
Ruby St. G40 M19 53
Ruchazie Pl. G33 K21 38
Ruchazie Rd. G32 L21 38
Ruchill Pl. G20 G15 21
Ruchill St. G20 G15 21
Ruel St. G44 O16 51
Rufflees Av., Barr. Q 8 59
Rugby Av. G13 F10 18
Rullion Pl. G33 K21 38
Rumford St. G40 M18 52
Rupert St. G4 J15 35
Rushyhill St. G21 H19 23
  Cockmuir St.
Ruskin La. G12 H15 21
Ruskin Pl. G12 H14 20
  Great Western Rd.
Ruskin Sq., Bish. E19 11
Ruskin Ter. G12 H15 21
Ruskin Ter. G73 N19 53
Russel Pl., Linw. L 1 28
  Gilmerton Rd.
Russell Cres. G81 B 6 4
Russell Cres., Bail. M26 56
Russell Dr., Bear. C12 7
Russell Rd., Clyde. C 6 4
Russell St. G11 J13 34
  Vine St.
Russell St., John. M 1 44
Russell St., Pais. K 5 30
Rutaerford Av., Chr. & C25 14
  Waterside
  Chryston Rd.
Rutherford La. G2 K16 35
  Hope St.
Rutherglen Rd. G5 L17 36
Ruthven Av., Giff. R14 62
Ruthven La. G12 H14 20
  Downside St.

Entry	Ref	Pg
Ruthven Pl., Bish.	F20	23
Ruthven St. G12	H14	20
Rutland Cres. G51	L15	35
Rutland La. G51	L15	35
Govan Rd.		
Rutland Pl. G51	L15	35
Ryan Rd., Bish.	E19	11
Ryan Way G73	Q20	65
Rye Cres. G21	G20	23
Rye Rd. G21	G20	23
Rye Way, Pais.	N 3	45
Ryebank Rd. G21	G20	23
Ryecroft Dr., Bail.	L25	40
Ryedale Pl., G15	D10	6
Ryefield Av., John.	N08	43
Ryefield Rd. G21	G19	23
Ryehill Gdns. G21	G20	23
Ryehill Pl. G21	G20	23
Ryehill Rd. G21	G20	23
Ryemount Rd. G21	G20	23
Ryeside Rd. G21	G19	23
Rylands Av. G32	M24	55
Rylands Gdns. G32	M24	55
Rylees Cres. G52	K 9	32
Rylees Pl. G52	L 9	32
Rylees Rd. G52	L 9	32
Ryvra Rd. G13	G11	19
Sackville Av. G13	G12	19
Sackville La. G13	G12	19
Sackville Av.		
Saddell Rd. G15	D10	6
St. Abbs Dr., Pais.	N 4	45
St. Andrews Av., Bish.	E18	10
St. Andrews Av., Both.	R28	69
St. Andrews Cres. G41	M15	51
St. Andrews Cres., Pais.	J 5	30
St. Andrews Cross G41	M16	51
St. Andrews Drive G41	N14	50
St. Andrews La. G1	L17	36
Gallowgate		
St. Andrews Rd. G41	M15	51
St. Andrews Rd., Renf.	J 8	31
St. Andrews Sq. G1	L17	36
St. Andrews St. G1	L17	36
St. Anns Dr., Giff.	R14	62
St. Blanes Dr. G73	P18	64
St. Bothwells Cres.,	N 4	45
Pais.		
St. Brides Av., Udd.	O29	57
St. Brides Rd. G43	O14	50
St. Brides Way, Both.	Q28	69
St. Catherines Rd.,	R14	62
Giff.		
St. Clair Av., Giff.	Q14	62
St. Clair St. G20	J15	35
Woodside Rd.		
St. Conval Pl. G43	O13	50
Shawbridge St.		
St. Cyrus Gdns., Bish.	E20	11
St. Cyrus Rd., Bish.	E19	11
St. Enoch Sq. G1	L16	35
St. Enoch Wynd G2	K16	35
Argyle St.		
St. Fillans Rd. G33	G23	25
St. Georges Cross G3	J16	35
St. Georges Pl. G2	J16	35
St. Georges Rd.		
St. Georges Rd. G3	J16	35
St. Germains, Bear.	D12	7
St. Helena Cres.,	C 8	5
Clyde.		
St. Ives Rd., Chr.	D27	15
St. James Av., Pais.	K 4	29
St. James Pl., Pais.	L 6	30
Love St.		
St. James Rd. G4	K17	36
St. James St., Pais.	L 6	30
St. Johns Ct. G41	M15	51
St. Johns Quad. G41	M15	51
St. Johns Rd. G41	M15	51
St. Johns Ter. G12	J15	35
Southpark Av.		
St. Jospehs Pl. G40	L18	36
Abercromby St.		
St. Kenneth Dr. G51	K12	33
St. Kilda Dr. G14	H12	19
St. Leonards Dr., Giff.	Q14	62
St. Margarets Pl. G1	L17	36
Bridgegate		
St. Mark St. G32	L21	38
St. Marnock St. G40	L19	37
St. Marys La. G2	K16	35
West Nile St.		
St. Marys Rd., Bish.	E18	10
St. Mirren St., Pais.	M 6	46
St. Monance St. G21	G18	22
St. Mungo Av. G4	K17	36
St. Mungo Pl. G4	K17	36
St. Mungo St., Bish.	F18	22
St. Mungos Rd. G67	C 2	70
St. Ninian St. G5	L17	36
St. Ninians Cres., Pais.	N 6	46
Rowan St.		
St. Ninians Rd., Pais.	N 6	46
St. Peters La. G2	K16	35
Blythswood St.		
St. Peters St. G4	J16	35
St. Ronans Dr. G41	N14	50
St. Ronans Dr. G73	P20	65
St. Stephens Av. G73	Q20	65
St. Stephens Cres. G73	Q21	66
St. Valleyfield St. G21	H18	22
Ayr St.		
St. Vincent Cres. G3	K14	34
St. Vincent Cres. La. G3	K15	35
Corunna St.		
St. Vincent La. G2	K16	35
Hope St.		
St. Vincent Pl. G1	K17	36
St. Vincent St. G2	K15	35
St. Vincent Ter. G3	K15	35
Salamanca St. G31	L20	37
Salen St. G52	L12	33
Salisbury Pl. G12	H14	20
Great Western Rd.		
Salisbury Pl., Dalm.	C 6	4
Salisbury St. G5	M16	51
Salkeld St. G5	M16	51
Salmona St. G22	H16	21
Saltaire Av., Udd.	P28	69
Saltmarket G1	L17	36
Saltmarket Pl. G1	L17	36
King St.		
Saltoun Gdns. G12	H14	20
Roxburgh St.		
Saltoun La. G12	H14	20
Ruthven St.		
Saltoun St. G12	H14	20
Salvia St. G72	P21	66
Sanda St. G20	H15	21
Sandaig Rd. G33	L24	39
Sandbank Av. G20	G14	20
Sandbank Dr. G20	G14	20
Sandbank St. G20	G14	20
Sandbank Ter. G20	F14	20
Sandeman St. G11	J12	33
Sandend Rd. G53	O10	48
Sanderling Pl., John.	O08	43
Sandfield St. G20	G15	21
Maryhill Rd.		
Sandford Gdns., Bail.	L25	56
Scott St.		
Sandgate Av. G32	M23	55
Sandhaven Rd. G53	O10	48
Sandholes, Pais.	M 5	46
Sandholm Pl. G14	G 9	18
Sandholm Ter. G14	G 9	18
Sandiefauld St. G5	M17	52
Sandiefield Rd. G5	M17	52
Sandmill St. G21	J19	37
Sandra Rd., Bish.	E20	11
Sandringham Dr., John.	O 1	44
Glamis Av.		
Sandringham La. G12	H14	20
Kersland St.		
Sandwood Cres. G52	L10	32
Sandwood Rd.		
Sandwood Path G52	L10	32
Sandwood Rd. G52	L10	32
Sandy Rd. G11	J13	34
Sandy Rd., Renf.	J 8	31
Sandyford Pl. G3	K15	35
Sauciehall St.		
Sandyford Place La. G3	J15	35
Elderslie St.		
Sandyford Rd., Renf.	K 7	31
Sandyford St. G3	K14	34
Sandyhills Cres. G32	M22	54
Sandyhills Dr. G32	M22	54
Sandyhills Gro. G32	N23	55
Hamilton Rd.		
Sandyhills Pl. G32	M22	54
Sandyhills Rd. G32	M22	54
Sandyknowes Rd.,	D 3	71
Cumb.		
Sanguhar Gdns., Blan.	R25	68
Sanilands St. G32	L22	38
Annick St.		
Sannox Gdns. G31	K19	37
Saracen Gdns. G22	G17	22
Saracen Head La. G1	L17	36
Gallowgate		
Saracen St. G22	H17	22
Sardinia La. G12	H14	20
Great George St.		
Sardinia Ter. G12	H14	20
Cecil St.		
Saucel Lonend, Pais.	M 6	46
Saucel St., Pais.	M 6	46
Saucelhill Ter., Pais.	M 6	46
Sauchenhall Rd., Chr.	C27	15
Sauchiehall St. G3	K15	35
Saughs Av. G33	G21	24
Saughs Dr. G33	G21	24
Saughs Gate G33	G21	24
Saughs Pl. G33	G21	24
Saughs Rd. G33	G21	24
Saughton St. G32	K21	38
Savoy Arcade G40	M18	52
Main St.		
Savoy St. G40	M18	52
Sawfield Pl. G4	J16	35
Garscube Rd.		
Sawmill Rd. G11	J12	33
Sawmillfield St. G4	J16	35
Saxon Rd. G13	F11	19
Scadlock Rd., Pais.	L 4	29
Scalpay Pl. G22	F17	22
Scalpay St. G22	F17	22
Scapa St. G23	F15	21
Scapa St. G40	M19	53
Springfield Rd.		
Scaraway Dr. G22	F17	22
Scaraway Pl. G22	F17	22
Scaraway St. G22	F17	22
Scaraway Ter. G22	F17	22
Scarba Dr. G43	P13	62
Scarrell Dr. G45	Q19	65
Scarrell Rd. G45	Q19	65
Scarrell Ter. G45	Q19	65
Schaw Rd., Pais.	L 7	31
Schipka Pass. G1	L17	36
Gallowgate		
School Av. G72	P22	66
School Rd. G33	G24	25
School Rd., Pais.	L 9	32
School Wynd, Pais.	L 6	30
Schoolfield La., Bish.	E19	11
Scioncroft Av. G73	O20	53
Scone St. G21	H17	22
Sconser St. G23	E15	9
Scorton Gdns., Bail.	M24	55
Scotland St. G5	L15	35
Scotland St. W. G5	L14	34
Scotsblair Av., Lenz.	C23	13
Scotsburn Rd. G21	H20	23
Scotstoun Mill Rd. G11	J14	34
Patrick Bridge St.		
Scotstoun Pl. G14	H11	19
Scotstoun St.		
Scotstoun St. G14	H11	19
Scott Av., John.	O09	43
Scott Dr., Bear.	C11	7
Scott Rd. G52	K 9	32
Scott St. G3	J16	35
Scott St., Bail.	M25	56
Scott St., Dalm.	D 6	4
Scotts Rd., Pais.	M 8	47
Sea Path G53	P 9	60
Sea Pl. G53	P 9	60
Seafar Rd., Cumb.	D 2	70
Seafield Dr. G73	Q20	65
Seaforth Cres., Barr.	Q 7	59
Seaforth La., Chr.	E28	15
Burnbrae Av.		
Seaforth Rd. G52	K10	32
Seaforth Rd. N. G52	K10	32
Seaforth Rd. S. G52	K10	32
Seaforth Rd., Clyde.	E 7	5
Seagrove St. G32	L20	37
Seamill St. G53	P 9	60
Seamore St. G20	J15	35
Searfe Av., Linw.	L 1	28
Killin Dr.		

Southbrae La. G13   G12 19
Milner Rd.
Southcroft Rd. G73   N18 52
Southcroft St. G51   K13 34
Southdeen Av. G15   D10 6
Southdeen Rd. G15   D10 6
Southend Rd., Clyde.   C 7 5
Southern Av. G73   P19 65
Southesk Av., Bish.   E18 10
Southesk Gdns., Bish.   D18 19
Southfield Av., Pais.   O 6 46
Southfield Cres. G53   O11 49
Southfield Rd., Cumb.   C 1 70
Southinch Av. G14   G 9 18
Southinch La. G14   G 9 18
Tweedvale Av.
Southlea Av. G46   Q13 62
Southlock St. G21   H18 22
Southmuir Pl. G20   G14 20
Southpark Av. G12   J14 34
Southpark La. G12   H15 21
Glasgow St.
Southpark Ter. G12   J15 35
Southpark Av.
Southview Ct. G64   F18 22
Southview Dr., Bear.   C11 7
Southview Pl., Bish.   G27 27
Southview Ter. G64   F18 22
Southview Ter., Bish.   F18 22
Southwold Rd., Pais.   L 9 32
Southwood Dr. G44   P17 64
Spateston Rd., John.   O08 43
Spean St. G44   O16 51
Speirs Pl., Linw.   K 1 28
Speirs Rd., John.   M 1 44
Spence St. G20   F14 20
Spencer Dr. G78   O 2 44
Spencer St. G13   F12 19
Spencer St., Clyde.   D 7 5
Spey Av., Pais.   N 3 45
Spey Dr., Renf.   J 9 32
Almond Av.
Spey Pl., John.   O08 43
Spey Rd., Bear.   E11 7
Spey St. G33   K21 38
Spiers Rd., Bear.   D13 8
Spiersbridge Av., Thorn.   Q12 61
Spiersbridge La. G46   Q12 61
Spiersbridge Rd., Thorn.   R12 61
Spiersbridge Ter. G46   Q12 61
Spindlehowe Rd., Udd.   P27 69
Spingburn Way G21   H18 22
Spinners La., Clyde.   B 7 5
Faifley Rd.
Spinners Row, John.   N08 43
Spittal Rd. G73   Q18 64
Spittal Ter. G72   R25 68
Spoutmouth G1   L17 36
Spring La. G5   M17 52
Lawmoor St.
Springbank Rd., Pais.   K 5 30
Springbank St. G20   H15 21
Springbank Ter., Pais.   K 5 30
Springboig Av. G32   L23 39
Springboig Rd. G32   K23 39
Springburn Rd. G21   G18 22
Springburn Way G21   H18 22
Springfield Av., Bish.   F19 23
Springfield Av., Pais.   M 8 47
Springfield Av., Udd.   P27 69
Springfield Cres., Bish.   F19 23
Springfield Dr., Bail.   R 9 60
Springfield Park Rd. G73   P20 65
Springfield Pk., John.   N 1 44
Springfield Rd. G40   M19 53
Springfield Rd., Barr.   S 8 59
Springfield Rd., Bish.   E19 11
Springfield Rd., Cumb.   B 3 71
Springfield Sq., Bish.   F19 23
Springhill Gdns. G41   N15 51
Springhill Rd., Bail.   L24 39
Springhill Rd., Barr.   R 7 59
Springkell Av. G41   M14 50
Springkell Dr. G41   M13 50
Springkell Gate G41   N14 50
Springside Pl. G15   D10 6
Springvale Ter. G21   H18 22
Hillkirk Pl.
Spruce Av., Blan.   S26 68
Spruce Av., John.   N 1 44
Spruce Dr., Lenz.   C22 12
Spruce Rd., Cumb.   B 4 71

Spruce St. G22   G17 22
Spynie Pl., Bish.   E20 11
Squire St. G14   J12 33
Staffa Av., Renf.   J 8 31
Staffa Dr., Pais.   O 6 46
Staffa Rd. G72   Q21 66
Staffa St. G31   K19 37
Staffa Ter. G72   Q21 66
Staffin Dr. G23   E14 8
Staffin St. G23   E15 9
Stag St. G51   K14 34
Stair St. G20   H15 21
Stamford St. G40   L19 37
Stamperland Av., Clark.   S15 63
Stamperland Dr., Clark.   S15 63
Stamperland Gdns., Clark.   S15 63
Stamperland Hill, Clark.   S15 63
Stanalane St. G46   Q12 61
Standburn Rd. G21   F20 23
Stanely Av., Pais.   N 4 45
Stanely Cres., Pais.   O 4 45
Stanely Dr., Pais.   N 5 46
Stanely Rd., Pais.   N 5 46
Stanford St., Clyde.   E 8 5
Stanhope Dr. G73   P20 65
Stanley Dr., Bish.   D19 11
Stanley Pl., Blan.   R26 68
Stanley St. G41   L15 35
Stanley Street La. G41   L15 35
Milnpark St.
Stanmore Rd. G42   O16 51
Stark Av., Clyde.   C 6 4
Startpoint St. G33   K22 38
Station Gdns., Bail.   M26 56
Station Rd. G20   F14 20
Station Rd. G33   G22 24
Station Rd. Step. G33   G23 25
Station Rd., Bail.   M26 56
Station Rd., Bear.   D11 7
Station Rd., Blan.   R27 69
Station Rd., Both.   R28 69
Station Rd., Chr.   G26 26
Station Rd., Giff.   Q14 62
Fenwick Rd.
Station Rd., Kilb.   N07 42
Station Rd., Pais.   M 4 45
Station Rd., Renf.   H 8 17
Station Rd., Udd.   P27 69
Station Way, Udd.   P28 69
Mansefield Dr.
Station Wynd G78   N 7 42
Steel St. G1   L17 36
Steeple Sq., Kilb.   M07 42
Steeple St.
Steeple St., Kilb.   M07 42
Stenton St. G32   K21 38
Stepford Path G33   K25 40
Stepford Rd.
Stepford Pl. G33   K24 39
Stepford Rd. G33   K24 39
Stephen Cres., Bail.   L24 39
Stephenson St. G52   K 9 32
Stepps Rd. G33   J23 39
Stepps Rd., Lenz.   E24 13
Steppshill Ter. G33   G23 25
Stevbrae, Lenz.   C24 13
Stevenson St. G40   L18 36
Stevenson St., Dalm.   D 6 4
Stevenson St., Pais.   M 6 46
Stewart Av., Renf.   J 7 31
Stewart Ct., Barr.   Q 8 59
Stewart St.
Stewart Dr., Bail.   L28 41
Coatbridge Rd.
Stewart Dr., Clyde.   C 7 5
Stewart Rd., Pais.   O 6 46
Stewart St. G4   J16 35
Stewart St., Barr.   Q 8 59
Stewart St., Dalm.   D 6 4
Stewarton Dr. G72   P21 66
Stewarton Rd., Thorn.   R12 61
Stewartville St. G11   J13 34
Stirling Av., Bear.   E12 7
Stirling Dr. G73   P19 65
Stirling Dr., Bear.   C11 7
Stirling Dr., Bish.   D18 10
Stirling Dr., John.   N08 43
Stirling Dr., Linw.   L 1 28
Stirling Fauld Pl. G5   L16 35
Stirling Gdns., Bish.   D18 10
Stirling Rd. G4   K17 36

Stirling St., Cumb.   B 3 71
Stirling Way, Renf.   J 8 31
York Way
Stirrat St. G20   G14 20
Stirrat St., Pais.   K 4 29
Stobcross Rd. G3   K15 35
Stobhill Rd. G21   F18 22
Stobo St. G31   L19 37
Stobs Dr., Barr.   P 7 59
Stobs Pl. G34   J26 40
Stock St., Pais.   N 6 46
Stockholm Cres., Pais.   M 6 46
Stockiemuir Av., Bear.   B11 7
Stockwell Pl. G1   L17 36
Stockwell St. G1   L17 36
Stoddard Sq., John.   M 2 44
Glenpatrick Rd.
Stonefield Av. G12   G14 20
Stonefield Av., Pais.   N 6 46
Stonefield Cres., Pais.   N 6 46
Stonefield Dr., Pais.   N 6 46
Stonelaw Dr. G73   O19 53
Stonelaw Rd. G73   O19 53
Stoneside Dr. G43   P13 62
Stoneside Sq. G43   P13 62
Stoney Brae, Pais.   L 6 30
Stoneyetts Cotts., Chr.   D27 15
Stony Brae, Pais.   O 6 46
Stonyhurst St. G22   H16 21
Stonylee Rd., Cumb.   C 3 71
Storie St., Pais.   M 6 46
Stormylands St., Barr.   R 8 59
Stornoway St. G22   F17 22
Stow Pl., Pais.   M 6 46
Stow St., Pais.   M 6 46
Strachur St. G22   F16 21
Straiton St. G32   K21 38
Stranka Av., Pais.   M 5 46
Stranraer Dr. G15   E11 7
Moraine Av.
Stratford St. G20   G15 21
Strathallan La. G12   J14 34
Highburgh Rd.
Strathallan Ter. G12   J14 34
Caledon St.
Strathallon Pl. G73   Q20 65
Ranald Gdns.
Strathbran St. G31   M20 53
Strathcarron Pl. G20   G14 20
Gelnfinnan Rd.
Strathcarron Rd., Pais.   N 7 47
Strathclyde Dr.   O19 53
Strathclyde Path, Udd.   P27 69
Strathclyde St. G40   N19 53
Strathclyde Vw. G71   R28 69
Strathcona Dr. G13   F12 19
Strathcona Gdns. G13   F13 20
Strathcona Pl. G73   Q20 65
Strathcona St. G13   G12 19
Strathdee Av., Clyde.   C 7 5
Strathdee Rd. G44   R15 63
Strathdon Av. G44   R15 63
Strathdon Av., Pais.   N 5 46
Strathdon Dr. G44   R15 63
Strathendrick Dr. G44   Q15 63
Strathmore Av., Blan.   R26 68
Strathmore Av., Pais.   M 8 47
Strathmore Gdns. G12   J15 35
Gibson St.
Strathmore Gdns. G73   Q20 65
Strathmore Rd. G22   F16 21
Strathord Pl., Chr.   D28 15
Strathord St. G32   M22 54
Strathtay Av. G44   R15 63
Strathview Gdns., Bear.   D11 7
Strathview Gro. G44   R15 63
Strathview Pk. G44   R15 63
Strathy Pl. G20   G14 20
Glenfinnan Rd.
Strathyre Gdns., Bear.   C13 8
Strathyre Gdns., Chr.   E28 15
Heathfield Av.
Strathyre St. G41   O15 51
Stratton Dr., Giff.   R13 62
Strauss Av., Clyde.   E 9 6
Stravanan Av. G45   R17 64
Stravanan Rd. G45   R17 64
Stravanan St. G45   R17 64
Strenabey Av. G73   Q20 65
Striven Gdns. G20   H15 21
Stroma St. G21   J19 37
Stromness St. G5   M16 51

Street	Grid	Page
Thornwood Ter. G11	J12	33
Thornyburn Dr., Bail.	M26	56
Thornyburn Pla., Bail.	M26	56
Three Ell Rd. G51	K14	34
Govan Rd.		
Threestonehill Av. G32	L22	38
Thrums Av., Bish.	E20	11
Thrums Gdns., Bish.	E20	11
Thrush Pl., John.	O08	43
Thrushcraig Cres., Pais.	N 6	46
Thurso St. G11	J14	34
Dumbarton Rd.		
Thurston Rd. G52	L10	32
Tibbermore Rd. G11	H13	20
Tillet Oval, Pais.	K 5	30
Tillie St. G20	H15	21
Tillycairn Dr. G33	J23	39
Tilt St. G33	J21	38
Tintagel Gdns., Chr.	D27	15
Tinto Dr., Barr.	S 8	59
Tinto Rd. G43	P14	62
Tinto Rd., Bear.	C10	6
Tinto Rd., Bish.	E20	11
Fintry Cres.		
Tinto Sq., Renf.	J 7	31
Ochil Rd.		
Tinwald Av. G52	L 9	32
Tinwald Path G52	L10	32
Tiree Av., Pais.	O 5	46
Tiree Av., Renf.	J 8	31
Tiree Ct., Cumb.	D 1	70
Tiree Dr., Cumb.	D 1	70
Tiree Gdns., Bear.	C10	6
Tiree Rd., Cumb.	D 1	70
Tiree St. G21	J20	37
Tirry Way, Renf.	J 9	32
Morriston Cres.		
Titwood Rd. G41	N14	50
Tiverton Av. G32	M23	55
Tobago Pl. G40	L18	36
Tobago St. G40	L18	36
Tobermory Rd. G73	R20	65
Todburn Dr., Pais.	O 6	46
Todd St. G31	K20	37
Todholm Rd., Pais.	N 7	47
Todholm Ter., Pais.	N 7	47
Toll La. G51	L14	34
Paisley Rd. W.		
Tollcross Rd. G31	L20	37
Tolsta St. G23	E15	9
Tontine La. G1	L17	36
Bell St.		
Tontine Pl. G73	Q21	66
Toppersfield, John.	O08	43
Torbreck St. G52	L12	33
Torbrex Rd., Cumb.	C 3	71
Torburn Av., Giff.	Q13	62
Tordene Path, Cumb.	B 1	70
Binniehill Rd.		
Torgyle St. G23	E14	8
Tormore St. G51	L11	33
Tormusk Dr. G45	Q19	65
Tormusk Rd. G45	Q19	65
Torness St. G11	J14	34
Torogay Pl. G22	F18	22
Torogay St. G22	F17	22
Torogay Ter. G22	F17	22
Toronto Wk. G32	O23	55
Torphin Cres. G32	L22	38
Torphin Wk. G32	L22	38
Torr Rd., Bish.	E20	11
Torr St. G22	H17	22
Torran Rd. G33	K24	39
Torrance Rd., Bish.	C20	11
Torrance St. G21	H18	22
Torridon Av. G41	M13	50
Torrin Rd. G23	E14	8
Torrington Av., Giff.	S13	62
Torrington Cres. G32	M23	55
Torrisdale St. G42	N15	51
Torryburn Rd. G21	H20	23
Torwood La., Chr.	E28	15
Burnbrae Av.		
Torglen Rd. G73	O18	52
Torglen St. G5	N17	52
Toward Rd. G33	K23	39
Tower Av., Barr.	Q 8	59
Tower Cres., Renf.	J 7	31
Tower Dr., Renf.	J 7	31
Tower Pl., John.	N 1	44
Tower Rd., John.	N09	43
Tower St. G41	L15	35
Tower Ter., Pais.	M 5	46
Towerhill Rd. G13	E11	7
Towerhill Ter. G21	H19	23
Broomfield Rd.		
Towerside Cres. G53	N10	48
Towerside Rd. G53	N10	48
Towie Pl., Udd.	P27	69
Townhead Rd., Gart.	J28	41
Townhead Ter., Pais.	M 5	46
Townmill Rd. G31	K18	36
Townsend St. G4	J17	36
Tracy St. G43	O14	50
Tradeston St. G5	L16	35
Trafalgar St. G40	M18	52
Trafalgar St., Dalm.	D 6	4
Trainard Av. G32	M21	54
Tranent Pl. G33	K21	38
Traquair Av. G78	O 3	45
Traquair Dr. G52	M10	48
Treeburn Av., Giff.	Q13	62
Trees Park Av., Barr.	Q 7	59
Trefoil Av. G41	O14	50
Tresta Rd. G23	F16	21
Trident Way, Renf.	J 8	31
Newmains Rd.		
Trinity Av. G52	M11	49
Trinity Dr. G72	Q23	67
Trinley Brae G13	E11	7
Trinley Rd. G13	E11	7
Tronda Pl. G33	K24	39
Tronda Rd. G33	K24	39
Trondra Path G33	K24	39
Trongate G1	L17	36
Troon St. G40	M19	53
Trossachs Rd. G73	R20	65
Trossachs St. G20	H16	21
Troubridge Av., John.	O07	42
Troubridge Cres. G78	N07	42
Troubridge Cres., John.	O07	42
Truce Rd. G13	F10	18
Truro Rd., Chr.	D27	15
Tryst Rd. G67	C 2	70
Tudor La. S. G14	H11	19
Orleans Av.		
Tudor Rd. G14	H12	19
Tudor St., Bail.	M24	55
Tufthill Av., Bish.	E18	10
Tufthill Gdns., Bish.	E18	10
Tullis Ct. G40	M18	52
Tullis St. G40	M18	52
Tulloch St. G44	P16	63
Tullochard Pl. G73	Q20	65
Tummel St. G33	J21	38
Tummel Way, Pais.	N 3	45
Tunnel St. G3	K15	35
Turnberry Av. G11	H13	20
Turnberry Dr. G72	P18	64
Turnberry Gdns., Cumb.	A 2	71
Eastfield Rd.		
Turnberry Pl. G73	P18	64
Turnberry Rd., G11	H13	20
Turnbull St. G1	L17	36
Turnlaw Rd. G72	R22	66
Turnlaw St. G5	M17	52
Turret Cres. G13	F11	19
Turret Rd. G13	F11	19
Turriff St. G5	M16	51
Tweed Av., Pais.	N 3	45
Tweed Cres. G33	J21	38
Tweed Cres., Renf.	H 9	18
Tweed Dr., Bear.	D11	7
Tweed Pl., John.	O08	43
Tweedsmuir Cres., Bear.	B12	7
Tweedsmuir Rd. G52	M10	48
Tweedsmuir, Bish.	E20	11
Tweedvale Av. G14	G 9	18
Tweedvale Pl. G14	G 9	18
Twinlaw St. G34	J26	40
Tylney Rd., Pais.	L 8	31
Tyndrum Rd., Bear.	C13	8
Tyndrum St. G4	J17	36
Tyne St. G14	J11	33
Tynecastle Cres. G32	K22	38
Tynecastle Pl. G32	K22	38
Tynecastle St. G32	K22	38
Tynwald Av. G73	Q20	65
Uddingston Rd., Both.	Q28	69
Uig Pl. G33	L24	39
Uist St. G51	K12	33
Ulundi Rd., John.	N09	43
Ulva St. G52	L12	33
Unden Pl. G13	F12	19
Underwood La., Pais.	L 5	30
Underwood Rd. G41	O15	51
Tantallon Rd.		
Underwood Rd. G73	P20	65
Underwood Rd., Pais.	L 5	30
Union Pl. G1	K16	35
Gordon St.		
Union St. G1	K16	35
Union St., Clyde.	F 8	17
Unity Pl. G4	J16	35
St. Peters St.		
University Av. G12	J14	34
University Gdns. G12	J14	34
University Pl. G12	J14	34
Unsted Pl., Pais.	M 7	47
Uphall Pl. G33	K21	38
Upland Rd. G14	H11	19
Upper Bourtree Ct. G73	Q20	65
Upper Bourtree Dr.		
Upper Bourtree Dr. G73	Q19	65
Upper Glenburn Rd.,	C11	7
Bear.		
Ure Pl. G4	K17	36
Montrose St.		
Urquhart Cres., Renf.	J 8	31
Urrdale Rd. G41	L13	34
Usmore Pl. G33	L24	39
Vaila Pl. G23	F15	21
Vaila St.		
Vaila St. G23	F15	21
Vale Wk., Bish.	F20	23
Valetta Pl., Dalm.	D 5	4
Valeview Ter. G42	O16	51
Vallay St. G22	F17	22
Valley Vw. G72	P23	67
Caledonian Circuit		
Valleyfield St. G21	H18	22
Van St. G31	L20	37
Vancouver Pl., Dalm.	D 5	4
Vancouver Rd. G14	H11	19
Vanguard St., Clyde.	E 8	5
Vanguard Way, Renf.	J 8	31
Varna La. G14	H12	19
Varna Rd. G14	H12	19
Veitchs Ct., Clyde.	C 6	4
Dumbarton Rd.		
Vennacher Rd., Renf.	H 7	17
Vennard Gdns. G41	N15	51
Vere St. G22	H17	22
Vermont Av. G73	O19	53
Vermont St. G41	L15	35
Vernon Dr., Linw.	L 1	28
Verona Av. G14	H11	19
Vesalius St. G32	L22	38
Vicarfield Pl. G51	K13	34
Vicarfield St.		
Vicarfield St. G51	K13	34
Vicarland Pl. G72	Q22	66
Vicarland Rd. G72	P22	66
Vicars Wk. G72	P22	66
Victoria Circus G12	H14	20
Victoria Cres. G12	H14	20
Dowanside Rd.		
Victoria Cres. La. G12	H14	20
Victoria Crescent Rd.		
Victoria Cres. Rd. G12	H14	20
Victoria Cross G42	N16	51
Victoria Rd.		
Victoria Dr. E., Renf.	J 8	31
Victoria Dr. S., Renf.	H 7	17
Victoria Park Corner	H11	19
G14		
Victoria Park Dr. N. G14	H12	19
Victoria Park Dr. S. G11	H11	19
Victoria Park Gdns. N.	H12	19
G11		
Victoria Park Gdns. S.	H12	19
G11		
Victoria Park La. N. G14	H11	19
Westland Dr.		
Victoria Park La. S. G14	H11	19
Westland Dr.		
Victoria Park St. G14	H11	19
Victoria Rd. G33	G23	25
Victoria Rd. G42	N16	51
Victoria Rd. G73	P19	65
Victoria Rd., Barr.	Q 7	59
Victoria Rd., Lenz.	D23	13
Victoria Rd., Pais.	N 5	46
Victoria St. G73	O19	53

Street	Grid	Pg
Victoria St., Clyde.	E 8	5
Victory Dr., Kilb.	M07	42
Glentyan Av.		
Viewbank, Thorn.	Q13	62
Viewfield Av., Bail.	L24	39
Viewfield Av., Bish.	F18	22
Viewfield Av., Blan.	R27	69
Viewfield Av., Lenz.	C23	13
Viewfield Dr., Bail.	L24	39
Viewfield Dr., Bish.	F18	22
Viewfield La. G12	J15	35
Gibson St.		
Viewfield Rd., Bish.	F18	22
Viewfield Rd., Coat.	M28	57
Viewfield Ter. G12	J15	35
Southpark Av.		
Viewmount Dr. G20	F14	20
Viewpark Av. G31	K19	37
Viewpark Dr. G73	P19	65
Viewpoint Pl. G21	G18	22
Viewpoint Rd. G21	G18	22
Viking Way, Renf.	J 8	31
Vanguard Way		
Villafield Av., Bish.	D19	11
Villafield Dr., Bish.	D19	11
Villafield Loan, Bish.	D19	11
Village Rd. G72	P24	67
Villiers Ct. G31	L18	36
Sword St.		
Vine St. G11	J13	34
Vinegarhill St. G31	L19	37
Vinicombe La. G12	H14	20
Vinicombe St.		
Vinicombe St. G12	H14	20
Vintner St. G4	J17	36
Violet St., Pais.	M 7	47
Virginia Bldgs. G1	K17	36
Virginia St.		
Virginia Ct. G1	K17	36
Virginia St.		
Virginia Pl. G1	K17	36
Virginia St. G1	K17	36
Viscount Av., Renf.	J 8	31
Voil Dr. G44	Q16	63
Vorlich Ct., Barr.	R 8	59
Vulcan St. G21	H18	22
Waddel Ct. G5	L17	36
Waddel St. G5	M17	52
Waldemar Rd. G13	F11	19
Waldo St. G13	F12	19
Walker Ct. G11	J13	34
Walker St.		
Walker Dr., John.	N 1	44
Walker Sq. G20	F14	20
Bantaskin St.		
Walker St. G11	J13	34
Walker St., Pais.	M 5	46
Walkerburn Rd. G52	M10	48
Walkinshaw Cres., Pais.	L 4	29
Ferguslie Park Av.		
Walkinshaw Rd., Renf.	H 5	16
Walkinshaw St. G40	M19	53
Walkinshaw St., John.	M09	43
Walkinshaw Way, Pais.	K 5	30
Broomdyke Way		
Wallace Av., John.	N 2	44
Wallace Pl., Blan.	R27	69
Wallace Rd., Renf.	J 7	31
Wallace St. G5	L16	35
Wallace St. G73	O19	53
Wallace St., Clyde.	F 7	17
Wallace St., Pais.	L 6	30
Wallacewell Cres. G21	G19	23
Wallacewell Cres., John.	N 1	44
Wallacewell Pl. G21	G19	23
Wallacewell Quad. G21	G20	23
Wallacewell Rd. G21	G19	23
Wallbrae Rd., Cumb.	D 3	71
Wallneuk Rd., Pais.	L 6	30
Wallneuk, Pais.	L 6	30
Incle St.		
Walls St. G1	K17	36
Walmer Cres. G51	L14	34
Walmer Ter. G51	L14	34
Paisley Rd. W.		
Walnut Cres. G22	G17	22
Walnut Cres., John.	N 1	44
Walnut Dr., Lenz.	C22	12
Walnut Pl. G22	G17	22
Walnut Rd. G22	G17	22
Walter St. G31	K20	37
Walton St. G41	O15	51
Walton St., Barr.	Q 8	59
Wamba Av. G13	F12	19
Wamba Pl. G13	F12	19
Wandilla Av., Clyde.	E 8	5
Wanlock St. G51	K13	34
Warden Rd. G13	F11	19
Wardhouse Rd., Pais.	O 5	46
Wardie Path G33	K24	39
Wardie Pl. G33	K25	40
Wardie Rd. G33	K25	40
Wardlaw Av. G73	O19	53
Wardlaw Dr. G73	O19	53
Wardlaw Rd., Bear.	E12	7
Wardpark Rd., Cumb.	A 4	71
Wardrop St. G51	K13	34
Wardrop St., Pais.	M 6	46
Ware Path G33	K25	40
Ware Rd. G33	K24	39
Warilda Av., Clyde.	E 8	5
Warp La. G3	K15	35
Argyle St.		
Warren St. G42	N16	51
Warriston Cres. G33	K20	37
Warriston Pl. G32	K22	38
Warriston St. G33	K20	37
Warroch St. G3	K15	35
Washington Rd., Renf.	K 6	30
Washington St. G3	K16	35
Wator Brae, Pais.	L 6	30
Smithhills St.		
Water Brae, Pais.	M 6	46
Forbes Pl.		
Water Rd., Barr.	Q 8	59
Waterfoot Av. G53	O11	49
Waterford Rd., Giff.	Q13	62
Waterloo La. G2	K16	35
Waterloo St.		
Waterloo St. G2	K16	35
Watermill Av., Lenz.	D23	13
Waterside La., Kilb.	N08	43
Kilbarchan Rd.		
Waterside St. G5	M17	52
Waterside Ter., Kilb.	N08	43
Kilbarchan Rd.		
Watling St., Udd.	O27	57
Watson Av. G73	O18	52
Watson Av., Linw.	L 1	28
Watson St., G1	L17	36
Watson St., Udd.	P27	69
Watt Rd. G52	K 9	32
Watt St. G5	L15	35
Wattlow Av. G73	P19	65
Waulkmill Av., Barr.	Q 8	59
Waulkmill St., Thorn.	Q12	61
Waverley Cres., Cumb.	D 1	70
Waverley Dr. G73	O20	53
Waverley Gdns. G41	N15	51
Waverley Gdns., John.	N 2	44
Waverley Pl., Udd.	R28	69
Waverley Rd., Pais.	O 3	45
Waverley St. G41	N15	51
Waverley Ter. G31	L19	37
Whitevale St.		
Waverley Way, Pais.	O 3	45
Waverley Rd.		
Waverley, Clyde.	E 8	5
Onslow Rd.		
Weardale La. G33	K23	39
Weardale St. G33	K23	39
Weaver La., Kilb.	M07	42
Glentyan Av.		
Weaver St. G4	K17	36
Weaver Ter., Pais.	M 7	47
Weavers Av., Pais.	M 4	45
Green Rd.		
Weavers Rd., Pais.	M 4	45
Green Rd.		
Webster St. G40	M19	53
Webster St., Clyde.	F 9	18
Wedderlea Dr. G52	L10	32
Weensmoor Pl. G53	Q10	60
Weensmoor Rd. G53	P10	60
Weeple Dr., Linw.	L 1	28
Weighhouse Clo., Pais.	M 5	46
Weir Av., Barr.	R 8	59
Weir Rd., Linw.	K 1	28
Weir St., Pais.	L 6	30
Weirwood Av., Bail.	M24	55
Weirwood Gdns., Bail.	M24	55
Welbeck Rd. G53	P10	60
Welfare Av. G72	Q23	67
Well Grn. G43	O14	50
Well Rd., Kilb.	M07	42
Well St. G40	L18	36
Well St., Pais.	L 5	30
Wellbank Pl., Udd.	P27	69
Church St.		
Wellbrae Ter., Chr.	E27	15
Wellcroft Pl. G5	M16	51
Wellfield Av., Giff.	Q13	62
Wellfield St. G21	H18	22
Wellhouse Cres. G33	K24	39
Wellhouse Path G33	K24	39
Wellhouse Rd. G33	K24	39
Wellington La. G2	K16	35
West Campbell St.		
Wellington Pl., Dalm.	D 5	4
Wellington Rd., Bish.	D20	11
Wellington St. E. G31	L20	37
Wellington St. G2	K16	35
Wellington St., Pais.	L 5	30
Calendonia St.		
Wellington Way, Renf.	J 8	31
Tiree Av.		
Wellmeadow Rd. G43	P13	62
Wellmeadow St., Pais.	M 5	46
Wellpark St. G31	K18	36
Wellpark St. G31	K18	36
Wells St., Clyde.	D 6	4
Wellshot Dr. G72	P21	66
Wellshot Rd. G32	M21	54
Wellside Dr. G72	Q23	67
Wemyss Gdns., Bail.	M25	56
Wendur Way, Pais.	K 5	30
Abbotsburn Way		
Wenloch Rd., Pais.	N 6	46
Wentworth Dr. G23	E15	9
West Av. G33	G23	25
West Av., Renf.	H 8	17
West Av., Udd.	P28	69
West Brae, Pais.	M 5	46
West Campbell St. G2	K16	35
West Campbell St., Pais.	M 4	45
West Chapelton Av., Bear.	D12	7
West Chapelton Cres., Bear.	D12	7
West Chapelton Dr., Bear.	D12	7
West Chapelton La., Bear.	D12	7
West Chapelton Av.		
West Coats Rd. G72	Q21	66
West Cotts., Gart.	H25	26
West Ct., Dalm.	D 6	4
Little Holm		
West Duntiblae Rd., Lenz.	B25	14
West George La. G2	K16	35
West Campbell St.		
West George St. G32	K16	35
West Graham St. G4	J16	35
West Greenhill Pl. G3	K15	35
West La., Pais.	M 4	45
West Lodge Rd., Renf.	H 7	17
West Nile St. G2	K16	35
West Princes St. G4	J15	35
West Regent La. G2	K16	35
Renfield St.		
West Regent St. G2	K16	35
West St. G5	L16	35
West St. G5	M16	51
West St., Clyde.	F 9	18
West St., Kilb.	M07	42
West St., Pais.	M 5	46
West Thomson St., Clyde.	D 7	5
Westbank La. G12	J15	35
Gibson St.		
Westbank Quad. G12	J15	35
Gibson St.		
Westbank Ter. G12	J15	35
Gibson St.		
Westbourne Cres., Bear.	C11	7
Westbourne Dr., Bear.	C11	7
Westbourne Gdns. La. G12	H14	20
Lorraine Rd.		
Westbourne Gdns. N. G12	H14	20
Westbourne Gdns. S. G12	H14	20